Children's Literature

REFERENCE SOURCES IN THE HUMANITIES

James Rettig, Series Editor

1986. **On the Screen: A Film, Television, and Video Research Guide.** By Kim N. Fisher. OP

1986. **Philosophy: A Guide to the Reference Literature.** By Hans E. Bynagle.

1987. **Music: A Guide to the Reference Literature.** By William S. Brockman. OP

1990. **Journalism: A Guide to the Reference Literature.** By Jo A. Cates.

1990. **Reference Works in British and American Literature. Volume I, English and American Literature.** By James K. Bracken.

1991. **Reference Works in British and American Literature. Volume II, English and American Writers.** By James K. Bracken.

1991. **Communication and Mass Media: A Guide to the Reference Literature.** By Eleanor S. Block and James K. Bracken. OP

1991. **Judaism and Christianity: A Guide to the Reference Literature.** By Edward D. Starkey. OP

1991. **Linguistics: A Guide to the Reference Literature.** By Anna L. DeMiller. OP

1992. **Reference Guide to Science Fiction, Fantasy, and Horror.** By Michael Burgess.

1994. **The Performing Arts: A Guide to the Reference Literature.** By Linda Keir Simons.

1995. **American Popular Culture: A Guide to the Reference Literature.** By Frank W. Hoffmann.

1996. **Classical Studies: A Guide to the Reference Literature.** By Fred W. Jenkins.

1997. **Philosophy: A Guide to the Reference Literature.** Second Edition. By Hans E. Bynagle.

1997. **Journalism: A Guide to the Reference Literature.** Second Edition. By Jo A. Cates.

1998. **Children's Literature: A Guide to Information Sources.** By Margaret W. Denman-West.

1998. **Reference Works in British and American Literature.** Second Edition. By James K. Bracken.

Children's Literature

A Guide to Information Sources

Margaret W. Denman-West

1998
Libraries Unlimited, Inc.
Englewood, Colorado

LIBRARIES UNLIMITED, INC.
P.O. Box 6633
Englewood, CO 80155-6633
1-800-237-6124
www.lu.com

Production Editor: Stephen Haenel
Copy Editor: Beth Partin
Proofreader: Matthew Stewart
Typesetter: Michael Florman

Library of Congress Cataloging-in-Publication Data

Denman-West, Margaret W., 1926-
    Children's literature : a guide to information sources / Margaret
W. Denman-West.
    xiv, 187 p. 17x25 cm. -- (Reference sources in the humanities series)
    Includes bibliographical references and index.
    ISBN 1-56308-448-1
    1. Children's literature--Bibliography. I. Title. II. Series.
Z1037.D35 1998
[PN1009.A1]
016.8088'99282--dc21   98-10177
                                                                  CIP

Authors are the eyes and ears of the past, the present, the future, definite and indefinite. We create worlds that were, are, and might be. We are the real magic makers, and please remember that the word magic *comes from the word* magus *or* mage, *which means wise one. The gifts we bear are stories. Filled with imagination. Mage-magic-image-imagination: a mantra for teachers and librarians.*

—Jane Yolen
Personal communication with the author

Contents

Acknowledgments ix
Introduction xi

Chapter 1: Guides to Award-Winning Books 1
    Awards, Honors, and Prizes 1
    The Newbery and Caldecott Awards 4
    Individual Awards for Children's Literature 6

Chapter 2: Recommended Reading 7
    Best Books 7
    Gifted and Reluctant Readers 22
    Picture Books/Movable Books 25
    For Reading Out Loud! 29
    Children with Special Needs 35
    Booklets and Pamphlets 41

Chapter 3: Multicultural Literature 45
    General Reference Sources 45
    African American Literature 53
    Hispanic/Latino Literature 56
    Jewish Literature 57
    Native American Literature 58
    The Literature of Other Cultures 61

Chapter 4: Subject Bibliographies 65
    General Subject Bibliographies 65
    The Social Sciences 75
    The Sciences 82

Chapter 5: Reference Books 87
    General Reference Sources 87
    Dictionaries/Encyclopedias/Guides 90
    Indexes 92
    Series and Sequels 99
    Commercial Bibliographies 100
    Guides to Issues 102
    Reviews of Children's Literature 103
    Textbooks 105

Chapter 6: Biographies 107

Chapter 7: Core Periodicals/Multimedia Reviews 119
    Periodical Guides 119
    Professional Journals 120
    Book-Reviewing Journals 124
    Children's Book Reviews in Major Newspapers 126

Chapter 8: Nonprint Media 129
 General Reference Sources 129
 Reference Sources on CD-ROM 134
 Reviewing Sources for Nonprint Media 135

Chapter 9: Special Collections of Children's Literature 137
 Directories 137
 A Selective List of Research Collections 138
 A Representative List of Centers 140

Chapter 10: Professional Associations 143

Chapter 11: The Information Superhighway via the Internet . . 151
 Print Reference Sources 151
 The Internet 152

Author/Title Index 163
Subject Index 181

Acknowledgments

I want to express my sincere appreciation to all who helped make this publication possible.

Lucille Van Vliet began it all by urging me to "take the step." When I finally decided to give it a try, family, friends, and colleagues gave me the confidence to keep going. The one person without whom I would never have made it is my daughter-in-law, Heidi Denman. Among many other "helps," she willingly and graciously edited my entries and acted as chauffeur to libraries and conferences as I searched for every possible source to be incorporated into the bibliography. I also want to thank the staff of the following local libraries who went "over and beyond" to help me locate books: the Cooperative Children's Book Center at the University of Wisconsin at Madison; the West Park branch of the Cleveland Public Library; the Children's Book Room of the Cleveland Public Library; and the children's librarians at Fairview Park Public Library, a branch of Cuyahoga County Public Library. This acknowledgment would not be complete without expressing my gratitude to the series editor, James Rettig, for his patience and understanding. Although we have never met, he figuratively "held my hand" as I struggled through the writing process. Thanks, Jim.

Introduction

Some Books are to be tasted,
others to be swallowed,
and some few to be chewed and digested.
—Sir Francis Bacon, 1561-1626
Of Studies

Children's Literature: A Guide to Information Sources, a bibliography of bibliographies and other information sources, was developed with professionals and laypeople in mind. As a guide to more than 400 information sources pertaining to literature for children, it is organized to enable researchers, teachers, librarians, parents, and others working with children to locate information using a variety of formats, including books, nonprint media, professional journals, and, through use of the newest technology, the Information Superhighway via the Internet and CD-ROM. Entries range from theoretical discourses to descriptive and evaluative bibliographies on special topics. Copyright dates are limited, with some exceptions, to books published between 1985 and 1997. Some books indicated in *Books in Print* as "out of print" are included because the titles cited are current enough to be located on the shelves of many public and school libraries. More than 300 of the books cited have been personally reviewed and individually evaluated. Every effort was made to locate and include all relevant bibliographies of children's books, appropriate reference sources, professional associations, and representative research centers.

It was not until the latter part of the nineteenth century and the beginning of the twentieth century that literature written for and about children was considered a literary form worthy of recognition. In fact, it was not unusual for nineteenth-century authors who also wrote children's books to use pseudonyms to conceal their true identity. The emergence of writers such as Louisa May Alcott, Mark Twain, Beatrix Potter, and illustrators such as Randolph Caldecott, Kate Greenaway, Arthur Rackham, and Walter Crane gave rise to the Golden Age of Children's Literature. From the 1920s to the 1960s children's literature came into its own. New authors made their appearance; different techniques in illustrating books, novel approaches to formatting stories, and broader-based story content became commonplace. "Dick and Jane" books were slowly replaced by books with more realism in content and characterizations. Authors like Dr. Seuss and Judy Blume came upon the scene, revolutionizing the traditional approach to writing for children. Innovative illustrators such as Maurice Sendak and Leo and Diane Dillon shook up conservative concepts of the art of illustrating children's books. The 1960s heralded an even more shocking era of realism in children's books. References and characterizations of children who are "different"—mentally, physically, and, yes, even in the color of their skin—began to make a significant impact on the content of children's books. Once-taboo topics are now integral elements in children's books; divorce, death, single parents, violence, AIDS, and other similar, controversial topics are no longer avoided. However, the pendulum appears to be swinging back. Incidences of censorship are growing in number; classics such as *Huckleberry Finn* and *Alice in Wonderland* are being challenged, along with Sendak's Caldecott Honor book, *In the Night Kitchen,* and Katherine Paterson's Newbery Medal winner, *Bridge to Terabithia.* As we approach the beginning of the twenty-first century, one wonders what new challenges to children's literature will have to be faced.

In the late 1970s, reviewing and evaluating the newest published books on the market, using *School Library Journal, Horn Book, Booklist,* and other reviewing media, was fairly simple. Due to the popularity of children's books in the retail marketplace as well as in school and public libraries, the publishing industry has responded by increasing the volume of new titles and reissues of old favorites coming off the presses. A recent study indicates that the biggest new market being targeted in the children's book publishing industry is grandparents, other family members, and friends. Another outcome of the growing volume of books available has been an increase in the publication of bibliographies of children's and young adult books. Bibliographies cover every subject from "best books" for children to very specialized topics such as twins in children's books; cat, dog, and horse stories; myths; classics; and single parents.

Trends come and go. An example was the burgeoning market for book reviewing, critiquing, and recommending titles for and about the handicapped child (now identified as the special child) in response to PL94-142, the mainstreaming in education law passed in 1975. Although some bibliographies of books on the special child are being updated, bibliographies of new books are rare. The most current trend is for books with multicultural themes. To encourage one culture to have a clear and positive understanding of another culture, recognition and acceptance of the rich diversity among people everywhere must be emphasized. Books are a medium through which these goals can be accomplished. Because stereotyping has been all too prevalent in children's books over the decades (and alas, still exists), guides to appropriate selections for purchase and recreational reading are important. Selective bibliographies now available provide excellent guides to fulfill this need. No doubt another trend will soon be in the making. What will it be?

CHAPTER OVERVIEWS

Whatever the trends and challenges ahead, teachers, librarians, parents, and others who work with children will want to consult the resources described and evaluated in this guide to educate themselves and to serve children's best interests. It has been organized to satisfy a wide variety of interests and to serve the needs of a diverse audience. The scope of each chapter is sketched below to serve as a guide to direct the reader's path through the contents.

The first two chapters are guides to bibliographies of "the best of the best." The bibliographies of award-winning books provided in chapter 1 are informative and range from references to multiple awards given for children's literature to Newbery and Caldecott award information and lists of international awards.

Bibliographies of titles selected as "best books" in chapter 2 vary from those produced in a special format, such as picture books or movable and pop-up books, to specialized topics, such as books for reading aloud, books for the gifted child, books for reluctant readers, and books about or to be used with the special needs child.

The third chapter, dedicated to multicultural literature, includes bibliographies of children's books for, by, and about African Americans, Native Americans, Hispanics/Latinos, Asian Americans, and other cultures.

Chapter 4 lists subject bibliographies. It is a melding of recommended books on a variety of specialized topics, including alphabet and counting books; the classics; the worlds of fantasy and mythology; exciting, funny, and scary books; humor; twins; and dog, cat, and horse stories. Bibliographies of children's books dealing with themes such as adoption, single-parent families, death and dying, ecology, survival themes, and other sensitive issues are covered. History, geography, and science bibliographies are located here.

Chapters 5 through 8 cover various reference formats. Chapter 5 includes general references, dictionaries, encyclopedias, indexes, series and sequels, guides to issues, sources of literary reviews, and textbooks.

Bibliographies of biographies, one of the most popular reading genres for elementary children, are located in chapter 6. Titles relating specifically to authors and illustrators of children's books are, for the most part, in formats that make them as easily used by children as by adults. The use of photographs of the biographees in these books lends an especially interesting element to many of the biographical sketches.

Chapter 7 is a guide to periodicals, professional journals, indexes to book reviews in newspapers, and other sources. Chapter 8 covers nonprint media, including the CD-ROM.

Chapter 9 is a representative list of research centers and special collections of children's literature. We are all familiar with the specialized collections of memorabilia for presidents, sports figures, movie stars (who can forget Elvis?), but how many are aware of the great many outstanding collections of children's literature housed in college and university libraries, public libraries, and other institutions across the United States? The collections reflect various aspects of literature for children, from the historical development of the genre to collections that cover special features, such as toys, dolls, and stuffed animals. Perhaps the most interesting items are the collections of authors' manuscripts, illustrators' drawings, and other items related to their books, illustrations, and writing. Collections of this nature offer researchers personal insight into the lives of authors and illustrators who have made an impact on literature for children. Teachers, librarians, parents, and children have a chance to get to know the author or illustrator. This list is not intended to be comprehensive or even evaluative; it is intended to be representative only.

Chapter 10 is a list of twenty-two professional associations related to children, books, and reading. In addition to a brief description of each association, addresses, telephone numbers, and, where available, e-mail or World Wide Web addresses or both are included.

Last, but in no way the least, is the chapter on the Information Superhighway. This new path to information is ever-changing; so the intent is to identify representative sites on the World Wide Web and applicable listservs. Chapter 11 introduces the reader to the almost unwieldy quantity of information related to children and books that is at the fingertips of those with computers, a modem, and access to the Internet. Although each site listed was checked before it was placed on the list, it is possible that when the reader checks out the sites, some will be gone and new ones will have been added. We are merely at the cutting edge of what the next century may bring to the world through technology. Sources of information related to children's literature no doubt will be out there "riding the waves." It is all very exciting; however, I must give you fair warning: Surfing the Net can be addictive.

I enjoyed researching this topic and hope this publication will make searching for the many interesting, informative, multisubject, and multiformat resources related to children and books easier.

Chapter 1

Guides to Award-Winning Books

AWARDS, HONORS, AND PRIZES

1. Children's Book Council (CBC). **Children's Books: Awards & Prizes: Including Prizes and Awards for Young Adult Books, 1996 ed.** New York: Children's Book Council, 1996. 496p. indexes. ISBN 0-933633-03-3. ISSN 0069-3472.

    This publication was initially begun as a series of information sheets pertaining to prize-winning children's books. In response to interest in the enterprise, it was expanded to book-length format designed as a source of information related to excellence in literature for children. With each new edition, the editors continue to be responsive to the information needs of practitioners and the general public.

    The text is organized into the following categories: U.S. awards selected by adults; U.S. awards selected by young readers; awards granted in Australia, Canada, New Zealand, and United Kingdom; and selected international and multinational awards. Within each category, awards are identified and defined. The entries include the donor, the criteria, and a description of the award granted. The substantial subject index provides an additional enhancement for the user. The details this publication provides and the ease with which the information is located identify it as a valuable addition to any library. The researcher may also want to refer to the Jones title (see entry 7) for more in-depth information on awards presented in the United States and to the Criscoe (entry 2) and Smith (entry 8) titles for more information on international awards.

2. Criscoe, Betty, and Philip J. Lanasa III. **Award-Winning Books for Children and Young Adults, 1990-1991.** Metuchen, NJ: Scarecrow, 1993. 714p. illus. indexes. ISBN 0-8108-2597-X.

    This guide to awards granted for children's and young adult books in English-speaking countries of the world describes 230 awards, thirty-two of which were introduced for the first time in this edition. The scope includes authors and illustrators who have received recognition for the body of their works, for awards for individual titles, and for meritorious service to youth.

    Entries, arranged alphabetically by author, provide bibliographic citations, brief biographies, and a selective bibliography of pertinent reviews and articles. The four appendixes provide sources of specialized and useful information for the reader. The indexes are organized into seven categories that provide multiple access points for the user. The impressive coverage and the ease of use of this publication recommend it highly and give reason to hope that an update is soon forthcoming.

3. Helbig, Alethea K., and Agnes Regan Perkins. **Dictionary of American Children's Fiction, 1990-1994: Books of Recognized Merit.** Westport, CT: Greenwood Press, 1997. 496p. index. ISBN 0-315-28763-5.

The purpose of this work is to provide information about award-winning books published during the years 1990-1994 for children and young adults. The entries, alphabetically arranged by author, include a substantial plot summary incorporating critical comments in the review. Among the interesting components integrated into the annotations are comments about the characters in the book and how they influence the story. With the addition of biographical information and listings of other works by the authors, Helbig and Perkins have produced a helpful, easy-to-use guide to meritorious literature for children. They have published similar dictionaries for British children's books (entry 4) and children's fiction from Australia, Canada, India, and New Zealand (entry 5). The other dictionaries of American fiction are listed below.

3.1. Helbig, Alethea K., and Agnes Regan Perkins. **Dictionary of American Children's Fiction, 1859-1959: Books of Recognized Merit.** Westport, CT: Greenwood Press, 1985. 666p. index. ISBN 0-313-22590-7.

3.2. Helbig, Alethea K., and Agnes Regan Perkins. **Dictionary of American Children's Fiction, 1960-1984: Recent Books of Recognized Merit.** Westport, CT: Greenwood Press, 1986. 930p. index. ISBN 0-313-25233-5.

3.3. Helbig, Alethea K., and Agnes Regan Perkins. **Dictionary of American Children's Fiction, 1985-1989: Books of Recognized Merit.** Westport, CT: Greenwood Press, 1993. 320p. index. ISBN 0-313-27719-2.

4. Helbig, Alethea K., and Agnes Regan Perkins. **Dictionary of British Children's Fiction: Books of Recognized Merit.** Westport, CT: Greenwood, 1989. 1650p. indexes. ISBN 0-313-22591-5.

Helbig and Perkins have provided an outstanding reference source to British fiction for children. They selected titles of recognized distinction published in Great Britain between 1678 and 1985. Each title is entered in dictionary format; authors, titles, characters, and settings are interfiled. The brief, critical evaluations enhance the value of the publication. This volume is a fine addition to children's reference works.

5. Helbig, Alethea K., and Agnes Regan Perkins. **Dictionary of Children's Fiction from Australia, Canada, India, New Zealand, and Selected African Countries: Books of Recognized Merit.** Westport, CT: Greenwood, 1992. 608p. index. ISBN 0-313-26126-1.

This is a companion to Helbig and Perkins's *Dictionary of American Children's Fiction* (see entries 3-3.3) and *Dictionary of British Children's Fiction* (see entry 4). The authors have included books that have received recognition as "outstanding" by professional associations and award committees. The *Dictionary* catalogs, annotates, and evaluates 263 books, authored by 164 twentieth-century authors. More than 700 alphabetical entries are arranged in dictionary format; they include authors, titles, illustrators, and subjects. The title entry provides the most complete information. Following the bibliographic citations are plot summary annotations, critical evaluations, descriptions of characters and settings, identification of special motifs, names of sequels, and lists of awards. Appendixes provide a list of books and authors by country and a list of books classified by award(s) received. Any children's literature collection would be enhanced by this valuable, comprehensive coverage of meritorious children's books from English-speaking countries besides the United States and Great Britain.

6.   Helbig, Alethea K., and Agnes Regan Perkins, eds. **The Phoenix Award of the Children's Literature Association: 1990-1994.** Lanham, MD: Scarecrow, 1996. 282p. ISBN 0-8108-3191-0.

This is an update of the 1993 edition honoring distinguished children's literature. The Phoenix Award was established in 1985 as a way to honor praiseworthy books written for children published in the previous twenty years that did not receive a major award. To correct this oversight, the Phoenix Awards are presented annually to the authors of children's books deserving of recognition for exemplary literary quality. The books being spotlighted represent a variety of genres and styles. Winners are listed in chronological order and each entry contains a brief plot summary with critical comments; a copy of the acceptance speech; the text of papers presented in recognition of the award-winning and honor book; a bibliography of the author's children's books; and biographical information. Because the books included are still read and enjoyed by children everywhere, this is a valuable addition to any library collection.

7.   Jones, Dolores Blythe. **Children's Literature Awards and Winners: A Directory of Prizes, Authors and Illustrators.** 3rd ed. Detroit: Neal-Schuman with Gale, 1994. 671p. indexes. ISBN 0-8103-6900-4. ISSN 0749-3096.

The author has combined organization of information and comprehensive indexes to help the reader locate information. The directory is arranged into four sections: a directory of awards, including the sponsoring organizations; a section on the history and purpose of each award, with criteria for selection; an author/illustrator section with biographical information; and selected bibliographies for further reading. The four separate indexes are arranged alphabetically by awards, subjects, authors/illustrators, and titles. The thoroughness with which Jones has researched information on awards for children's literature is commendable. This would be a valuable reference source for any collection.

8.   Smith, Laura. **Children's Book Awards International: A Directory of Awards and Winners, from Inception Through 1990.** Jefferson, NC: McFarland, 1992. 671p. indexes. ISBN 0-89950-686-0.

The international scope and the comprehensive coverage of this guide provide information on children's book awards that are less well known and often difficult to locate, together with those that are universally recognized. The alphabetically arranged directory provides data about approximately 11,000 awards and their winners. In conjunction with the names of the award winners and book titles, entries include such information as the sponsoring organization, date of the award's inception, the name of the contact person, criteria for selection, what constitutes the award, and the purpose of the award. Indexes are by author, title, illustrator, and sponsor.

The magnitude and scope of this publication is impressive. The Children's Book Council publication (see entry 1) provides similar information; however, it is not as comprehensive.

THE NEWBERY AND CALDECOTT AWARDS

9.   Ammon, Bette D., and Gale W. Sherman. **Handbook for the Newbery Medal and Honor Books, 1980-1989.** Hagerstown, MD: Alleyside Press, 1991. 276p. illus. indexes. ISBN 0-913853-15-1.

Locating an annotated list of the Newbery award winners is basically a simple task, but Ammon and Sherman have given us more than just factual information about the award. A brief history of the Newbery Award introduces the text, followed by suggested reading strategies for using literature in the classroom. The thirty-six award-winning entries, alphabetically arranged, provide the bibliographic citation, genre, themes, readability, interest level, reviews, author and illustrator information, and a plot summary. Each entry includes ideas for enrichment activities to stimulate the reader's enjoyment and interaction with the text. The ideas are designed to help in planning programs that will stretch the child's creative and imaginative talents and call upon higher-level thinking skills. A bibliography of other books with similar content/themes is provided. The appendix, which furnishes location information for the resources and materials suggested in the enrichment activities, is particularly noteworthy.

For the teacher/library media specialist or the parent seeking to turn children on to books and reading, Ammon and Sherman provide a warehouse of ideas. In view of the emerging technologies and computerized information bases now available, an update is desirable.

10.   Association for Library Service to Children (ALSC). **The Newbery and Caldecott Awards: A Guide to the Medal and Honor Books.** 1996 ed. Chicago: American Library Association, 1996. 145p. illus. indexes. ISBN 0-8389-3460-9. ISSN 1070-4493.

The current edition of the highly respected ALSC series continues as a favorite first choice for those seeking brief information about the prestigious Newbery and Caldecott Medal and Honor Book selections awarded annually. An introductory essay titled "Frederick G. Melcher: A Remembrance" was written by his grandson, Frederick Melcher II. Sections on terms, definitions, and the significance of the awards provide answers to many often-asked questions. Entries are arranged chronologically from the inception of each award—1922 for the Newbery Award and 1938 for the Caldecott Award. Each entry includes the title, author, publisher, and a brief annotation. Portraits of the award winners and photographs of the front cover of the award-winning books accompany the entries for the recent winners. Indexes are arranged by author/illustrator and title. This easy-to-use, inexpensive paperback is a must for all libraries serving children.

11. Brown, Muriel W., and Rita Schock Foudray. **Newbery and Caldecott Medalists and Honor Book Winners: Bibliographies and Resource Materials Through 1991.** 2nd ed. Jim Roginski, ed. New York: Neal-Schuman, 1992. 511p. indexes. ISBN 1-55570-118-3.

This is an easy-to-use guide to the 327 authors and illustrators who were awarded the Newbery and Caldecott Medals and those who received the Honor Book awards. Entries, arranged alphabetically by author, include the standard bibliographic citation, an annotation, the location of the original manuscript, suggested background reading, and articles about each award recipient. This valuable reference source is a guide for the serious researcher and the interested layperson.

12. Comfort, Claudette Hegel. **Distinguished Children's Literature: The Newbery & Caldecott Winners—The Books and Their Creators.** Minneapolis, MN: T. S. Denison, 1993. 260p. illus. ISBN 0-5130-1965-0.

Although this is not a scholarly publication, its oversized physical format and the simple, easy-to-read annotations provide a reference work children can search independently. Winners of the Newbery and Caldecott Awards and honor recipients are arranged in chronological order, and each title entry consists of a complete bibliographic citation, a brief plot summary, and some biographical information. The many illustrations enhance the text. The lack of an index does not appear to be a drawback in using the book.

13. Kingman, Lee, ed. **Newbery and Caldecott Medal Books, 1976-1985.** Boston: Hornbook, 1986. 321p. illus. indexes. ISBN 0-87675-004-8.

The reader seeking information about the Newbery and Caldecott Award books for the years 1976 to 1985 will find this an excellent authority. The editor's preface refers to changes in themes and issues reflected in children's books, for example, current events that have an impact on the unstable world of today's youth. In spite of changes seen in the themes and vocabularies of many current books published for children, Kingman emphasizes that the basic purpose and criteria for honoring distinguished American children's books with a Newbery or Caldecott Medal remain the same.

Each entry includes the standard bibliographic citation, a lengthy, well-written, easy-to-follow plot summary, biographical information with portrait, and the text of the recipient's acceptance speech. The inclusion of essays on literature for children by Barbara Bader, Ethel Heins, and Zena Sutherland, highly respected experts in the field of literature for children, provides an additional element of excellence.

14.   Sharkey, Paulette Bochnig. **Newbery and Caldecott Medal and Honor Books in Other Media.** Jim Roginski, ed. New York: Neal-Schuman, 1992. 160p. indexes. ISBN 1-55570-119-1.

In response to interest in alternative ways for children to enjoy the award-winning Newbery and Caldecott books, their texts and illustrations have been converted to diverse media formats, including video and audiocassettes, filmstrips, large print books, Braille, posters, postcards, television programs, and even bookmarks. Medal and Honor Books that have been produced in an alternate format are in the bibliography. In some instances multiple formats are available for a single title, each of which is included with complete bibliographic information. Available taped interviews with the award-winning authors and illustrators are also included. Because computers have virtually become standard equipment in schools and homes, a listing of CD-ROMs related to children's books, authors, and illustrators is needed for inclusion in any planned update.

INDIVIDUAL AWARDS
FOR CHILDREN'S LITERATURE

15.   Smith, Henrietta M. **The Coretta Scott King Awards Book: From Vision to Reality.** Chicago: American Library Association, 1994. 113p. illus. portraits. index. ISBN 0-8389-3441-2.

The year 1994 was celebrated as the anniversary date for two very important events in the history of African American culture: the fortieth anniversary of the *Brown v. Board of Education of Topeka* Supreme Court decision and the twenty-fifth anniversary of the Coretta Scott King Awards. In 1970 Glydon Flynt Greer, a school librarian, began the initial steps toward increasing the American public's awareness of children's books by and about African Americans. The result was the inauguration of the Coretta Scott King Awards, granted in recognition of outstanding contributions to literature for children by African American authors and illustrators. The name selected for the award was chosen to honor Mrs. Coretta Scott King for her courage and determination in working for peace. Smith has chosen a distinctive approach to depict how the goal of the Coretta Scott King Awards has been accomplished and, at the same time, provide interesting bibliographic access to the medal and honor recipients. In the section discussing the author awards, the author's name and the title of the book for which the award was received are entered in reverse chronology from the most recent winner to the year 1970, when the first awards were presented. Brief plot summaries are given with critical comments to help the user understand those qualities for which the recognition was given. Nestled about halfway into the listing of award winners is an interesting essay, "Conversation with Patricia McKissack," twice a Coretta Scott King Awards recipient. Nineteen color plates from both medal and honor book winners introduce a section discussing books recognized for their illustrations. Each entry incorporates, in addition to the plot summaries, brief descriptions of the illustrations and comments on the artistic style and techniques used in producing the illustrations. Biographical sketches, with portraits, of sixty-one of the award and honor winners precede the author and title index.

Chapter 2

Recommended Reading

BEST BOOKS

16. **Adventuring with Books: A Booklist for Pre-K–Grade 6.** Julie Jenson and Nancy L. Roser, eds. 10th ed. Urbana, IL: National Council of Teachers of English for the Committee on the Elementary School Booklist, 1992. 603p. indexes. ISBN 0-8141-0079-1.

The specified purpose of this reference source is to help teachers, librarians, and parents introduce books of exceptional literary quality, artistic merit, and strong appeal to children from preschool age through sixth grade. The use of children's books in the classroom is currently emerging as the heart of language arts programs and is also becoming an integral part of other school curricula. Guides to selection of quality literature, such as this publication, are essential tools.

Jenson and Roser reviewed books published between 1988 and 1992, seeking to discover popular themes, newer art techniques, and subjects not previously addressed in the world of children's literature, such as "cultural diversity" and "environmental concerns." A well-designed table of contents allows the user to access the many topics easily. Two thousand books are classed into thirteen age-level groupings with numbers assigned sequentially within each chapter to the alphabetically entered authors. Standard bibliographic citations, descriptive annotations, and interest levels are included. Appendixes list awards for children's literature and a directory of publishers. Although the entries are succinct, they are also informative. In view of the fact that *Adventuring with Books* is in its tenth edition, its importance to the world of books and reading is self-evident.

The eleventh edition is now available: *Adventuring with Books: A Booklist for Pre-K–Grade 6.* Wendy K. Sutton, ed. 11th ed. Urbana, IL: National Council of Teachers of English for the Committee on the Elementary School Booklist, 1997. 401p. indexes. ISBN 0-8141-0080-5.

17. Apseloff, Marilyn Fain. **They Wrote for Children Too: An Annotated Bibliography of Children's Literature by Famous Writers for Adults.** New York: Greenwood, 1989. 202p. indexes. ISBN 0-313-2598-1-X.

Apseloff's guide to recommended best books for children takes a unique approach. She identifies books for children written by prominent literary figures known primarily as writers of adult literature; they range from Beowulf to Dylan Thomas. Literature formats include poetry, novels, picture books, drama, biography and autobiography, informational literature, fantasy, mythology, legends,

realistic fiction, and adventure fiction. Initial organization of entries is by time periods: pre-nineteenth century, nineteenth century, and twentieth century. Within
each time period, entries are divided first by genre and then alphabetically by
author. The reader will be surprised to discover the names of many authors with
whom they are familiar as writers of adult books.

18.   Arbuthnot, May Hill, et al. **Children's Books Too Good to Miss.**
New York: University Press, 1979. 87p. index. illus. ISBN
0-8295-0287-4.

May Hill Arbuthnot is renowned for her contributions to the world of literature for children. Her depth of understanding of books and children and her
knowledge of what children enjoy reading has been demonstrated in her textbooks
for the study of children's literature. The authors identify a list of books whose appeal never diminishes, many of which are considered classics. Books selected are
those they believe every child should experience, without regard for date of publication. A good balance between the old and new has been achieved. A selective,
easy-to-use list of quality children's books has been provided in this small but
valuable publication. Although the copyright date is more than fifteen years old,
the titles are still appropriate for today's children.

19.   Association for Library Service to Children (ALSC). **Notable Children's Books: 1976-1980.** Chicago: American Library Association, 1986. 70p. indexes. ISBN 0-8389-3333-5.

In this update of ALSC's *Notable Children's Books*, the Reevaluation
Committee deleted titles that did not stand the test of time and many new titles
were added. Selections made by the committee are books that are worthy of note;
exhibit creativity; have good plot development; are of literary quality; demonstrate
originality of text and illustrations; reflect clarity of text; and, to be sure, appeal to
children. The 290 books listed are organized into the following categories: biography, fantasy, information, poetry, realism, and traditional literature. The guide is
well organized for ease of use. The moderate price and the quality of the books recommended make this guide a valuable addition to any library collection.

20.   Barker, Keith, ed. **Information Books for Children.** 2nd ed.
Brookfield, VT: Scholar Press, 1995. 283p. indexes. ISBN
1-85982-072-2.

With the burgeoning number of new children's books published annually,
selecting the most appropriate source to use in locating specific information is a
difficult and time-consuming task. To provide a guide for making appropriate selections, the author has classified approximately 1,500 informational books written for children ages three to sixteen into twelve subject areas, using the Dewey
Decimal Classification system as a guide. Each entry provides bibliographic data,
a descriptive and evaluative annotation, published reviews of the book, and recommended age levels. Added features are author and photographer profiles and
author, title, and subject indexes.

21. Barstow, Barbara, and Judith Riggle. **Beyond Picture Books: A Guide to First Readers.** 2nd ed. New Providence, NJ: R. R. Bowker, 1995. 501p. index. ISBN 0-8352-3519-X.

Making the transition from picture books to first readers can be a challenge to both the young reader and the adult offering reading guidance. This reference book helps bridge that gap. First readers, defined as books at first- and second-grade-level readability, are characteristically part of a series, use large print, are usually well illustrated, and contain short sentences with appropriate grade-level vocabulary. Barstow and Riggle have selected books that are well-written, accurate and attractive and whose subject matter reflects the interests of this age group. The second edition of *Beyond Picture Books* describes 2,495 titles, 85 percent of which are new to the list. The entries, assigned location numbers, are arranged alphabetically by author. A standard bibliographic citation is followed by recommended subject headings, readability level, and a brief annotation. As an extra treat, a list of the 200 most outstanding first readers is presented. Indexes by subject, title, illustrator, and readability level complete the book. This reference source is now available on the Bowker CD-ROM, *Children's Reference PLUS.* The overall quality of this publication distinguishes it as a valuable reference source for any collection.

22. Carr, Jo, comp. **Beyond Fact: Nonfiction for Children and Young People.** Chicago: American Library Association, 1982. 224p. ISBN 0-8389-0348-7.

Carr decries the lack of attention that nonfiction receives in homes, schools, and public libraries. Although studies have shown that more nonfiction than fiction books are checked out from school library media centers, a review of the recipients of awards and honors reflects the infrequency with which nonfiction titles are chosen. The author uses clever, interest-grabbing chapter titles to introduce her bibliographies of recommended nonfiction books. The following chapter headings illustrate her approach to "hooking children" on nonfiction: "Books as Instruments of Intelligence"; "Science: The Excitement"; "History: The Past Realized, Remembered and Enjoyed"; "Biography: Facts Wanted"; "Controversy: An Active, Healthy Skepticism." Each chapter begins with a discussion of the topic and its appeal to children. Bibliographic citations and annotations accompany each title.

Although McElmeel's nonfiction bibliography (see entry 47) is more current, Carr's discussion of nonfiction as a major reading interest of children should not be overlooked. The two books could well be used in conjunction with one another.

23. Cascardi, Andrea E. **Good Books to Grow On: A Guide to Building Your Child's Library from Birth to Age 5.** New York: Warner Books, 1985. 130p. indexes. ISBN 0-446-38173-Xpa.

The author believes that a child who early in life is provided with the opportunity to learn to love books and reading will become a lifetime reader. She seeks to challenge parents to action by providing suggestions for choosing books for the first five years of the child's life. Recommended books are categorized into six chapters, which are organized by age groupings. Bibliographic citations, followed by an

annotation, are arranged alphabetically by author. Subsequent chapters include information for locating the recommended books, a complete list of the Caldecott
Medal winners and Honor Books, and a bibliography of sources used by the author
in her research. Although the goal of this work was well met, an update is needed.

24.   **Choices: A Core Collection for Young Reluctant Readers.** Peg
       Glisson and Sharon Salluzzo, eds. Vol. 3. Evanston, IL: John Gor-
       don Burke, 1994. 272 p. indexes. ISBN 0-93427-230-1.
       This bibliography focuses on books to be used to encourage reluctant read-
ers, defined as individuals who are able to read but are not motivated to do so, to
become "eager readers." Of the 500 titles listed in volume 1,275 are retained in
volume 2. A major criterion used in the selection process was that books must have
high interest levels, such as books about vampires, mystery books, and high-
adventure books. In fact, a high interest level often took priority over quality of
writing; however comic book types of literature are not included. The books recommended reflect topics and titles that are appealing to capable but less-than-
enthusiastic readers; books listed under subject headings such as "Guaranteed
Hits" and "Attention Grabbers" are bound to draw their attention. Although the information contained in *Choices* is very useful, the format and small size of the
print detract somewhat from its ease of use.
       A new volume is scheduled for 1997: *Choices: A Core Collection for
Young Reluctant Readers.* Beverly Fahey and Maureen Whalen, eds. Vol. 4. Evan-
ston, IL: John Gordon Burke, 1997. ISBN 0-93427-236-0.

25.   Colborn, Candy. **What Do Children Read Next? A Reader's
       Guide to Fiction for Children.** Detroit, MI: Gale Research, 1994.
       1135p. illus. index. ISBN 0-8103-8886-3.
       Colborn has designed an advisory guide to help match readers from grades
one to eight with books that mirror their interests and inspire them to read. An
overview essay furnishes a brief history of children's literature and describes current trends in writing for children. With popular reading interests in mind, the
1,928 books listed in the section entitled "Other Books You Might Like" were selected to encourage young readers to explore new authors and new titles. More
than half the books were published within the last five years, and the remainder
have stood the test of time. In addition to standard bibliographic information, each
entry includes the period and geographical locale of the story, character names,
character descriptions, and a brief plot summary. Adding to the merit of this work
are ten indexes that reflect a variety of information, such as a time period index and
a locale index. The reader will find it difficult to set aside this fascinating book.

26.   Cullinan, Bernice E. **Let's Read About Finding Books They'll
       Love to Read.** New York: Scholastic, 1993. 182p. ISBN
       0-590-47462-6.
       According to the author, each child experiences his or her own unique way
of becoming a reader. It is incumbent upon adults working with children to discover and build upon that process. They need to know how to use it to open the
reading world to the child and to hook him or her into becoming a lifetime reader.

Chapters 1 through 6 are discussions of ways in which the adult can establish an environment to encourage and facilitate achieving this goal. Subsequent chapters are bibliographies, intended for children from preschool to age twelve, with book recommendations for "books they'll love." Although most of the titles included in the list are current publications, books that remain popular with children today also are included. Readers will, no doubt, find books on the list that they considered their favorites in their childhood.

27. Donavin, Denise Perry, ed. **Best of the Best for Children: Books, Magazines, Videos, Audio, Software, Toys, Travel.** New York: Random House, 1992. 366p. indexes. ISBN 0-679-40450-3; 0-679-74250-6pa.

In the preface the editor explains that children need to have the opportunity to read, see, hear, and interact with books to help them grow intellectually and to stimulate their creative skills. The impact of emerging technologies is seen as a major influence on children's interests and tastes; they are experiencing a world quite different from that into which their parents were born. To reflect the changing world of the printed medium, the publishing industry has responded by developing alternative formats through which children can approach the new and wonderful adventures found in books and reading. The intent of this work is to furnish a selective list of books available in print and nonprint formats and to identify other formats that can be used to bring children and good books together.

Chapters are organized by type of medium. Within each chapter, entries are first listed according to age levels and then alphabetically by title. In addition to the bibliographic citation, pertinent details indicate why that title was selected for the bibliography. Critical comments address both the quality of the production and its "child-appeal." The indexes are well organized and contain good cross references.

This guide's convenient format makes it easy for users to follow any book title from its first entry in the bibliography to other formats in which it has been produced, such as video and audiocassette. With the ever-increasing number of children's books becoming available on video, current bibliographies of this type will continue to serve as good guides for selecting and evaluating quality items.

28. Elleman, Barbara, ed. **Children's Books of International Interest.** 3rd ed. Chicago: American Library Association for the Association of Library Service to Children, 1984. 101p. indexes. ISBN 0-8389-3314-9.

Elleman's book evolved as a means of promoting and strengthening international understanding and interaction through publicizing literature for children. It serves as a selective guide to more than 300 books produced in the United States and that have been recommended for translation into other languages. An important criterion used in the selection process is the identification of books that children the world over can appreciate and that also promote understanding of the United States by children of other countries. Selection guidelines require titles of high quality with universal themes, titles with quality child-appeal, and those that depict the American way of life. Titles are organized into broad categories carefully selected to reflect the major reading interests of children, for example, folklore, fiction, biography, poetry, history, people and places, and science and nature. Entries consist of the standard bibliographic citation, a brief annotation with critical evaluations, and a recommended age level. A directory of publishers; a combined author, illustrator, and title index; and a separate subject index complete the text.

29. Estes, Sally, ed. **Popular Reading for Children, III: A Collection of *Booklist* Columns.** Chicago: American Library Association, 1992. 64p. indexes. ISBN 0-8389-7599-2.

This is the third in a series of compilations of "popular reading" columns from *Booklist*, the American Library Association's review periodical. This edition covers seven years of the popular reading lists for children, from 1985 to 1992. Each list is devoted to a single subject and has a catchy title such as "Eerie Reading," "Beasts and More," "Shades of the Past," and "Chucklebait." The primary criteria used in the selection of entries are their appeal to children and the appropriateness or relevance of the subject matter. Standard books and classics are accompanied by more recently published books. Books within each category are further divided into broad age groups, and each standard bibliographic citation is followed by an annotated plot summary that includes interesting critical comments.

This book is an excellent, inexpensive handbook for teachers, parents, and librarians interested in guiding the "eager young reader" to appealing as well as quality titles.

30. Ettlinger, John R. T., and Diana L. Spirt. **Choosing Books for Young People: A Guide to Criticism and Bibliography: 1976-1984.** Vol. 2. Phoenix, AZ: Oryx, 1984. 168p. ISBN 0-89774-247-8.

This bibliography of bibliographies lists books that evaluate children's literature and that recommend informational, instructional, and recreational books. It is a key to 415 books, published between 1977 and 1984, that select, describe, and criticize books for children and youth. Bibliographic citations and brief annotations are provided for each entry. The determination of the value and usefulness of each title as a reference source is furnished.

31. Gillespie, John T., and Corinne J. Naden, eds. **Best Books for Children: Preschool Through Grade 6.** 5th ed. New Providence, NJ: R. R. Bowker/Reed Reference, 1994. 1411p. indexes. ISBN 0-8352-3455-X.

The editors of this new edition of the highly regarded Best Books for Children series have maintained the high standards established in previous editions. In addition to the 15,647 individually selected and evaluated books cited, more than half of which are new to this edition, the editors have incorporated suggestions for recreational and curricular activities for a variety of age levels. Books are categorized into eight major subject headings and then subdivided more specifically. Each book, entered alphabetically by author, is numbered sequentially and includes a complete bibliographic citation, a one-line description, and citations to at least two reviews. Indexes are by author, illustrator, title, subject, and grade level.

The extensive number of entries in this edition may at first appear overwhelming, but in its function as a comprehensive contemporary source of recommendations for best books, it is a leader in the field. A sixth edition is currently in process.

This reference source is now available on the Bowker CD-ROM, *Children's Reference PLUS.*

32. Hearne, Betsy. **Choosing Books for Children: A Commonsense Guide.** rev. ed. New York: Delacorte, 1990. 228p. illus. index. ISBN 0-385-30084-0; 0-385-30108-1pa.

Books are a bridge that can connect the developing minds of young children to the exciting world around them. To help the parent and teacher build this bridge, the author has provided some commonsense guidelines to use in the selection of children's books. The chapters are organized by topics with titles ranging from picture books to teenage titles. In addition to the annotated list of recommended books, each chapter contains guidelines for selecting other books with similar themes.

The author's understanding of children and her knowledge of techniques to encourage them to become lifetime readers, regardless of age, is evident throughout. The quality of the ideas presented and her encouragement and enthusiasm for choosing the "right" book are noteworthy.

33. **High Interest—Easy Reading: An Annotated Booklist for Middle School and Senior High School.** Patricia Phelan, ed. Urbana, IL: National Council of Teachers of English, 1996. 115p. indexes. ISBN 0-8141-2098-2pa.

The National Council of Teachers of English, recognizing the need to identify books that encourage nonreaders and reluctant readers to develop good reading habits, formed a revision committee to update an earlier publication by the council. The committee selected books using the following criteria: the book is appropriate for a wide range of ages; the plots generate excitement and suspense, have likable characters, and have plenty of adventure. Approximately 300 books are entered under nineteen well-defined categories, including such titles as "Growing Up," "Issues of Our Times," and "Sports." Entries, arranged alphabetically by author, include a bibliographic citation and an annotation. Author and title indexes provide quick access for the user. Appendixes include award-winning books and a directory of publishers.

34. Hobson, Margaret, and Jennifer Madden. **Children's Fiction Sourcebook.** 2nd ed. Brookfield, VT: Scholar Press, 1995. 342p. indexes. ISBN 1-85982-083-8.

Approximately 150 of the best and most popular children's authors and their books have been included in this publication designed to serve as a guide to English-language fiction for children ages six to thirteen years. Although the bias is toward authors of the United Kingdom, all English-speaking countries are well represented. Author entries, listed alphabetically, include biographical information and awards received. Books by each author are entered in reverse chronological order. Discussion of classics, series, awards, and television tie-ins are located in the remaining chapters. Because children often become enthusiastic about reading everything by a favorite author, the author entry approach is especially useful. Hobson and Madden have generated a valuable one-stop source for recommendations of children's books.

35.   International Reading Association (IRA). **Kids' Favorite Books: Children's Choices: 1989-1991.** Newark, DE: International Reading Association/Children's Book Council, 1992. 96p. index.

More than 2,000 children at various test sites participate in the reading program to evaluate approximately 500 recently published books. Their reactions are assessed, and the final selections are narrowed to about 100 titles. The selections are published annually in the "Children's Choices" section of IRA's publication *The Reading Teacher. Kids' Favorite Books* is the compilation of three years of "Children's Choices." Entries are separated into recommended reading levels, starting with beginning readers and moving on to older readers, with a "catch-all" section for titles labeled as appropriate for all ages.

This inexpensive booklet is a great idea for a gift. Engaging children in the process of identifying their own "favorites" is sure to appeal to young readers.

36.   International Reading Association (IRA). **More Kids' Favorite Books: A Compilation of Children's Choices: 1992-1994.** Newark, DE: International Reading Association/Children's Book Council, 1995. 132p. indexes. illus. ISBN 0-87207-130-8.

"Children's Choices" is an annual list of new children's books that children from around the United States have chosen as their favorites (see entry 35). *More Kids' Favorite Books*, a compilation of the annual lists, provides more than 300 titles of "favorites" for children from ages four to thirteen. Reading-level groupings range from picture books, beginning readers, and developing readers to books for young adults. Each entry provides bibliographic information, an annotation, and information on illustrations. The indexes are by author, illustrator, and title.

37.   International Reading Association (IRA). **Teachers' Favorite Books for Kids: Teacher's Choices, 1989-1993.** Newark, DE: International Reading Association, 1994. 100p. indexes. illus. ISBN 0-87207-389-0.

Teachers' Favorite Books for Kids is a compilation of five years of the annual "Teachers' Choices" list selected by the Teachers' Choice Committee of the International Reading Association. The selection process involves teachers and librarians around the United States. Every book is read and rated by six or more people, and many are read by as many as 200 teachers and librarians. The ratings are collected and collated by the committee and published in annotated form in November issues of *The Reading Teacher*. The goal is to identify books that introduce students to ideas and issues and encourage them to ask questions about the world in which they live. Each book is evaluated for merit in style, content, structure, beauty of language, and quality of presentation. More than 150 books have been chosen and classified by primary, intermediate, and advanced age levels. A bibliographic citation and an annotation accompany each book entry.

This is an excellent selection of recommended books published within the last few years. The quality of the recommendations and the booklet's nominal cost distinguish it as a must-purchase item for every library serving children. Other booklets produced by the IRA are *Children's Choices* (see entries 35 and 36) and *Young Adult Choices.*

38. Kobrin, Beverly. **Eyeopeners! How to Choose and Use Children's Books About Real People, Places and Things.** New York: Viking Penguin, 1988. 317p. illus. indexes. ISBN 0-670-82073-3; ISBN 0-14-046830-7pa.

Only occasionally are bibliographies devoted to recommended nonfiction books. *Eyeopeners!* responds to this deficiency. The introduction provides inspiration and guidance for the user, with clues to serve as guides in the selection of nonfiction books. The 500 nonfiction titles for which there are critical reviews are organized into 61 categories that extend across a variety of issues. Some of the issues, such as sex, racism, and substance abuse, are controversial in nature. Each entry includes a brief annotation and tips to help parents and teachers construct interesting activities with which to extend the topic. The Quick-Link index is a detailed subject, author, title, and illustrator index. This very practical bibliography should prove to be a valuable addition to school and public library collections.

39. Kobrin, Beverly. **Eyeopeners II: Children's Books to Answer Children's Questions About the World Around Them.** New York: Scholastic, 1995. 305p. indexes. ISBN 0-590-48402-8.

In *Eyeopeners II* Kobrin maintains her goal of opening the eyes of children to good nonfiction books. She suggests that the more than 800 books she includes are "a delight to look at, a pleasure to read, and a source of fascinating information." She sought imaginative, enriching, and informative books. Teachers and library media specialists are her target audience, but she suggests that parents and other caregivers will reap benefits as well. The titles are entered under 50 topics that appeal to children's interests, running the gamut from AIDS and airplanes to wolves, jackals, foxes and words. Many entries are accompanied by tips for useful and fun follow-up activities for parents as well as teachers and library media specialists. The author's style of presentation, selection of interesting and informative titles, and her personal reflections establish this as a valuable reference source for anyone working with children and reading.

40. Landsberg, Michele. **Reading for the Love of It: Best Books for Young Readers.** New York: Prentice Hall, 1987. 327p. indexes. ISBN 0-13-579822-1.

The author of this interesting guide aspires to encourage adults to discover how good literature can enhance a child's life. This selective bibliography of books that will open up a world of discovery to children fulfills her goal. Selections were carefully chosen to a balance of boys and girls as central characters. Chapter headings include "Books to Encourage the Beginning Reader," "First Novels," "Liberating Laughter," "The Quest for Identity," and five other thematic titles. Each entry includes an annotation and recommended age level. Although selections were made based on quality rather than popularity, it is gratifying to observe that the majority of titles listed are, indeed, popular choices with children. A newer edition is available, also by Landsberg: *Reading for the Love of It: Best Books for Young Readers.* New York: Prentice Hall, 1989. 227p. indexes. ISBN 0-13-755125-8.

Another recommended reading guide by the same author, primarily for use by parents, is *Michele Landsberg's Guide to Children's Books: With a Treasury of More Than 350 Great Children's Books* (New York: Penguin Books, 1985).

41.   Liggett, Twila C., and Cynthia Mayer Benfield. **The Reading Rainbow Guide to Children's Books: The 101 Best Titles.** New York: Citadel Press, 1994. 248p. illus. indexes. ISBN 1-55972-222-3; 0-8065-1493-0pa.

From its inception, the goal of the Reading Rainbow program has been to bring the world of literature and the magic of the written word to children through the medium of television. Discovery of new horizons and new worlds of enjoyment can come by way of televised book presentations as well as by way of the traditional print format.

Following a brief introduction to the behind-the-scenes world of Reading Rainbow, the author explains how the "101 best" titles were selected from the more than 400 Reading Rainbow books. Entries are arranged into nineteen content/theme headings, including "Multicultural" and "Physically Challenged." Within each entry is a bibliographic citation, an annotation, a description of the lead-in for the Reading Rainbow televised version, and a picture of the book cover. A complete Reading Rainbow book list is included as well as indexes by author, title, and subject. Reading Rainbow book choices have proved, over the years, to be of the highest caliber, and this selection of the best is impressive.

The new, updated edition of the Reading Rainbow guide by Liggett and Benfield is now available: *The Reading Rainbow Guide to Children's Books: The 101 Best Titles.* rev. ed. New York: Citadel Press, 1996. illus. indexes. ISBN 0-8065-1796-4.

42.   Lindskoog, John, and Kathryn Lindskoog. **How to Grow a Young Reader: A Parents' Guide to Books for Kids.** Wheaton, IL: Harold Shaw, 1989. 182p. index. ISBN 0-87788-353-X.

In the preface the authors state that through books one learns the wonder of the ordinary and the joy of sharing the thoughts and experiences of all kinds of people. To help parents offer this exciting experience to children, the authors have developed a browsing guide to the best for children in all the following categories: poetry—"Rhyme and Reason"; fantasy—"Flights of Fancy"; classics—"Tried and True"; realistic fiction and biography—"Steps in Time"; picture books—"Open Eyes"; and Christian values—"Open Hearts." Descriptive and evaluative comments follow each title.

43.   Lipson, Eden Ross. *The New York Times* **Parent's Guide to the Best Books for Children.** Rev. and updated. New York: Times Books/Random House, 1991. 464p. illus. indexes. ISBN 0-8129-1889-4.

Lipson's book is designed to alleviate the difficulty in choosing the right book for a child, especially in view of the great number of new children's books published annually. Using the Children's Book Section of the *New York Times*, Lipson has identified 101 books published in the United States as the "best." Selection criteria is not based on awards or prizes received, but rather on "intrigue and delight." The list is a compilation of classics, long-time favorites, and distinguished and popular new titles. Recommendations apply to children of all ages and all genres of books. Selections, made by a panel of judges, are organized into six broad book categories: wordless, picture book, storybook, early reading, middle reading, and young adult reading books. Titles, entered alphabetically by author, are assigned sequential numbers. Entries include the standard bibliographic citation, plot summaries with introspective comments, details of special recognitions received, and references to similar or related titles. A comprehensive subject index accompanies the author and title indexes. This interesting, well-organized book should be in every library serving children.

44.   Mahoney, Ellen, and Leah Wilcox. **Ready, Set, Read: Best Books to Prepare Preschoolers.** Metuchen, NJ: Scarecrow, 1985. 348p. indexes. ISBN 0-8108-1684-9.

To help parents select books to encourage preschool children to develop positive attitudes toward reading, the authors have prepared a bibliography of recommended books and suggestions to help parents involve their children in the reading experience. They contend that sharing the pleasure of good stories and illustrations sets the stage for a lifetime love of reading and is also a bonding experience between the child and parent. The text is organized into five sections on the progressive stages of child growth and development, from infancy to the four- and five-year-old stage. Within each stage are listed stories, poetry, songs, language activities, and games to use with the stories. Among the titles recommended are both classics and recent publications. Parents/caregivers are given guidelines for implementing good preparatory reading programs.

45.   McElmeel, Sharron L. **Educator's Companion to Children's Literature, Volume 1: Mysteries, Animal Tales, Books of Humor, Adventure Stories, and Historical Fiction.** Englewood, CO: Libraries Unlimited, 1995. 151p. ISBN 1-56308-329-9.

46.   McElmeel, Sharron L. **Educator's Companion to Children's Literature, Volume 2: Folklore, Contemporary Realistic Fiction, Fantasy, Biographies, and Tales from Here and There.** Englewood, CO: Libraries Unlimited, 1996. 160p. ISBN 1-56308-330-2.

Although these volumes are directed toward teachers and school library media specialists, the bibliographies will be equally useful to public librarians and parents. In each volume, book annotations are organized into chapters with titles reflecting the genres identified in the volume subtitle. Chapters are introduced by interesting and provocative discussions of each genre. Entries provide bibliographic information and plot summaries. Biographical vignettes of well-known authors offer many interesting sidelights.

McElmeel's approach to integrating literature and learning to "turn kids on" to reading is appropriate for use by the neophyte as well as the professional in the field of children's literature. (See entry 47 for an additional bibliography by the author.)

47.   McElmeel, Sharron L. **Great New Nonfiction Reads.** Englewood, CO: Libraries Unlimited, 1995. 225p. illus. indexes. ISBN 1-56308-228-4.

Children's natural curiosity about the world in which they live can be encouraged and extended through reading. Therefore it is important that they have access to "the latest and greatest" informational literature. Nonfiction books are no longer the dry, factual, frequently pedantic texts of the past; the newest generation of nonfiction books are more visually attractive and more interesting in format and text. The author has selected more than 100 recently published books with subjects ranging from adoption to karate to wounds and injuries. The chapter entitled "The World of Information Literature" provides recommended guidelines for selecting and using nonfiction literature. The subsequent chapter, "Seeking Information," discusses informational literature in variant formats. An additional 500 nonannotated but recommended titles are listed under one of the more than 100 topics reflecting the most prevalent informational interests of children. Complete bibliographic information is given for each featured title and includes a notation indicating its target audience by age designations. The annotation is followed by a feature entitled "Connections" that lists references to other books with the same or similar topics. The last chapter presents biographical sketches of twenty-two people who have gained prominence and have made significant contributions to society.

McElmeel's guide to current nonfiction serves as an excellent purchasing guide for building nonfiction collections in public and private libraries and also serves as a guide for children seeking information on a special topic.

48.   McGovern, Edythe, and Helen Muller. **They're Never Too Young for Books: A Guide to Children's Books for Ages 1 to 8.** Buffalo, NY: Prometheus Books, 1994. 342p. ISBN 0-87975-858-9.

Adults who strongly believe in the value of reading to the very young know that the process of selecting appropriate books is very important. Differentiation between books of high caliber and those of mediocre quality is improved when established criteria, such as those provided by these authors, are used. Part 1 of the text discusses ways to establish and achieve an amicable environment for children that encourages them to become enthusiastic about books and reading. Part 2 opens with suggestions for establishing a reading program and continues with an extensive bibliography of recommended books, categorized primarily by content/theme. Entries, which are alphabetized by title, provide bibliographic information followed by a brief descriptive annotation. The last section is a bibliography of recommended books for reading aloud. The more than 230 pages of bibliographic citations of approved books provide an excellent source of recommended reading to use with children. Although there is no index, and the format differs somewhat from most bibliographies, this publication provides an easy-to-use guide to book selection for young children.

49. Nodelman, Perry, ed. **Touchstones: Reflections on the Best in Children's Literature.** Vol. 1. Metuchen, NJ: Scarecrow Press with the Children's Literature Association (CLA), 1985. 315p. index. ISBN 0-8108-2561-9.

50. Nodelman, Perry, ed. **Touchstones: Fairy Tales, Fables, Myths, Legends and Poetry: Reflections on the Best in Children's Literature.** Vol. 2. Metuchen, NJ: Scarecrow Press with the Children's Literature Association (CLA), 1987. 236p. index. ISBN 0-8108-2562-7.

51. Nodelman, Perry, ed. **Touchstones: Picturebooks: Reflections on the Best in Children's Literature.** Vol. 3. Metuchen, NJ: Scarecrow Press with the Children's Literature Association (CLA), 1989. 191p. index. ISBN 0-8108-2568-5.
   Nodelman has edited a three-volume set of reflections on distinguished children's books. Each volume is composed of traditional classics and treasured books that he feels everyone should read. The intent of the publication is to give children (and their parents) a sense of familiarity with these highly esteemed books. Discursive essays are written by professionals in the field of children's literature. Volume 1 opens with Matthew Arnold and closes with a discussion of Laura Ingalls Wilder's books. Titles are entered alphabetically by author, accompanied by standard bibliographic information, a plot description, and critical comments by the editor. The entire set is scholarly and will enhance any library collection.

52. Oppenheim, Joanne F., Barbara Brenner, and Betty D. Bolgehold. **Choosing the Right Book for the Right Child at the Right Time.** New York: Ballantine, 1986. 345p. indexes. ISBN 0-345-32683-0.
   An interesting and well-developed discussion of children's literature, entitled "Book Connections," introduces the reader to the importance of finding the right book for a child. The subsequent section is a bibliography of recommended books for children, organized into seven age-level groupings that range from books for babies to books for children ages ten to twelve. Each entry includes brief bibliographic information and a descriptive and evaluative annotation. The concluding section is a purchasing guide to resources for locating the recommended titles cited in the bibliography.

53. Oppenheim, Joanne F., and Stephanie Oppenheim. **The Best Toys, Books and Videos for Kids 1997: 1,000+ Kid-Tested Classics and New Products.** New York: Prima, 1996. 297p. indexes. ISBN 0-76150-705-1.

The focus of this annual publication is explained in its subtitle. The authors have selected "the best of the new, as well as those we consider blue-chip classics." They comment that selecting the best is especially difficult because of the current marketing trend of introducing an increasing number of family-oriented media for the general public. This guide endeavors to be a child-oriented guide to items that have received top-rated recognition in reviewing sources. The main section of the guide is a listing of items by media format, including toys, books, videos, audio (great music and stories), and computer software/CD-ROMs, with subsections under each broad format heading. Entry titles, organized by one of four age groups, are followed by brief annotations. Nonprint media entries include the producer and price. The last chapter is a list of toys for special needs children. Also provided are a list of available top-rated mail-order catalogs and some safety guidelines for using nonprint media with children. A subject, title, and brand-name index completes the work.

The goal of the authors—to produce an easy-to-use, inexpensive guide to reduce the guesswork for those seeking to select "the best for the dollar"—is well met.

54. Spencer, Pam. **What Do Young Adults Read Next? A Reader's Guide to Fiction for Young Adults.** Detroit: Gale Research, 1994. 816p. indexes. ISBN 0-8103-8887-1.

Although the title indicates that this is a reading guide for young adults, a review of the recommended titles discloses a great many books that are appropriate, as well as popular, with upper elementary-age students. The author's objective is to identify and recommend books that reflect the interests of both the reluctant reader and the avid reader. In addition to the entries for 1,500 titles published between 1988 and 1992, listed alphabetically by author, are guides to "other books you might like." Ten indexes provide access to books, using such standard approaches as author, title, subject as well as less common topics such as periods, geographical locations, names of characters, and even character descriptions. This book is worth serious consideration for any library collection used by children.

55. Sutherland, Zena, Betsy Hearne, and Roger Sutton, eds. **The Best in Children's Books.** Chicago: University of Chicago Press, 1991. 492p. indexes. ISBN 0-226-78054-3.

Since the Center for Children's Books was established in 1945 at the University of Chicago, it has served as an eminently respected, authoritative source for review and evaluation of the literary quality of books for children. The University's *Bulletin of the Center for Children's Books* is considered a major review and selection tool. This text is a compilation of 1,046 of the "best books" chosen from issues of the *Bulletin of the Center* between 1985 and 1990. Elements of the selection process include seeking qualities in children's books that foster perceptive thinking and content and formats that appeal to the curiosity of children. Entries are numbered sequentially and listed alphabetically by author. A complete biblio-graphic citation, a recommended age/grade level, and a well-written annotation make up each entry. This work, similar to the Gillespie and Naden book (entry 31), will serve as an invaluable tool for establishing a list of the most highly recom-mended books for children of all ages.

56.   Thomas, James L. **Play, Learn, and Grow: An Annotated Guide to the Best Books and Materials for Very Young Children.** New Providence, NJ: R. R. Bowker, 1992. 439p. indexes. ISBN 0-8352-3019-8.

A team of sixty-four librarians and early childhood education specialists were selected to review and examine more than 5,000 books and other materials for young children. Their goal was to provide a guide to exemplary print and non-print media to be used by parents, librarians, and teachers working with the very young. The final list contains 1,074 titles divided into the following eight catego-ries: concept/counting/alphabet books, folklore/fairy tales, informational books, periodicals, participation and manipulation books, poetry/nursery rhymes/songs, storybooks, and wordless books. Each bibliographic entry includes genre, recom-mended age levels, a brief annotation, reviewing sources, and a purchase priority to serve as a guide in the selection process. Five indexes, including a purchase pri-ority index and a format index, make locating entries easy. Individuals working to bring very young children and books together will find this a worthwhile and infor-mative book.

57.   White, Valerie. **Choosing Your Children's Books: 2 to 5 Years.** Atlanta: Bayley and Musgrave, 1994. 78p. illus. index. ISBN 1-882726-15-4; 1-882726-10-3pa.

58.   White, Valerie. **Choosing Your Children's Books: 5 to 8 Years.** 2nd ed. Atlanta: Bayley and Musgrave, 1994. 78p. illus. index. ISBN 1-882726-13-8; 1-882726-11-1pa.

59.   White, Valerie. **Choosing Your Children's Books: 8 to 12 Years.** Atlanta: Bayley and Musgrave, 1994. 78p. index. ISBN 7-882726-14-6; 1-882726-12-Xpa.

White has produced a series of guides to selecting the best in children's books. Each is a guide to books with the highest-quality writing style, story line, and illustrations. The guides, intended for parents, teachers, and children, are sim-ple, up-to-date, and inexpensive. Each is targeted to a relatively narrow age group and includes books that appeal to the interests and readability levels of the children within that group. One hundred and fifty fiction books, with full bibliographic cita-tions, are entered under one of thirteen subject sections ranging from adventure novels to sports.

60.   Wilson, George, and Joyce Moss. **Books for Children to Read Alone: A Guide for Parents and Librarians.** New York: R. R. Bowker, 1988. 184p. indexes. ISBN 0-8352-2346-9.

This guide incorporates books embodying concepts that appeal to children and whose vocabulary and sentence structure encourage independent reading. The authors maintain that reading alone helps children build self-confidence and establishes a sense of achievement. To affirm their opinions, the authors asked young readers to examine and react to a preselected group of books. The children's responses were analyzed to determine reader interest and readability levels, and their personal comments were integrated into the annotations. More than 350 titles, both fiction and nonfiction, are organized into seven chapters by age levels from early childhood to grade three. The contents are arranged for ease of use and provide many helpful guides for recommending read-alone books.

61.   Winkel, Lois, and Sue Kimmel. **Mother Goose Comes First: An Annotated Guide to Best Books and Recordings for Your Preschool Child.** New York: Henry Holt, 1990. 194p. indexes. ISBN 0-8050-1001-7.

In a society that annually publishes thousands of new books for children, differentiating quality books from mediocre ones is difficult. To rectify this concern, Winkel and Kimmel have developed a practical, easy-to-use guide for people working with preschool children. Broad genre/subject themes, such as nursery rhymes and lullabies, folktales, contemporary classics, and concept books, are used as chapter titles. Entries in each category, arranged alphabetically by author, include the bibliographic citation, a brief description of the text, and typical age ranges. A notation is made when the title is available on tape, including the names of performers. Indexes are by author, illustrator, title, and performer. Readers who recognize that the earlier a child is introduced to books and reading, the more likely he or she is to become a lifetime reader will find this an especially valuable reference resource.

GIFTED AND RELUCTANT READERS

Gifted Readers

62.   Baskin, Barbara H., and Karen Harris. **Books for the Gifted.** New York: R. R. Bowker, 1980. 263p. index. ISBN 0-8352-1161-4; 0-8352-1428-1pa.

One of the most common traits of children identified as "gifted" is a love of reading. Locating books that nurture and challenge their interest, intellect, and curiosity is often difficult. The authors have generated an excellent selection of about 200 books they regard as appropriately intellectually demanding for the gifted child. In the preliminary chapters Baskin and Harris discuss the problem of identifying gifted students and some concerns regarding the expectations and treatment, especially in schools, of these "special" children. Excellent criteria to be used in selecting books are provided in chapter 3. Remaining chapters are bibliographies of recommended books for toddlers to children age twelve. Entries include a bibliographic citation and lengthy descriptive and evaluative annotations. A review of the titles indicates that most of them have the potential for challenging readers by confronting them with abstract concepts and ambiguity and by requiring higher-level reasoning skills. This book is not intended to be exhaustive but rather a beginning.

63.   Hauser, Paula, and Gail A. Nelson. **Books for the Gifted Child.** Vol. 2. New York: R. R. Bowker, 1988. 244p. index. ISBN 0-8352-2467-8.

This volume, covering books published from 1980 to 1987, expands and updates the Baskin and Harris book (see entry 62). The 195 books included focus on cognitively demanding literature that addresses and encourages the reader's imagination and aesthetic sensitivity. Preliminary chapters discuss various aspects of gifted children, such as their attitudes, interests, and need for guidance. The closing chapter presents a selective guide to "Intellectually Challenging Books." Each entry is arranged alphabetically by author and provides a bibliographic citation, recommended age level, and a lengthy descriptive and evaluative annotation. Indexes are by title, subject, and reading level.

This reference source is now available on the Bowker CD-ROM, *Children's Reference PLUS.*

64.   Polette, Nancy. **Books and Real Life: A Guide for Gifted Students and Teachers.** Jefferson, NC: McFarland, 1984. 117p. indexes. ISBN 0-89950-119-2pa.

Polette describes some of the characteristics of gifted children such as reading at an accelerated level; having long attention spans; expressing themselves maturely; adapting easily; and enjoying questioning, reasoning, and probing. She has developed a selective bibliography of realistic books that deal with real-life problems, such as death, illness, family problems, and low self-esteem. In the selection process she sought books that open up discussion, provide problem-solving experiences, approach a situation in a unique way, and are written so that solutions to a problem are not easily apparent.

65.   Polette, Nancy. **Picture Books for Gifted Programs.** Metuchen, NJ: Scarecrow, 1981. 220p. index. ISBN 0-8108-1467-7.

The passing of Public Law 94-142 in 1975, a mandate for mainstreaming special needs children, at the same time brought about a greater awareness of the special needs of the gifted child. Recognizing the dearth of books for gifted children, Polette took a leadership role in the development of guidelines for identifying books for the gifted child and in the generation of bibliographies to serve those working with gifted children. In her introduction she states that picture books embody every productive and critical thinking skill. Building on that statement, she divides her bibliography of recommended picture books into five thinking-skill categories that reflect cognitive development, including visual communication skills, oral communication skills, productive thinking skills, and critical thinking skills. Each category begins with a discussion of the process to be used to develop that skill through literature, followed by an annotated bibliography of relevant book titles. Each entry, arranged alphabetically by author, is critiqued, including Polette's personal comments on its value as a challenge to the gifted child.

The author provides an inventory of good ideas and approaches to encourage children to use critical thinking skills, accompanied by a reservoir of picture books that even today are read enthusiastically by children. Because the picture book continues to be a favorite form of literature for children, an update of this excellent reference source would be enthusiastically received.

Reluctant Readers

66.   Brown, Dorothy. **A World of Books: An Annotated Reading List for ESL/EFL Students.** Washington, DC: Teaching English to Speakers of Other Languages, 1988. 70p. ISBN 0-939791-32-3.

Brown's *A World of Books* is an informational guide to recommended fiction and nonfiction books appropriate for children for whom English is a second language and those for whom English is a foreign language. The number of children and young adults entering public schools in the United States with no, or very minimal, English-speaking skills is escalating. This list, prepared as a response to the special needs of these students, contains titles of books to help them make the transition from their native tongues to the English language and, at the same time, to offer them recreational reading opportunities. A bibliographic entry, plot description, and recommended reading level are provided for each book. The appendixes contain information for locating the books, cross references to book topics and genres, and book titles listed under either the section for short and easy books or the section for advanced readers.

The usefulness of this bibliography in schools experiencing an influx of families from non-English-speaking countries cannot be overstated.

67.   LiBretto, Ellen V., ed. **High/Low Handbook: Encouraging Literacy in the 1990s.** 3rd ed. New York: R. R. Bowker, 1990. 290p. indexes. ISBN 0-8352-2804-5.

The third edition of this beneficial reference source for locating reading materials for the reluctant or disabled reader continues its tradition of excellence. The core collection of more than 400 titles represents a wide variety of topics. A well-organized, easy-to-use checklist of evaluative criteria serves as a guide for the user. Materials include books, periodicals, and computer software. Entries for non-English-speaking people learning English as a Second Language are also provided. Title, subject, reading level, and interest level indexes provide location information. The *High/Low Handbook* is now available on the Bowker CD-ROM, *Children's Reference PLUS.*

This guide presents a beneficial collection of books and other media that are of high interest but not so challenging that the reluctant reader or person with poor reading skills will lose interest.

68.   Pilla, Marianne Laino. **The Best High/Low Books for Reluctant Readers.** Englewood, CO: Libraries Unlimited, 1990. 100p. indexes. ISBN 0-87287-532-6.

The goal of this bibliography is to provide a list of high-quality, easy-to-read, high-interest books with low vocabulary levels, both fiction and nonfiction, to recommend for recreational reading to reluctant readers in grades 3 to 12. The 374 entries are carefully selected to entice the reluctant reader to enjoy reading as a leisurely, pleasurable pastime. The author examined each title for content interest, appealing artwork, a comfortable format, an easy-to-read typeface, and a large variety of subjects. Bibliographic citations include annotations, recommended age levels, reading interest levels, and subject headings.

69.   Ryder, Randall J., Bonnie G. Graves, and Michael F. Graves. **Easy Reading: Book Series and Periodicals for Less Able Readers.** Newark, DE: International Reading Association, 1989. 90p. index. ISBN 0-87207-234-7.

The genre of high-interest/easy-reading books was created specifically for students with poor or no reading skills, according to the authors. Books published to meet the needs of these students are often published as a series, with similar topics, settings, and characters. They tend to have themes that reflect sports, romance, and mysteries. Also available are general-interest periodicals that reflect upper elementary grade interests but are written at a second-grade reading level. The purpose of this bibliography is to provide a convenient reference for selecting high-interest/low-vocabulary materials in a variety of formats for these children. The overview section describes the selection process and criteria used in identifying recommended book series and periodicals. The bibliography contains reviews for forty-four series and fifteen periodicals, listed alphabetically by publisher and then by major series or periodical title. Following the bibliographic information, each entry contains three or four descriptive paragraphs, the first of which is a general description of the series or periodical. The next three paragraphs provide supplementary materials, a critical evaluation, and a list of the materials provided with the series.

PICTURE BOOKS/MOVABLE BOOKS

70.   Cianciolo, Patricia. **Picture Books for Children.** 4th ed. Chicago: American Library Association, 1997. 213p. illus. index. ISBN 0-8389-0701-6.

Cianciolo contends that picture books are to be considered "a genre apart from any other kind of literature." Picture books are enjoyed by people of all ages, from the six-month-old child through grandparents reading to their grandchildren. The author's introduction, "The Picture Book: A Distinct Kind of Literary Art," provides many thought-provoking concepts. One of special interest is that on current trends in the writing and illustrating of picture books. The subject categories into which *Picture Books for Children* is organized present fundamental concerns of children. Chapter titles are "Me and My Family," "Other People," "The World I

Live In," and "The Imaginative World." Each chapter combines realistic fiction and fanciful tales, informative books, and verse. Entries, numbered consecutively from 1 to 272, are entered alphabetically by author, followed by an evaluative annotation. Once again, Cianciolo has written an outstanding guide to picture books that will appeal to parents as well as professionals working with children.

71. Hall, Susan. **Using Picture Storybooks to Teach Literary Devices: Recommended Books for Children and Young Adults.** Phoenix, AZ: Oryx, 1990. 168p. index. ISBN 0-89774-582-5.

According to the author, quality picture books, with their simple, visual format, are able to effectively illustrate many literary devices often found in books written for children and young adults. In the first section of the text, Hall discusses picture storybooks as literature, advocating their use to teach literary elements, such as simile, metaphor, and pun, at the elementary and secondary school levels. In the second part of the text, she supplies an alphabetically arranged list of thirty literary terms, including alliteration, hyperbole, and parody. As each term is defined, a list of appropriate picture books that incorporate the literary device is presented. For each of the 275 books included, bibliographic information is supplied, followed by a brief plot summary and an example of how the literary term is illustrated in the book.

This is a well-conceived and functional bibliography. It reflects substantial research and sensitivity to literary terminology. Perusing the text and observing how the literary devices are identified in the picture storybooks mentioned is an enjoyable experience.

A second volume is available, also by Hall: *Using Picture Storybooks to Teach Literary Devices: Recommended Books for Children and Young Adults.* Vol. 2. Phoenix, AZ: Oryx, 1994. 256p. index. ISBN 0-89774-849-2.

72. Lima, Carolyn, and John A. Lima. **A to Zoo: Subject Access to Children's Picture Books.** 4th ed. New Providence, NJ: R. R. Bowker, 1993. 1158p. illus. indexes. ISBN 0-8352-3201-8.

Increased emphasis on early childhood education has encouraged interest in picture books. The authors have defined picture books as those in which the illustrations occupy as much as or more space than the text and whose vocabulary and concepts are suitable for preschool ages through grade two. Picture book illustration has not always been considered an art form, but an improved quality of artwork in current picture books for children has become evident, leading to its acceptance as a significant form of artistic expression. The interesting introduction, "Genesis of the English-Language Picture Book," has been updated, and recent titles have been added.

Selecting judiciously from the thousands of picture books available is much easier as the result of this tome. *A to Zoo* contains more than 14,000 fiction and nonfiction titles recorded under approximately 800 subject headings. The subjects used reflect many current trends in children's picture books, for example pop-ups and board books. Even crossover books, those that appeal to adults at one level and to children at another, are included. Contents are arranged into three sections. The first comprises an alphabetical list of subject headings, including numerous cross-references, that reflect library terms and common "looking for" questions asked of librarians by children. The second section is the list of picture books arranged under one of the subject headings, entered alphabetically by author and followed by titles of his or her picture books. The last section is the bibliographic citation for every book listed, arranged alphabetically by author. An illustrator index lists titles and authors as a guide to distinguishing works with identical titles but different illustrators. *A to Zoo* is now available on the Bowker CD-ROM, *Children's Reference PLUS*. A new edition is planned for release in 1998.

This book is a pleasure to use; the design and illustrations are appealing. It is highly recommended as a valuable addition to any collection in which picture books are paramount.

73.   Marantz, Sylvia S. **Picture Books for Looking and Learning: Awakening Visual Perceptions Through the Art of Children's Books.** Phoenix, AZ: Oryx, 1992. 208p. index. ISBN 0-89774-716-X.

According to Marantz, artists draw from their own visual and emotional experiences to develop their creative expressions. The author aspires to encourage children to build their own imaginative creations through well-illustrated children's picture books that inspire them to see alternative ways of visualizing the world around them. Marantz's goal is to help adults gain confidence in appreciating the art of children's picture books by guiding them in the process, advising them about what "to see" in the illustrations, showing them the way to probe their own visual art values, and urging them to question and seek understanding of what they see in picture book illustrations. The author uses an interesting format to accomplish her goal of urging readers to look at art critically and to appreciate it for its "message." The forty-three award-winning books chosen for review and discussion are entered by age levels and, within each age group, are entered alphabetically by illustrator. Elements of design in each of the books are analyzed and thoroughly discussed. Well-known illustrators, such as Maurice Sendak and Ezra Jack Keats, are not included because their art has been discussed extensively elsewhere. Readers will, however, be familiar with most of the illustrators Marantz has selected; they include, among others, award-winning illustrators Ed Young and Steven Gammell and other illustrators popular with young children, such as Tomie dePaola and Steven Kellogg. A special effort is made to include books valuable in developing children's cultural awareness. Appendixes provide references to other sources of information on art in children's books.

The style and content of this text will intrigue diverse readers, that is, those reading it from the purview of the artist and those whose interest lies primarily in the topic as it relates to literature for children.

74.   Marantz, Sylvia S., and Kenneth A. Marantz. **The Art of Children's Picture Books: A Selective Reference Guide.** 2nd ed. New York: Garland, 1993. 320p. index. ISBN 0-8153-0937-6.

The second edition includes all of the material from the first edition and adds books that have been published up to the first half of 1993. The introduction presents the authors' viewpoints on the role of illustrations in picture books. They imply that illustrations of a book should be perceived and valued as a form of visual art and that book illustrations can symbolically convey meanings and feelings that words alone are unable to do. Artistic techniques, shapes, and media used can create feeling, manipulate opinions, and interpret the text. The Marantzes have applied approximately 450 children's picture books to illustrate their assumptions. They also specify other books, articles, and audiovisual materials that confirm their position. Indexes are by artist, author/editor/compiler, and source of title.

The authors' enthusiasm for the artistic elements of picture books is interesting, and their well-written, provocative discussions will engage the reader's critical thinking skills.

75.   Marantz, Sylvia S., and Kenneth A. Marantz. **Multicultural Picture Books: Art for Understanding Others.** Worthington, OH: Linworth, 1994. 150p. illus. index. ISBN 0-938865-22-6.

When illustrations reflect the art as well as the culture of the country in which the story is set, children have a greater understanding and appreciation of that culture. The authors have again kindled the reader's thinking skills in this book, dedicated to both the art form and multicultural literature. A 1997 supplement is now available. (See entry 132 for the complete annotation.)

76.   Montanaro, Ann R. **Pop-up and Movable Books: A Bibliography.** Metuchen, NJ: Scarecrow Press, 1993. 558p. indexes. ISBN 0-8108-2650-X.

Pop-ups and movable books, popular during the nineteenth and early twentieth centuries, are experiencing a resurgence of interest, exemplified by the recent increase in the number of reproductions being sold in bookstores everywhere. To help in the identification of these unique books and to provide guidance in gathering historical information about many of them, Montanaro has recorded approximately 1,600 English-language books containing movable illustrations and published between the 1850s and 1991. These three-dimensional picture books come in a variety of formats that include pop-ups, fan-folded, lift the flap, peep shows, rotating wheels, tab-operated, and transformations (slot illustrations). The introduction presents an interesting history of this type of picture book, from century-old books to those with current and often more complex formats. Entries, arranged alphabetically by title, provide a bibliographic citation, dates that can be verified, and a content description.

This publication provides difficult-to-find information in an easy-to-use format. Persons interested in nineteenth-century books and their illustrations will find this to be a bonanza.

77. Nodelman, Perry, ed. **Touchstones: Picturebooks: Reflections on the Best in Children's Literature.** Vol. 3. Metuchen, NJ: Scarecrow Press with The Children's Literature Association (CLA), 1989. 191p. index. ISBN 0-8108-2568-5.

This volume of Nodelman's *Touchstones* series honors distinguished children's picture books. It is a collection of analytical essays written by people well known in the field of children's literature. It examines traditional classics and treasured books that fall in the must-read category. The intent of this publication is to give children (and their parents) a sense of familiarity with these highly reputed books. The entire set is scholarly and will enhance any library collection (see entries 49-51).

78. Polette, Nancy. **Picture Books for Gifted Programs.** Metuchen, NJ: Scarecrow Press, 1981. 220p. index. ISBN 0-8108-1461-7.

In her introduction, the author states that picture books embody productive and critical thinking skills and that cognitive development in early childhood is enhanced by parents sharing picture books with the very young. Picture books are not only for the very young, however. The talent and creative genius of illustrators of picture books stimulate creative and innovative thinking for children of all ages. (See entry 65 for the complete annotation.)

79. Richey, Virginia H., and Katharyn E. Puckett. **Wordless/Almost Wordless Picture Books: A Guide.** Englewood, CO: Libraries Unlimited, 1992. 223p. index. ISBN 0-87287-878-3.

Richey and Puckett state that the art and technique of creating wordless picture books require special creative skills. An illustrator must be able to create visual representations that communicate plot and characters and also transmit to the reader the mood of the story. The authors have selected 685 children's picture books that illustrate this difficult blending of picture and mood in such a way that the wordless book can be used successfully with the very young and also the early elementary age child. It is suggested that older children will also find them valuable as a stimulant for creative writing ideas. Entries, arranged alphabetically by author, provide the bibliographic citation and a brief annotation. In addition to the title, illustrator, and subject indexes are those for format, series, and "Use of Print" ("Almost Wordless—Dialog," "Almost Wordless—Labels," etc.).

FOR READING OUT LOUD!

80. Blishen, Edward, comp. **Children's Classics to Read Aloud.** New York: Kingfisher Books, 1991. 255p. illus. ISBN 1-85697-825-7.

Although this is not a bibliography by definition, it does provide book recommendations for readers seeking guidance in selecting "the best classics" for reading aloud. Twenty great classics cherished by children for generations have been identified by the author. From each of these, he extracts episodes ideal for oral reading. An examination of the titles included reveals that the books selected were chosen to please a variety of tastes. Excerpts, which are included in the text, come from such diverse titles as Kenneth Grahame's *Wind in the Willows* and E. B. White's *Charlotte's Web*; from J. R. R. Tolkien's *The Hobbit* to Lewis Carroll's *Alice in Wonderland*; or from Jack London's *Call of the Wild* to Frances Hodgson Burnett's *The Secret Garden*. What a gem! This is a wonderful way to turn children on to books and reading and will appeal to children of all ages.

81.   Bodart, Joni Richards. **Booktalking the Award Winners 3.** Bronx, NY: H. W. Wilson, 1997. 192p. indexes. ISBN 0-8242-0898-6.

This is the newest offering in the *Booktalking* series by Joni Bodart. She is a strong advocate for using this process to inspire reading through short presentations designed to hook children on reading. It is an attention-grabbing method that will pique the curiosity of the listener and kindle his or her desire to find out "what happens next." Bibliographies are presented by award, theme, genre, and age groupings. Selections for booktalking include such sources as the Margaret L. Batchelder award, John Newbery awards and Honor Books, Coretta Scott King award, and other national and international awards. Approximately 200 books are covered by the bibliography. An index to all three of the *Booktalking the Award Winners* series is now available.

82.   **Books to Read Aloud with Children of All Ages.** Boston: Child Study Children's Book Committee at Bank Street College, 1994. 56p.

The Child Study Children's Book Committee has been reviewing children's books for more than seventy-five years. Every few years they update and re-issue this small but valuable selection guide. The committee reviewed more than 3,500 children's books published annually and identified a select number of the best to be incorporated in this publication. When a child asks, "Will you read to me?" parents and caregivers can feel confident that they have made a good choice when using this inexpensive guide. The approximately 350 entries, which include a brief bibliographic citation and a single-line description, also include poetry and verse, informational books, and holiday books.

83.   Freeman, Judy. **Books Kids Will Sit Still For: The Complete Read-Aloud Guide.** 2nd ed. New York: R. R. Bowker, 1990. 660p. illus. index. ISBN 0-8352-3010-4.

Research studies indicate that the most effective way to encourage children to become good readers is to read to them. With this in mind, Freeman has developed this selection guide to present the "whys" and "hows" of reading aloud. Based on recommendations from parents, librarians, and teachers, she has compiled a book list that will inspire exciting read-aloud programs. The author offers 101 ways to celebrate books, including storytelling, dramatics, and booktalks. Her graded, annotated list of 201 book titles is described as "tried and true." Each entry contains the standard bibliographic information, subject headings, the number of chapters in each book, and the number of sittings required to complete the reading.

This is a remarkable text. Nothing has been left to guesswork. Ideas, guide-lines, recommendations for book titles, suggestions for presentation, plus excellent indexing provide valuable information for a read-aloud program.

84. Freeman, Judy. **More Books Kids Will Sit Still For: A Read-Aloud Guide.** New Providence, NJ: R. R. Bowker, 1995. 869p. illus. indexes. ISBN 0-8352-3520-3; 0-8352-3731-1pa.

Although *More Books Kids Will Sit Still For* is an all-new text, the format and purposes are modeled after the 1990 edition. Introductory chapters serve as manuals for read-aloud programs, including creative ideas for celebrating reading. The more than 3,500 annotated titles of read-aloud books, all of which have been child-tested, occupy about four-fifths of the text. Books are arranged in eight age-level categories and, within each category by subject. The text is well illustrated and a delight to read. It should be high on the list for use by adults working with children. This publication is now available on the Bowker CD-ROM, *Children's Reference PLUS.*

85. Gillespie, John T., and Corinne J. Naden. **Middleplots 4: A Book Talk Guide for Use with Readers 8-12.** New Providence, NJ: R. R. Bowker, 1994. 434p. indexes. ISBN 0-8352-3446-0.

Gillespie and Naden believe the best way to bring good books and children together is by delivering books via tantalizing and seductive booktalks. Books selected for this guide are organized under eight themes that guide the user from adventure and mystery stories to the lives of interesting people. Entries, arranged alphabetically by author, include bibliographic information, a lengthy plot summary, thematic material, booktalk material, reviews, and other recommended titles. In addition to the author, title, and subject indexes for the current volume, indexes from the three previous volumes are cumulated to provide a complete listing of potential booktalk titles. The former title, *Introducing Bookplots*, has been succeeded by a four-volume set, including *Primaryplots* (see entry 94), *Middleplots*, *Juniorplots*, and *Seniorplots.*

Middleplots 4 is now available on the Bowker CD-ROM, *Children's Reference PLUS.*

86. Kimmel, Margaret Mary, and Elizabeth Segel. **For Reading Out Loud! A Guide to Sharing Books with Children.** Revised and expanded. New York: Dell, 1991. 279p. ISBN 0-440-50400-7.

Sharing books with children by reading to them continues to be an important activity in the early years of a child's life. The authors share some of the interesting comments they have received from parents, telling how read-aloud programs have influenced the lives of their children. The first six chapters are a series of essays discussing various aspects of the importance of reading aloud to children, regardless of age. The seventh chapter is a bibliography of 300 books recommended for reading aloud. With each book entry, entered alphabetically by title, is a brief plot description, interesting suggestions for activities relating to the story, and a recommended listening level. The last two chapters offer helpful cross-listings of titles by subject, length, type, and settings. Poetry selections and a selected bibliography of sources form the appendixes.

This is another inexpensive, informative, and easy-to-use book that will be a handy ready-reference for home, school, and library.

87.   **A List of Stories to Tell and Read Aloud.** 8th ed. New York: New York Public Library for the New York Public Library's Stories Committee, 1990. 104p. index. ISBN 0-87104-709-8.

This is an update of the New York Public Library's booklet of recommended story-time titles, some of which also appeared in the first edition published in 1927. The annotated list includes books, poetry, recordings, films, and videos on storytelling. The reasonably priced booklet is a good supplementary list for any library collection and a useful guide for parents or other individuals who are interested in reading and telling stories to children.

88.   McElmeel, Sharron L. **The Latest and Greatest Read-Alouds.** Englewood, CO: Libraries Unlimited, 1994. 210p. illus. indexes. ISBN 1-56308-140-7.

The scope and purpose of this text reflects the author's endeavors to provide currency and narrative appeal in the books she is introducing. Her belief in the value of reading as a learning experience for children is evidenced by citations of data relating to the benefits of reading aloud. Many practical and interesting tips are suggested to encourage independent reading. Chapter 1 lists fifty-seven picture books for children ages five to seven, arranged alphabetically by author, with descriptive and evaluative annotations. Chapter 2 continues with a list of more than 100 books recommended for reading aloud to primary age children. Annotations in this chapter are somewhat longer and include both listening levels and read-alone levels. The last chapter offers twenty-one steps that range from using a reading-aloud program to infusing reading-related activities and projects into learning programs.

This very useful and well-constructed guide and bibliography will be an especially helpful asset to those working with preschool and elementary school children.

89.   Rochman, Hazel. **Tales of Love and Terror: Booktalking the Classics, Old and New.** Chicago: American Library Association, 1987. 120p. index. ISBN 0-8389-0463-7.

Rochman contends that "Great books touch feeling and meaning." This is what many books labeled "classics" are able to do. Instead of turning off nonreaders by requiring them to read the classics, she suggests that we can lure them into becoming lifetime readers through booktalking. Her book selections, which may elicit raised eyebrows from some adults, are those that will pique the curiosity of young listeners. Rochman selects topics/themes that are popular with young people, identifies a selected list of representative titles, and then provides annotations and suggestions for booktalking each title. She has also appended to each topic more bibliographies of recommended books with similar themes. Books selected for possible booktalking activities represent an excellent blending of older, well-known classics with more current, popular books, many of which may well be destined to become tomorrow's classics. *Tales of Love and Terror* is now available on videocassette.

Although this approach to hooking children on reading may not work with all students, the high-interest approach the author suggests is very impressive and might bridge the gap of reading indifference for many young people.

90.   Russell, William F. **Classic Myths to Read Aloud.** New York: Crown, 1989. 264p. index. ISBN 0-517-58837-4.

Russell states in his introduction that myths have survived because people of disparate ages and cultures find inspiration from tales that influence their own lives. He reaches out to encourage enjoyment of classics by offering them in a read-aloud format. The myths are divided into two age-related sections: five years and up and eight years and up. Tales range from the story of Icarus and Daedalus for the younger children to the story of Helen of Troy for older children. Each entry begins with a plot synopsis, followed by an approximate reading time, vocabulary, and pronunciation guide. A two- to three-page discussion of each myth helps the reader find answers to questions that might be elicited from a read-aloud session. The paragraph entitled "A Few Words More" at the end of each myth discusses the origins of often-used words that appear in the tale.

This approach to bringing children and classical myths together is interesting and should generate some good discussions.

91.   Russell, William F. **Classics to Read Aloud to Your Children.** New York: Crown, 1984. 311p. ISBN 0-517-55404-6.

92.   Russell, William F. **More Classics to Read Aloud to Your Children.** New York: Crown, 1994. 264p. ISBN 0-517-88227-2.

This is an update and expansion of the earlier editions. Formats remain the same and share the goal of providing guidance for bringing children and myths together in a thought-provoking way. In recognition of the impact of reading on children in relation to their future success in school, Russell has developed a bibliography of classics to be read to children ages five to twelve. He advocates strongly that parents and teachers incorporate oral reading into planned family activities. To foster his suggestions, he has chosen classics that continue to be favorites over the years. To facilitate planning, he has provided guidelines for implementing reading sessions to create and hold the attention of children. Titles are entered at three age levels: children five and up, children eight and up, and children eleven and up. The books are followed by suggested poetry and holiday favorites.

Many parents and teachers will appreciate the excellent choices of children's classics and the beneficial guides provided.

93.   Sierra, Judy, and Robert Kaminski. **Multicultural Folktales: Stories to Tell Young Children.** Phoenix, AZ: Oryx, 1991. 126p. illus. ISBN 0-89774-688-0.

Folktales that have been handed down through oral tradition are natural read-aloud choices for children. They have continuously been a favorite form of story sharing and serve as a means of transmitting knowledge and encouraging children to appreciate cultures other than their own. (See entry 139 for the complete annotation.)

94. Thomas, Rebecca, L. **Primaryplots 2: A Book Talk Guide for Use with Readers Ages 4-8.** New Providence, NJ: R. R. Bowker, 1993. 431p. indexes. ISBN 0-8352-3411-8.

Primaryplots 2 has been updated and expanded in response to increasing interest in literature-based curricula, especially at the elementary level. Teachers and other educators need quality fiction and nonfiction literature suitable for incorporation into their literature-based lesson planning. This edition features 150 books published between 1988 and 1992 that serve as guides for booktalks, story programs, classroom activities, and reading guidance. Books are organized into eight chapters, each of which reflect popular reading interests of children. Bibliographic citations include a plot summary, suggested activities, and a list of more recommended titles with similar themes. In response to current themes in literature, the publishers of this volume increased the number of titles with multicultural themes. Extensive indexes add to the book's usefulness. *Primaryplots 2* is now available on the Bowker CD-ROM, *Children's Reference PLUS.*

This is a gold mine for teachers, library media specialists, parents, and others working with primary age children. Book selections reflect both popular and high-quality choices and activities that are practical and creative.

95. Trelease, Jim. **Hey! Listen to This: Stories to Read Aloud.** New York: Viking, 1992. 414p. ISBN 0-670-83691-5.

In this update of the 1989 edition, Trelease strengthens his claim that certain stories weather the test of repeated reading better than others. After examining Trelease's reading choices and accompanying comments, it is easy to understand why he has achieved national acclaim for his work with children and reading. His recommended selections, inserted in the text, include myths and legends, fairy and folktales, religion, humor, fantasy, history, and biography. Some selections are a single story and others are chapters from a familiar tale. An introduction, brief notes, and titles of related books accompany the entry for each of the forty-eight books he cites. Biographical information and personal comments made by some of the authors reveal interesting sidelights about their books. Chapter titles used for the twelve categories selected are clever and provocative, such as "Gigantic Creatures," "Children of Courage," and "Orphans of the Storm." The format is bound to pique the curiosity of readers, and related comments provide an additional element of interest. Trelease's guide is a great read as well as a valuable reference source.

96. Trelease, Jim. **The Read-Aloud Handbook.** 4th ed. New York: Penguin, 1993. 387p. indexes. ISBN 0-14-046971-0.

Once again Trelease offers to us his read-aloud guides to the world of children and books. The importance of reading aloud to children seems to be a "standard" he carries in his quest to convince parents and teachers to join his crusade. In the first half of this edition, Trelease cites research implying that reading to a child is the "single most important factor in developing a lifetime reader." His fourth edition includes updated statistics, new research, and recently published titles. It contains selections of the best read-alouds from the more than 15,000 new books published since the last edition. The second half of the book, his "Treasury of

Read-Alouds," is a guide to recommended books ranging from picture books to novels. They are organized into nine categories, with bibliographic information and descriptive and evaluative annotations. The reader should be sure to read Trelease's humorous essay, "Doomsayers," located in the appendix. It is evident that Trelease has done it again!

CHILDREN WITH SPECIAL NEEDS

For purposes of this bibliography, "special needs" has been defined as any disability that impairs functioning in some way, whether temporary or permanent.

97. Anderson, Marcella F. **Hospitalized Children and Books: A Guide for Librarians, Families, and Caregivers.** 2nd ed. Metuchen, NJ: Scarecrow, 1992. 136p. index. ISBN 0-8108-2519-8.

The introduction points to the importance of a patient/family library center in the pediatric section of a hospital. Anderson not only discusses how it provides a valuable service to hospitalized children, but she also provides guidelines for ways in which the library can develop an outreach program. Her basic bibliography of books recommended as appropriate for children in a hospital setting will help establish a high-quality book collection. Included are titles for programs such as a story hour and a time for reading aloud. Book-related activities are described, and appropriate filmstrips are suggested. The growing number of chronically ill children in hospitals makes the availability of library media resources specifically for youth imperative. Anderson's guide will help make a program of this nature much easier to implement.

98. Azarnoff, Pat. **Health, Illness, and Disability: A Guide to Books for Children and Young Adults.** New York: R. R. Bowker, 1983. 259p. indexes. ISBN 0-8352-1518-0.

Although the copyright date of *Health, Illness, and Disability* is more than ten years old, many of the books are still found on library shelves and on reading lists for children. This guide serves as a referral to children's books in which the protagonists deal in some way with health problems, illnesses, or disabilities. The extensive bibliography is entered alphabetically by author, followed by the bibliographic citation and a brief annotation. The subject index is organized into eight major subject classes, providing location guides as specifically as possible.

The Friedberg (entries 106, 107) and Robertson (entry 112) titles, both R. R. Bowker publications, extend and expand this guide to working with special needs children.

99.   Baskin, Barbara H., and Karen H. Harris. **More Notes from a Different Drummer: A Guide to Juvenile Fiction Portraying the Disabled.** New York: R. R. Bowker, 1984. 495p. illus. indexes. ISBN 0-8352-1871-6.

Creating a receptive climate for special needs children has been a major challenge for the public schools. Lack of understanding of some of the characteristics of special needs children and preconceived attitudes toward their "differentness" often create barriers to their successful integration into the regular classroom. Books are recognized as avenues that promote understanding and acceptance and diminish negative attitudes.

Baskin and Harris wrote their first bibliography, *Notes from a Different Drummer* (New York: R. R. Bowker, 1977), as an informational guide to be used to help mitigate these difficulties. They described and critiqued both fiction and nonfiction books written between 1940 and 1975 that portray disabled children. The new edition extends the initial efforts, but some significant changes have been made. On the premise that the fiction genre permits the widest freedom of expression and perception of values, the authors limited entries to works of fiction. The introductory chapter addresses the areas in contemporary society in which special needs people are now more actively participating. This is followed by discussion of the strengths and weaknesses of mainstreaming in schools. The authors have prepared criteria to use in selecting books to achieve a worthy collection of literature portraying the special needs child. The heart of this work is the more than 425 pages dedicated to annotated guides to juvenile fiction published between 1976 and 1980 in which special needs characters are portrayed. Each citation identifies the disability of the character, and the annotation contains a lengthy analysis of the story. Each entry also contains a discussion of elements related to the disability and how attitudes about the impairment are conveyed. This publication is now available on the Bowker CD-ROM, *Children's Reference PLUS.*

The authors have once again provided an exceptionally fine reference source to books dealing with special needs children. The Robertson publication (entry 110) updates this edition; however, it is not intended to supersede it, but rather to augment it with more recent titles.

100.   Carlin, Margaret F., Jeannine L. Laughlin, and Richard D. Saniga. **Understanding Abilities, Disabilities, and Capabilities: A Guide to Children's Literature.** Englewood, CO: Libraries Unlimited, 1991. 141p. indexes. ISBN 0-87287-717-5.

The goal of *Understanding Abilities . . .* is to present a listing of print and nonprint media on disabling conditions portrayed in literature for children. The bibliography includes fiction and nonfiction books, films, and videos written and produced since 1982. Children for whom the books are intended range in age from preschool through adolescence. The nine chapter titles identify the major handicapping conditions; within each chapter the entries are listed under either "Books" or "Films." Bibliographic information is followed by a plot summary in which the book is evaluated for both literary merit and appropriateness of the portrayal of the identified disability. The selective list of recommended books on disabilities is well organized for ease of use.

101. Cuddigan, Maureen, and Mary Beth Hanson. **Growing Pains: Helping Children Deal with Everyday Problems Through Reading.** Chicago: American Library Association, 1988. 165p. indexes. ISBN 0-8389-0469-6.

Cuddigan and Hanson, a librarian and a nurse, respectively, have identified thirteen life experiences that children increasingly must confront today. They carefully reviewed and critically judged over 2,000 titles in their quest to locate appropriate books to guide and nurture children through times of stress and crisis. The life experiences chapter titles are: "Behavior"; "Child Abuse and Neglect"; "Death and Dying"; "Difficult Situations"; "Emotions and Feelings"; "Family" (which includes divorce and separation); "Fears"; "Friendship"; "Hospitalization and Other Illnesses"; "Safety and Safety Issues"; "Self-Concepts/Self Esteem"; "Sexual Equality"; and "Understanding Society" (which includes poverty and cultural diversity). Each of the thirteen topics is introduced by a thematic discussion setting the tone of the chapter and raising the consciousness of the reader. A listing of books dealing sensitively with each issue is an integral part of each chapter.

This is an especially interesting reference source; it addresses topics from which we often prefer to shy away. The titles cited are well chosen and appropriate; they are carefully selected to approach diverse life experiences in today's society.

102. Dreyer, Sharon Spredemann. **The Best of** *Bookfinder*: **A Guide to Children's Literature About Interests and Concerns of Youth Aged 1-18.** Circle Pines, MD: American Guidance Service, 1992. 451p. indexes. ISBN 1-88671-440-0.

Dreyer's three-volume publication *The Bookfinder* (see entry 103) has proved to be an invaluable informational reference tool for bibliotherapy. She has selected 676 children's books from the original three-volume set and categorized them under more than 450 psychological, developmental, and behavioral topics of high interest and importance to children and young people. She updates the lengthy summaries and evaluations located in the original text. Subject headings and citations to other formats in which the book can be found, including paperback, audio books, videos, and Braille are added features. The 100-page subject index, with cross-references to the three-volume set, is a major asset to this newer version of the original Bookfinder series.

103. Dreyer, Sharon Spredemann. **The Bookfinder, Volume 4: When Kids Need Books: Annotations of Books Published 1983 Through 1986.** Circle Pines, MN: American Guidance Service, 1989. 642p. indexes. ISBN 0-913476-50-1.

This is a continuation of Dreyer's highly regarded guide to books to help children cope with many problems, physical and emotional, with which they may come in contact or that they may experience themselves, in today's society. It is written in the belief that children who read about other children who have solved similar problems may be able to see alternatives for themselves. It indexes and annotates reviews of 731 children's books published between 1983 and 1986. The books selected have been categorized according to more than 450 psychological, behavioral, and developmental topics. Each entry contains bibliographic information, subject headings, and an annotation. The first paragraph of each entry is a book synopsis; the second is a commentary on the theme and message of the book. Recommendations of other books relating to the same topic are included in each entry. The indexes are by author, title, and subject.

This is an especially useful tool for school libraries and public libraries and is often used by counselors and bibliotherapists.

104.   Friedberg, Joan Brest, June B. Mullins, and Adelaide W. Sukiennik. **Accept Me As I Am: Best Books of Juvenile Nonfiction on Impairments and Disabilities.** New York: R. R. Bowker, 1985. 363p. indexes. ISBN 0-8352-1974-7.

Mainstreaming brought to the forefront the need for an awareness and understanding of children with disabilities. Literature has proven to be an agent capable of influencing attitudes and acceptance of impairments. The authors selected nonfiction titles considered authentic in their representation of disabling conditions and in which the portrayal of the disabled person is positive and nonstereotypical. Preliminary chapters discuss understanding disabilities and how to work with children with disabilities. The subsequent chapters are organized according to one of the following categories of disability: physical problems, sensory problems, cognitive or behavior problems, and multiple/severe and various disabilities.

This is a companion volume to the Baskin and Harris title, *More Notes from a Different Drummer: A Guide to Juvenile Fiction Portraying the Disabled* (see entry 99). Friedberg's updated version of this book (see entry 105) both supplements and extends this edition.

105.   Friedberg, Joan Brest, June B. Mullins, and Adelaide Weir Sukiennik. **Portraying Persons with Disabilities: An Annotated Bibliography of Nonfiction for Children and Teenagers.** 2nd ed. New Providence, NJ: R. R. Bowker, 1992. 385p. indexes. ISBN 0-8352-3022-8.

This all-new volume continues in the tradition of the 1985 edition, *Accept Me As I Am*, by the same authors (see entry 104). The goal of this edition is also to foster constructive attitudes toward human differences through encouraging parents, teachers, and librarians to select interesting, informative, and well-written nonfiction when working with children. The selections included are those published since 1984 and are chosen for preschool age children through the young adult years. The first four chapters discuss various aspects of working with disabled children. They describe recommended criteria for selecting nonfiction, explain how disabilities are dealt with in social and historical perspectives, make informative reference to various disabilities for better understanding of them, and detail patterns and trends in current nonfiction that apply in some way to disabilities. The last four chapters provide complete bibliographic citations for recommended books, arranged under broad categories of disabling conditions, followed by a descriptive and evaluative annotation. The categories are sequenced in the following order: books dealing with physical problems, including AIDS; books dealing with sensory problems; books dealing with cognitive and behavioral problems; and entries for books that deal with multiple and severe disabilities. This reference source is now available on the Bowker CD-ROM, *Children's Reference PLUS.*

The authors' book choices are excellent and the discussions and evaluations are impressive.

106.   Manna, Anthony L., and Cynthia Wolford Synons. **Children's Literature for Health Awareness.** Metuchen, NJ: Scarecrow, 1992. 659p. indexes. ISBN 0-8108-2582-1.

The preface's opening sentence states that this book is for those interested in promoting the holistic health of children. Health awareness cuts across many areas of a child's life, such as personal and emotional health, career opportunities, and, of course, physical well-being. To achieve this goal of health awareness, the authors have identified fiction and nonfiction children's books that address topics that answer specific health questions and concerns and also supplement the teaching of healthy lifestyles. The first three chapters discuss the relationship between children's literature and health education and the need for comprehensive health programs. Also provided is a guide for evaluating and selecting books that relate to particular health issues. In chapter 4 the authors describe specific children's books that reflect the goals and topics of health education. The subsequent chapter provides a methodology for using health-oriented literature with children, and the concluding chapter is an extensive bibliography of children's books that can be used to introduce children to good health behaviors. The bibliography is organized into twelve health issues, with a brief citation and a single-sentence description for each entry. The appendixes contain an annotated list of nonbook health-related resources.

The authors have demonstrated a remarkable ability to identify health issues in all genres of literature, including poetry, fantasy, folktales, and drama.

107.   Oppenheim, Joanne F., and Stephanie Oppenheim. **The Best Toys, Books and Videos for Kids 1997: 1,000+ Kid-Tested Classics and New Products.** New York: Prima, 1996. 297p. indexes. ISBN 0-76150-705-1.

A section of this guide to kid-tested classics and new products for children from birth to ten years of age is devoted to recommendations of toys, books, videos, audiocassettes (music and stories), and computer software/CD-ROMs for special needs children. Entries are arranged in categories reflecting the disability for which they are recommended. (See entry 53 for the complete annotation.)

108.   Pearl, Patricia. **Helping Children Through Books.** 3rd ed. Portland, OR: Church and Synagogue Library Association. 1990. 23p. index. ISBN 0-915324-28-8.

In response to the increasing problems facing children today, the author has provided a selective list of recommended fiction and nonfiction books appropriate for children from preschool to the sixth grade. A wide range of topics is addressed, including divorce, stepparents, single parents, drugs, adoption, handicaps, self-acceptance, moving, and death. Each entry includes a brief description and an evaluative statement. The focus is on books that present good role models and encourage self-sufficiency and courage.

109.   Rasinski, Timothy V., and Cindy S. Gillespie. **Sensitive Issues: An Annotated Guide to Children's Literature K-6.** Phoenix: Oryx, 1992. 277p. index. ISBN 0-89774-777-1.

The authors believe that children must be exposed to meaningful literature in order to become lifelong readers. Reading about sensitive issues can help children deal with many of the problems that may confront them in their own lives. Chapters 2 to 9 present annotated bibliographies of children's books published since 1975 that focus on the following issues: divorce, death and dying, substance abuse, nontraditional home environments, child abuse, prejudice and cultural differences, moving, and illness and disability. Each chapter opens with a discussion of issues, followed by a list of related books, which are summarized and critiqued. Suggested activities to heighten an understanding of the issue provide additional guidance for the user. This is an impressive, well-organized reference source.

110.   Robertson, Debra E. J. **Portraying Persons with Disabilities: An Annotated Bibliography of Fiction for Children and Teenagers.** 3rd ed. New Providence, NJ: R. R. Bowker, 1992. 482p. indexes. ISBN 0-8352-3023-6.

The 1975 Education for All Handicapped Children Act, PL94-142, created a new challenge for the public schools. The mainstreaming act requires equal access to educational opportunities for all, which includes appropriate library media for handicapped children attending classes in the regular classroom. It is important that librarians, teachers, and others working with children have access to library collections that include books reflecting appropriate characterizations of disabled people. The Friedberg book (see entry 105) lists appropriate nonfiction titles; Robertson uses the same format for presenting fiction titles. Although this publication serves as an update of the highly regarded Baskin and Harris bibliography (see entry 99), it is an all-new volume, repeating only a few of the most highly recommended titles from the earlier edition.

The broad disability categories for the nonfiction titles identified in the Friedberg book are repeated in this publication. More than 600 book titles are cited by the author. Each entry, annotated and evaluated, is entered under an appropriate impairment. Plots and themes present positive portrayals of the disability, and to the extent possible, a featured character in the book has the identified disabling condition. If a book is included in which the disabled character is depicted in a negative or nonappropriate manner, this is alluded to in the annotation. This reference source is now available on the Bowker CD-ROM, *Children's Reference PLUS*.

This is a highly recommended bibliography with which teachers, librarians, and parents should become familiar.

111.   Rudman, Masha Kabakow, Kathleen Dunne Gagne, and Joanne E. Bernstein. **Books to Help Children Cope with Separation and Loss: An Annotated Bibliography.** 4th ed. New Providence, NJ: R. R. Bowker, 1993. 514p. indexes. ISBN 0-8352-3412-6.

The high standards set by the earlier editions of *Books to Help Children Cope with Separation and Loss* is maintained in the fourth edition. Dealing with a personal loss through death, divorce, desertion, illness, accident, or war is a traumatic experience for anyone; for a child it is even more difficult. An essay updated from the 1989 edition discusses the impact of separation and loss on children and identifies the behaviors that often follow this kind of trauma. A second essay, also an update, discusses the use of books as a coping mechanism. It points to ways in which bibliotherapy has been used as a means of helping children overcome bereavement and trauma. The annotated bibliography of more than 740 books is arranged thematically. The half-page annotations are both descriptive and evaluative, noting the strengths and weaknesses of each book in relation to its value in helping children cope. Selected readings for adults are provided with each category. The appendix, a directory of organizations that can be contacted for help, is arranged alphabetically under twenty-five issue headings. The author, title, subject, interest level, and reading level indexes are comprehensive. This publication is now available on the Bowker CD-ROM, *Children's Reference PLUS*.

The authors have provided an excellent continuation of an outstanding and valuable publication.

112.   Sharkey, Paulette Bochnig. **Newbery and Caldecott Medal and Honor Books in Other Media.** New York: Neal Schuman, 1992. 142p. index. ISBN 1-55570-119-1.

Many books awarded Newbery and Caldecott recognition have been converted into nonprint formats, making access to these prestigious publications unhampered for children with disabilities. Media forms into which these books have been transformed include large print, Braille, talking books, and computer software. (See entry 14 for the complete annotation.)

BOOKLETS AND PAMPHLETS

Often large public library systems publish free booklets of recommended books for children and young adults. Some professional associations and libraries also publish inexpensive booklets of suggested reading for children. The following are representative agencies and examples of their free or inexpensive publications.

Professional Associations

113.   **Child Study Children's Book Committee at Bank Street College**
610 West 112th Street
New York, NY 10025

Children's Books of the Year is an annotated list of more than 600 titles selected from over 4,000 new books. Selections, made by a group of approximately thirty volunteers, reflect the interests of librarians, parents, and children. Popularity and quality of writing govern selection.

Paperback Books for Children contains approximately 600 books available in paperback editions written by noteworthy authors and illustrators. The age levels represented are preschool through fourteen.

Books to Read Aloud with Children of All Ages annotates about four hundred titles; included are well-known classics and books just newly arrived on the market (see entry 82).

114.   Children's Book Council, Inc. (CBC)
568 Broadway
New York, NY 10012

CBC Features is the newsletter of the Children's Book Council. The Council, official sponsors of National Children's Book Week, engages in reading development activities and works with other national organizations to promote books and reading.

Outstanding Science Trade Books for Children is an annual list sponsored by the National Science Teachers Association and the CBC Joint Committee.

Notable Children's Trade Books in the Field of Social Studies is an annual list sponsored by the National Council of Social Studies and the CBC Joint Committee.

See entry 394 for more information on CBC.

115.   International Reading Association (IRA)
800 Barksdale Road, Box 8139
Newark, DE 19714-8139

Children's Choices is a project of the International Reading Association/Children's Book Council Joint Committee. Schoolchildren from across the United States are given the opportunity to identify favorite books, and their choices are compiled and published annually as a source of child-tested recommendations.

Teachers' Choices is another self-selected list of recommended books. New trade books that encourage reader participation and that have been proven valuable in curriculum development and implementation are identified. (See also entry 37.)

For more information on IRA, see entry 401.

116.   Reading Is Fundamental, Inc. (RIF)
600 Maryland Avenue, SW, Suite 600
Washington, DC 20024-2569

Reading Is Fundamental is a nonprofit organization designed to help children discover the joy of reading. Their reading motivational program has been implemented all over the United States in schools, public libraries, and other organizations working with children. RIF produces numerous inexpensive pamphlets and booklets for purchase, each of which is oriented toward encouraging children to become lifetime readers. Sample titles include: *Reading Aloud to Your Children, Reading Is Fun!* and *Children Who Can Read, but Don't.*

See entry 407 for more information on RIF.

Representative Public Library Booklets/Pamphlets

117. The Cleveland Public Library
325 Superior Avenue
Cleveland, OH 44114-1271

Celebrate with Books is a twenty-two-page booklet that includes picture books, early readers, fiction and nonfiction, folklore, myths and fables, poetry and song, and more.

Reading As We Grow is, as the subtitle indicates, a list of books for parents and children from kindergarten through grade four. It contains fifteen pages of well-selected titles that are bound to become children's favorites.

A second booklet entitled *Reading As We Grow* follows the pattern of the first one and is for children in grades five through eight. This nineteen-page booklet focuses on books to help children with problems, such as growing up, divorce, single-parent families, adoption and foster care, latchkey children, understanding death, and more.

118. The New York Public Library: Office of Branch Libraries
55 Fifth Avenue
New York, NY 10016

Although the New York Public Library's pamphlets and booklets listing recommended books for children are not updated on a regular basis, they still serve as excellent guides to reading choices. Titles are selected by the New York Public Library staff and are recommended for children, parents, and librarians everywhere. Examples of titles available are *Children's Books*, a pamphlet; *The Black Experience in Children's Books* (see entry 142); *A List of Stories to Tell and Read Aloud* (see entry 87); *Libros en Español Para Pequenos*, recommended books in Spanish; and *Light a Candle! The Jewish Experience in Children's Books.*

Chapter 3

Multicultural Literature

GENERAL REFERENCE SOURCES

119.   Ada, Alma Flor, Violet J. Harris, and Lee Bennett Hopkins, eds. **A Chorus of Cultures: Developing Literacy Through Multicultural Poetry.** Carmel, CA: Hampton-Brown, 1993. 303p. illus. indexes. ISBN 1-56334-325-8.

This "chorus of cultures" is a combination of seasonal and theme-oriented poetry, indexes to serve as guides to locating these and similar poems quickly, and activities to help infuse multiculturalism into the classroom. The editors believe poetry can be used as a means of enabling children to gain a better understanding of diverse cultures. They have used theme-oriented poetry to serve as a springboard to a greater awareness and acceptance of other cultures. Introducing individual poems and anthologies about other cultures and by poets from diverse cultures provides a refreshing and interesting method of building awareness.

120.   Anderson, Vicki. **Cultures Outside the United States in Fiction: A Guide to 2,875 Books for Librarians and Teachers, K-9.** Jefferson, NC: McFarland, 1994. 414p. indexes. ISBN 0-89950-905-3.

Anderson identifies recommended fiction for children with settings in countries other than the United States. The books included reflect people of other lands and the unique aspects of their cultures. Books are entered alphabetically by author under one of 150 selected countries. Most of the titles chosen have been published since 1960, although some classics, such as stories by Rudyard Kipling, are included. Age levels for which the selections are made range from preschool to young adult. Each entry contains standard bibliographic information, a suggested grade level, a brief annotation, and subject headings. An excellent guide is the grade-level appendix, arranged by grade, then country, author, and title. Separate author, title, and subject indexes conclude this valuable reference source.

121.   Anderson, Vicki. **Immigrants in the United States in Fiction: A Guide to 705 Books for Librarians and Teachers, K-9.** Jefferson, NC: McFarland, 1994. 135p. indexes. ISBN 0-89950-906-1.

This bibliography contains fiction titles with themes reflecting the social life and customs of people who emigrated to the United States. Books selected mirror the diversity of customs and cultures; they impart the adversities many immigrants had to overcome, and they show respect for the contributions these people made to the historical development of our nation. Sequentially numbered titles are arranged alphabetically by author under sixty nationality/ethnic groupings. Reading levels range from preschool to young adult.

This well-organized major undertaking serves as a valuable guide to works of fiction that will help children gain a better understanding of the roles played by families who left their homes abroad and came to the "new land," making our country a stronger nation.

122.   Austin, Mary C., and Esther C. Jenkins. **Promoting World Understanding Through Literature, K-8.** Littleton, CO: Libraries Unlimited, 1983. 266p. indexes. ISBN 0-87287-356-0.

This bibliography serves as a valuable reference source for teachers and parents interested in promoting literature and an understanding of our multiethnic world. Chapters are arranged by the following cultures: blacks and African Americans; Mexicans and Mexican Americans; and Native North Americans, Indians, and Eskimos. Each ethnic group is introduced by a brief orientation to the culture, geography, and people. An overview of children's fiction and nonfiction literature identified with each culture includes an annotated bibliography, categorized by genre, and a list of additional recommended books. Author, title, and subject indexes complete this well-developed publication.

123.   Bishop, Rudine Sims, ed. **Kaleidoscope: A Multicultural Booklist for Grades K-8.** Urbana, IL: National Council of Teachers of English, 1994. 169p. illus. indexes. ISBN 0-8141-2549-3.

As the title suggests, Bishop sees our world as one made up of many colors, many cultures, and many philosophies. Children's books reflecting this multifaceted world have been carefully selected to focus on interracial and intercultural topics and relationships. Selections include the following cultures indigenous to the United States: African American, Asian American, Hispanic American/Latino, and Native American. The editor also covers the cultures in their native lands, including Africa, Asia, South and Central America, the Caribbean, Mexico, and Canada. Selections for the bibliography are based on the book's quality and contribution to a positive understanding and appreciation of people of different colors and cultures. In order to present an even more accurate picture of the many cultures of Africa, Bishop differentiates between the many African tribes whose environments and customs are dissimilar. She has included books portraying immigrations set in historical times, as well as recent immigrations such as those of the boat people and Cubans. Entries are arranged under nine topics and categorized by four age levels to help the reader select appropriate books. Good indexing and organization of information has generated a highly commendable reference source.

The second edition, also by Bishop, covers books from 1993 to 1995: *Kaleidoscope: A Multicultural Booklist for Grades K-8.* 2nd ed. Urbana, IL: National Council of Teachers of English, 1997. 220p. illus. indexes. ISBN 0-8141-2543-3.

124. Boyd, Alex, ed. **Guide to Multicultural Resources: 1997/1998.** Fort Atkinson, WI: Highsmith, 1997. 584p. indexes. ISBN 0-917846-83-4. ISSN 1050-4249.

This biennial publication is a concise directory and almanac to more than 3,600 sources of information related to multicultural resources. Its comprehensive nature qualifies it as a valuable guide for those seeking to offer a well-developed program of multicultural awareness for any age group. It is a guide to all manner of resources, including print resources, videos, and resources that can be accessed through the Internet. Cultures under which the resources are entered are African American, Asian American, Hispanic American, Native American, and Multicultural American. The introduction to each culture is written by an authority of that culture; included in each introduction is a summary of current trends within the culture. A special feature is the key to national organizations where contacts can be made.

125. Day, Frances Ann. **Multicultural Voices in Contemporary Literature: A Resource for Teachers.** Portsmouth, NH: Heinemann, 1994. 244p. photos. ISBN 0-435-08826-2pa.

Day celebrates the lives and works of thirty-nine multicultural authors and illustrators whose works reflect the great diversity of cultures in today's society. (See entry 292 for the complete annotation.)

126. Hayden, Carla D., ed. **Venture into Cultures: A Resource Book of Multicultural Materials and Programs.** Chicago: American Library Association, 1992. 165p. illus. index. ISBN 0-8389-0579-X.

In response to the growing interest in ensuring culturally authentic representations in children's books, the author has identified books that accurately mirror the multicultural population native to the United States, as well as those who have recently immigrated there. To assure ethnic authenticity, each of the seven chapters has been written by a member of the culture to which the chapter pertains. In addition to the annotated bibliographic information, programming ideas and a list of resources accompanies each chapter. Hayden has included a good variety of titles and formats, and her program ideas are well supported with guides for their use.

127. Helbig, Alethea K., and Agnes Regan Perkins. **This Land Is Our Land: A Guide to Multicultural Literature for Children and Young Adults.** Westport, CT: Greenwood, 1994. 401p. index. ISBN 0-313-28742-2.

This guide includes books written for preschool through high school age children published between 1985 and 1992. The authors identify four major U.S. ethnic groups and provide 570 annotations of multicultural literature for children. Additional books relating to multicultural literature are also listed. Chapter titles reflect the following cultures indigenous to the United States: African Americans, Asian Americans, Hispanic Americans, and Native Americans. Books are organized by genre, including fiction, oral tradition, and poetry. Each entry, arranged alphabetically by author, contains bibliographic information, age and grade level, and a one-paragraph descriptive and evaluative annotation. Indexes are arranged by title, writer, illustrator, grade level, and subject.

This is another invaluable source of information to use in helping children understand the literature of diversity in our culture.

128.   Kruse, Ginny Moore, and Kathleen T. Horning. **Multicultural Literature for Children and Young Adults: A Selected Listing of Books by and About People of Color, Vol. 1: 1980-1990.** 3rd ed. Madison, WI: Cooperative Children's Book Center with the Wisconsin Department of Public Instruction, 1991. 78p. index.

129.   Kruse, Ginny Moore, Kathleen T. Horning, and Megan Schliesman. **Multicultural Literature for Children and Young Adults: A Selected Listing of Books by and About People of Color, Vol. 2: 1991-1996.** Madison, WI: Cooperative Children's Book Center with the Wisconsin Department of Public Instruction, 1997. 120p. index. ISBN 0-931641-07-1.

A careful selection of books by and about African Americans, American Indians, Asian Americans, and Hispanic Americans is the focus of this compilation of multicultural literature. The authors have chosen books of high quality that are innovative in style and accurate in presentation of the cultures identified, and whose themes are of a significant nature and reflect unusual insight into people of color. The introduction is a discussion of the history of stereotypical portrayals of people whose cultures are nonwhite. According to the authors, nonstereotypical portrayals of people of color in children's books before the 1970s tended to be the exception rather than the rule. From the late 1960s forward, a rapid change resulting from a number of factors became apparent. Active encouragement of writers of color and recognition of their writing skills and artistic talents by the publishing industry began to play a significant role in the development of contemporary multicultural children's literature. The Kruse and Horning bibliography of multicultural literature reflects the emergence of culturally authentic children's books during the 1980s. The 475 books listed, which include picture books, fiction, poetry, and biography, are divided into sixteen subject-oriented sections, such as literature, history, the arts, and biographies. Each entry, alphabetically entered by author, includes the bibliographic citation, an annotation, and suggested age levels. Each section concludes with a helpful "see also" list of related titles. The sequence of four appendixes provides guides to authors and illustrators of color and to other multicultural resources. Because of the current emphasis on multicultural education in our schools, this concise, inexpensive bibliography should be available in every library serving children.

130.   Lindgren, Merri, ed. **The Multicolored Mirror: Cultural Substance in Literature for Children and Young Adults.** Fort Atkinson, WI: Cooperative Children's Book Center/Highsmith, 1991. 195p. illus. index. ISBN 0-917846-05-2.

This publication resulted from a conference, held in April 1991 at the University of Wisconsin at Madison and sponsored by the Cooperative Children's Book Center, which recognized the contributions of minority authors and illustrators to children's literature. The goal was to share ideas, evaluations, and information related to minorities reflected in children's books. Essays stress the need to recognize that values and self-esteem are transmitted through identification with one's culture, a quality that can be communicated through books that authentically "mirror" the culture. Specific titles were cited as good examples of these qualities. The essays are insightful, and the bibliographies were carefully chosen to reflect cultural authenticity.

131.　Manna, Anthony L., and Carolyn S. Brodie, eds. **Many Faces, Many Voices: Multicultural Literary Experiences for Youth.** Fort Atkinson, WI: Highsmith, 1992. 183p. illus. index. ISBN 0-917846-12-5pa.

The inaugural year of the annual Virginia Hamilton Conference at Kent State University in Ohio was 1985. The conference focus, cultural diversity in literature for young people, was established at that time. *Many Faces, Many Voices* contains many of the presentations given at the conferences over the intervening eight years. The term "cross-culturalism" is extended to encompass all cultures and social, political, and economic conditions that reflect the different cultures. Manna and Brodie selected keynote conference speeches and workshops that they feel set the tone of the conference and, at the same time, share a storehouse of ideas, experiences, and recommendations of the presenters. The reader is able to enter the world of the "teller" when reading Virginia Hamilton's reflections on life as an African American writer; he or she can journey with a Japanese American writer, have a look into Appalachia, and read interesting comments related to Jewish American juvenile literature. Each of the eleven chapters includes bibliographies of recommended juvenile literature with multicultural themes. An appendix lists additional multicultural trade books recommended by the advisory board of the conference. Each entry includes a bibliographic citation, an age/grade level, and a critical annotation.

This follow-up to the highly respected Virginia Hamilton Conference will be applauded by proponents of a better understanding of multicultural literature for children. The presentations and accompanying bibliographies are representative of the cross-cultural nature of the annual conference.

132.　Marantz, Sylvia, and Kenneth Marantz. **Multicultural Picture Books: Art for Understanding Others.** Worthington, OH: Linworth, 1994. 150p. illus. index. ISBN 0-938865-22-6.

When illustrations reflect the art, as well as the culture, of the country in which a story is set, children gain a greater understanding and appreciation of that culture. They learn to respect the artistic representational styles of other nationalities and develop a greater sense of identity with their own cultural styles. The first two sections of this book discuss using picture books to depict other cultures and provide guidelines for selecting multicultural picture books. Section 3 is organized into sixty-seven geographical areas. Within each geographical area, the reader finds bibliographies of recommended picture books whose illustrations are sensitive to the spirit of that area's culture. Other resources and information included in the text are an asset to this unique approach to the study of multiculturalism in children's picture books.

A new edition by the same authors is now available: *Multicultural Picture Books: Art for Understanding Others.* Worthington, OH: Linworth, 1997. 150p. illus. index. ISBN 0-938865-63-3.

133.   Miller-Lachmann, Lyn. **Global Voices, Global Visions: A Core Collection of Multicultural Books.** New Providence, NJ: R. R. Bowker, 1995. 870p. indexes. ISBN 0-8352-3291-3.

As a teacher, the author was concerned when she found it difficult to locate book titles for some of her students who asked for titles of books pertaining to their cultural backgrounds in order to have a better understanding of their own heritage. Since the 1980s, interest in multicultural education has created a plethora of books to fill what was, at one time, a major deficiency. Miller-Lachmann developed this core collection, applicable for all age groups, as a selective listing of significant and recommended works of fiction, nonfiction, and biography presenting multicultural themes and information. Books were reviewed for cultural honesty and authentic representations.

The introduction discusses our changing world and growing global interdependence. The first four chapters comprise works by and about African Americans, Asian Americans, Latinos, and Native Americans. The remaining chapters cover the rest of the world, organized by regions.

This was decidedly a monumental undertaking. The result is an excellent reference source for anyone seeking multicultural fiction and nonfiction books.

134.   Miller-Lachmann, Lyn. **Our Family, Our Friends, Our World: An Annotated Guide to Significant Multicultural Books for Children and Teenagers.** New Providence, NJ: R. R. Bowker, 1992. 710p. indexes. ISBN 0-8352-3025-2.

Children can learn to live together better when they understand each other's heritage and culture. To that end, the author identifies each major ethnic group and lists children's books in which positive cultural role-models are depicted. Her extensive introduction is both an excellent guide for using multicultural books and also a historical overview of the emergence of multicultural literature. Each chapter, individually authored, opens with a helpful introduction, followed by a list of recommended books arranged by age levels. The first four chapters cover ethnic groups within the United States: African American, Asian American, Hispanic American, and Native American. The remaining chapters comprise bibliographies of books for children to introduce them to the lands and cultures of people in Canada, Mexico and the Caribbean, Central and South America, Great Britain, Europe, Asia, Africa, Australia, the Pacific Islands—all countries and cultures of the world. This reference source is now available on the Bowker CD-ROM, *Children's Reference PLUS.*

The comprehensive coverage, the guides for use, and the well-organized indexes qualify this book as an excellent source of guidance to multicultural literature for children.

135.   Ramirez, Gonzalo, Jr., and Jan L. Ramirez. **Multiethnic Children's Literature.** Albany, NY: Delmar, 1994. 158p. illus. index. ISBN 0-8273-5433-9.

The authors designed their bibliography for teachers, library media specialists, parents, and others working with children from kindergarten through eighth grade. Their criteria led them to seek out books that are artistically competent, well written, and appropriate in their cultural depiction. Selections consist of a variety of genres and cultures, including Hispanic Americans, African Americans, Asian Americans, and Native Americans. Entries reflect traditional literature and stories with current settings. The literature of other countries is also included. Entries provide bibliographic information, including translator where appropriate; a plot summary; comments on the artistic quality of illustrations; and a list of related titles.

136.   Roberts, Patricia L., and Nancy Lee Cecil. **Developing Multicultural Awareness Through Children's Literature: A Guide for Teachers and Librarians, Grades K-8.** Jefferson, NC: McFarland, 1993. 216p. indexes. ISBN 0-89950-879-0.

The authors affirm that education and an opportunity to understand people of different ethnological backgrounds can have a positive effect on children's thinking and feeling about other cultures. Well-written multicultural literature for children can replace fears with acceptance, prejudice and stereotypical thinking with accurate representations, and unease with respect. The 240 titles, appropriate for elementary through junior high school students, include fiction, folk literature, and biographies. They are categorized into five major ethnic groups: African American, Asian American, European American, Latin American, and Native American. Target activities are provided to help children modify misconceptions and stereotypes. The organization of information, the selection of titles, and the follow-up activities provide a commendable informational reference source.

137.   Rochman, Hazel. **Against Borders: Promoting Books for a Multicultural World.** Chicago: American Library Association, 1993. 135p. illus. indexes. ISBN 0-8389-0601-Xpa.

When one culture has a clear, positive understanding of another culture, there is an appreciation of the richness of diversity and a respect for other ethnic groups. In her introduction Rochman states, "Multiculturalism means across cultures, against borders." She believes that the best books can break down borders. Her criteria for selection of books for this bibliography reflect her understanding of the need for acceptance of cultures other than her own and a sensitivity to factors that differentiate between stereotyped and authentic models, between sensationalism and reality. Part 1, "Themes: Journeys Across Cultures," addresses themes in multicultural literature. Issues are illustrated with discussions and evaluative comments, using representative multicultural books. Part 2, "Resources Going Global," is arranged into three sections: "Racial Oppression," "Ethnic U.S.A.," and "The Widening World." Books addressed in this section include fiction, nonfiction, poetry, and videos. The selections are from elementary to high school age levels. Comments in the annotations are primarily evaluative and are often very critical of the way a culture or ethnic group is portrayed.

Throughout the text, the author's comments and evaluation mirror her commitment to quality literature and her goal to promote understanding and acceptance of a multicultural world.

138.   Rothlein, Liz, and Terri Christman Wild. **Read It Again! Multicultural Books for the Primary Grades.** Glenview, IL: Scott, Foresman, 1993. 136p. illus. ISBN 0-673-36064-4.

In response to the growing diversity in ethnic and cultural populations in the United States, an ever-increasing number of new books attempt to accurately reflect these diverse factors. The authors recognize the importance of parents and educators encouraging children to accept and live in harmony with cultures others than their own; a way to achieve that goal is through the selection and use of well-written multicultural literature for children. Rothlein and Wild have identified twelve highly regarded books, each of which presents appropriate and accurate cultural representations, to use with children. They are arranged by the following broad classifications: "People of Asian Roots," "People of African Roots," "Hispanic People," and "Native Americans." Each selection is accompanied by guidelines for multicultural activities for parents and educators to use in working with children. The goal is to extend opportunities that lead to an appreciation of people of all races and cultures as well as strengthening pride in one's own heritage.

139.   Sierra, Judy, and Robert Kaminski. **Multicultural Folktales: Stories to Tell Young Children.** Phoenix, AZ: Oryx, 1991. 126p. illus. ISBN 0-89774-688-0.

Folktales that have been handed down through oral tradition are natural read-aloud choices for children. They have continuously been a favorite form of story sharing and serve as a means of transmitting knowledge and encouraging children to appreciate cultures other than their own. Sierra and Kaminski illustrate variants of the same folktale, for example the Cinderella tale, in diverse locales. The reader will easily recognize many of the tales, possibly told to him or her as a child, and perhaps will be surprised at the country from which the tale originated. Craft ideas, techniques for telling, participation ideas, and recommended resources all serve to contribute to the usefulness of this reference source.

140.   Thomas, Rebecca L. **Connecting Cultures: A Guide to Multicultural Literature for Children.** New Providence NJ: R. R. Bowker, 1996. 676p. indexes. ISBN 0-8352-3760-5.

Thomas states that through reading, children are able to understand the differences and similarities among people of different cultures. The purpose of this annotated bibliography of multicultural literature for children is to help build connections among all cultures. Entries include fiction, folktales, poetry, and songbooks for children from preschool to the sixth grade. Thomas has provided 1,637 entries, arranged alphabetically by author, with a bibliographic citation, a use level, subject headings, and a single-line descriptive annotation. The indexes are arranged by subject, use, culture, title, and illustrator. The subject index is especially extensive, covering 730 topics and subtopics.

141. Totten, Herman, and Risa Brown. **Culturally Diverse Library Collections for Children.** New York: Neal-Schuman, 1994. 299p. index. ISBN 1-55570-140-X.

Discussion of the need for greater understanding of diverse cultures is presented in the introduction. Libraries serving children should strive to provide and encourage the use of a culturally diverse collection. In this world in which contact with all nations and cultures is no longer uncommon, appreciation of dissimilar ideas and experiences is an essential ingredient to a peaceful world. Literature is a voice that can bring about better understanding and can perhaps even be an avenue through which cultural conflicts and misunderstandings can be avoided. Appropriate literature also emphasizes positive experiences that all people have in common, such as love, families, friendship, the search for oneself. The authors have identified children's books that encourage acceptance of diverse ethnic backgrounds. The chapters are categorized into the following cultures: Native American, Asian American, Hispanic American, and African American. The focus is on biographies, folklore, and fiction. Annotated entries are grouped first by recommended age level and then alphabetically by author. Bibliographic information and a brief story outline identifying characters and conflicts are provided. Reference sources, scholarly works, and nonfiction references are included. The index is an integrated author, illustrator, and title index. This is a very impressive, well-researched bibliography.

AFRICAN AMERICAN LITERATURE

142. **The Black Experience in Children's Books.** New York: New York Public Library, 1994. 64p. index. ISBN 0-87104-726-8.

In the introduction the compiler observes that there seems to be an encouraging, albeit still minimal, increase in the ethnic presence in children's books. More books by black authors and illustrators are appearing on "new books" lists. The entries in this small booklet are arranged geographically as follows: the United States, South and Central America, the Caribbean, Africa, and England. Within each geographical section, entries are arranged by format or content, such as picture books, folklore, biographies. Although the U.S. section is the most extensive, other geographical sections are well represented. Bibliographic information for each entry is followed by a one- or two-sentence annotation, just enough to reflect the plot of the book. The appendix offers an alphabetical listing of the black authors and illustrators. A list of the Coretta Scott King Awards is included, and an author, title, and illustrator index follows.

What a gem this small, inexpensive, yet very useful booklet is.

143. MacCann, Donnarae, and Gloria Woodward, eds. **The Black American in Books for Children: Readings in Racism.** 2nd ed. Metuchen, NJ: Scarecrow, 1985. 298p. indexes. ISBN 0-8108-1826-4.

The authors, concerned about the negative attitudes toward black culture and stereotyping in literature for children, have updated their 1972 publication of readings on racism. The discussions and evaluations of books located within the text are written by specialists in the field of children's literature. These authorities have analyzed children's books for quality and authenticity of representation of the black experience. Books that present good images of blacks, positive role models, and accurate perspectives on the black American in the history of our country have been selected. The books selected for the bibliography are those that can be reliably recommended as important in helping black children develop positive perceptions of themselves and that also present positive images of African American culture to all children, regardless of skin color or ethnic background.

Although this is primarily a handbook of readings on racism in children's books, many well-known and highly regarded books have been analyzed for their perspective on the black experience. It is valuable as a guide for thinking critically when reading aloud or recommending books portraying the black culture.

144.   Moll, Patricia Buerke. **Children & Books I: African American Story Books and Activities for All Children.** Tampico, FL: Hampton Mae Institute, 1991. 217p. illus. index. ISBN 0-96165-112-1.

This combined bibliography and activities book challenges the reader to establish a reading program that builds upon the natural, inherent love children have for books and reading. The author has created activities that encourage and expand this natural interest. The bibliographies are organized into seven general categories, with emphasis on African American culture. In conjunction with the standard bibliographic citation, Moll has included story time crafts and other activities as extensions of the reading experience. A special feature is the arrangement of titles and activities in developmental sequences from early stages to higher levels of development. The approximately ninety entries include both fiction and nonfiction titles. The chapter on authors and illustrators provides information to help introduce these artists to the children. Children of all races will be able to benefit from the recommendations and creative ideas presented; the book will enhance any library collection.

A newer edition by the same author is now available: *Children & Books I: African American Story Books and Activities for All Children.* 2nd ed. Tampico, FL: Hampton Mae Institute, 1994. 250p. illus. index. ISBN 0-96165-114-8.

145.   Rollock, Barbara. **Black Authors and Illustrators of Children's Books: A Biographical Dictionary.** 2nd ed. New York: Garland, 1992. 234p. illus. indexes. ISBN 0-8240-7078-X.

This biographical publication profiles black authors and illustrators whose works provide an integral study of the black creative presence in children's books. (See entry 305 for the complete annotation.)

146.   Sims, Rudine. **Shadow and Substance: Afro-American Experience in Contemporary Children's Fiction.** Urbana, IL: National Council of Teachers of English, 1982. 112p. ISBN 0-8141-4376-8.

Sims endeavors to encourage people working with children and books to make socially responsible book choices. She discusses the findings of a survey and content analysis of 150 books of realistic fiction about African Americans published between 1965 and 1979. The books were placed in four major categories:

realistic fiction without a social conscience; melting-pot books; culturally conscious fiction; and the image makers. An extensive bibliography of additional titles is also provided.

147.   Sullivan, Charles, ed. **Children of Promise: African-American Literature and Art for Young People.** New York: Harry N. Abrams, 1991. 126p. illus. index. ISBN 0-8109-3170-2.

Sullivan has brought together an anthology of the voices of the United States through poetry, paintings, folk songs, photographs, and excerpts from books, each of which reach out primarily to African Americans and their culture. Through the "voices" of Benjamin Banneker, W. E. B. Du Bois, and Arna Bontemps we feel the agony of the slave as well as the refusal to give up seeking freedom. We feel the pain through the poetry of Gwendolyn Brooks and Langston Hughes, the hope through the folk songs that express a sense of derision for some and for others a sense of joy amid despair, hope, and faith. We feel the impact of the lives of Harriet Tubman, Frederick Douglass, Booker T. Washington, and Martin Luther King, Jr., on the African American culture of today. Through the 100 poems, folk songs, and literary excerpts as well as the eighty-four illustrations, we follow the historical march of African Americans from the 1790s with Benjamin Banneker to the 1960s with Martin Luther King, Jr. to today with Jesse Jackson and other outstanding African American politicians and sports figures.

This may serve well as an inspiration to all youth. The African American emphasis, to be sure, is the major focus, but the promise children can attain knows no color lines.

148.   Williams, Helen E. **Books by African-American Authors and Illustrators: For Children and Young Adults.** Chicago: American Library Association, 1991. 270p. indexes. ISBN 0-8389-0570-6.

Williams has provided a representative selection of books by black writers and illustrators in response to the need to advance knowledge of and interest in the excellent contributions of black artists. The first three chapters, arranged by grade levels, include more than 1,200 titles entered alphabetically by author with annotations that identify cognitive abilities and skills reflected in the text. Chapter 4 describes and identifies the artistic contributions of black illustrators. In addition to standard bibliographic information, reviewing sources are provided. Appendixes include awards and prizes, a glossary of art terms, and a bibliography of sources used. The index is thorough and easy to use.

Evidence of extensive research is apparent in the extent and coverage Williams has provided. The currency and thoroughness of the content of this book distinguish it as a valuable reference source for all libraries.

HISPANIC/LATINO LITERATURE

149. Beilke, Patricia, and Frank J. Sciara. **Selecting Materials for and About Hispanic and East Asian Children and Young People.** Hamden, CT: Shoestring, 1986. 178p. index. ISBN 0-208-01993-6.

Beilke and Sciara provide guidelines for in-service programs on using appropriate criteria for selecting multicultural literature for children. The emphasis is on identifying cultural relevance in books for children and young people. The chapter devoted to the selection of Hispanic literature includes Mexican, Puerto Rican, and Cuban American cultures. The authors include selection criteria for Hispanic and East Asian cultures with guidelines for applying them. A selective list of books relating to the two very diverse cultures accompany each chapter.

150. Dale, Doris Cruger. **Bilingual Books in Spanish and English for Children.** Littleton, CO: Libraries Unlimited, 1985. 163p. indexes. ISBN 0-87287-477-X.

The author's purpose is to identify and evaluate children's books published between 1940 and 1982 in which the text is in both Spanish and English. She lists bibliographies, catalogs from trade publishers, and printed library catalogs from applicable school districts and universities. The second part of the guide is a bibliography of titles organized chronologically by ten-year increments. Titles are entered alphabetically by author within each ten-year grouping. The bibliographic information and annotations are written in English only. Reviews, where available, are included.

151. Day, Frances Ann. **Latina and Latino Voices in Literature for Children and Teenagers.** Portsmouth, NH: Heinemann, 1997. 228p. indexes. ISBN 0-435-07202-1.

The author presents highlights in the lives and careers of Latina and Latino writers who are considered established or emerging writers. (See entry 291 for complete annotation.)

152. **A Latino/Hispanic Heritage Series.** Metuchen, NJ and Lanham, MD: Scarecrow.

The Latino/Hispanic Heritage Series, authored by Isabel Schon and published by Scarecrow Press, serves as a guide to Latino/Hispanic culture. In recognition of the insufficiency of resources available to help librarians, teachers, and parents locate children's books written in Spanish, the author has compiled basic bibliographies of books appropriate for children in preschool through high school. Her goal is to guide young people toward an understanding and appreciation of the people and cultures of Central and South America, Puerto Rico, Spain and of Latino/Hispanic people in the United States. Her book lists contain titles that meet the informational, recreational, and personal interests of children. Books included are selected to reflect authenticity in representation of both Hispanic culture in Spanish-speaking countries and the Hispanic/Latino heritage in the United States. Included are reference works, fiction, nonfiction, easy books, and professional books. Entries are arranged first under country of origin and are then subdivided by genre. Annotations are both descriptive and evaluative. Noteworthy titles are identified with an asterisk, and perceived weaknesses are noted. To help the non-Spanish-speaking patron, titles are translated into English.

This series is a major contribution to libraries seeking to locate quality Hispanic literature for children. Current titles in the series are listed below.

> 152.1.   Schon, Isabel. **Basic Collection of Children's Books in Spanish.** Metuchen, NJ: Scarecrow, 1986. 240p. index. 0-8108-1904-X.

> 152.2.   Schon, Isabel. **A Hispanic Heritage: A Guide to Juvenile Books About Hispanic People and Cultures.** Metuchen, NJ: Scarecrow, 1991. 165p. indexes. ISBN 0-8108-2462-0.

> 152.3.   Schon, Isabel. **Books in Spanish for Children and Young Adults: An Annotated Guide.** Metuchen, NJ: Scarecrow, 1993. 305p. ISBN 0-8108-2622-4.

> 152.4.   Schon, Isabel. **A Latino Heritage: A Guide to Juvenile Books About Latino People and Cultures.** Lanham, MD: Scarecrow, 1995. 210p. ISBN 0-8108-3057-4.

> 152.5.   Schon, Isabel. **The Best of the Latino Heritage: A Guide to the Best Juvenile Books About Latino People and Cultures.** Lanham, MD: Scarecrow, 1996. 304p. ISBN 0-8108-3221-6.

153.   Schon, Isabel, ed. **Contemporary Spanish-Speaking Writers and Illustrators for Children and Young Adults: A Biographical Dictionary.** Westport, CT: Greenwood, 1994. 248p. index. ISBN 0-313-29027-X.

This is an excellent biographical guide to writers and illustrators of Spanish heritage who publish children's books in Spanish for Hispanic children. It is often difficult to locate biographical information in English-speaking countries on writers and illustrators whose native language is not English. The author has filled that gap for the Spanish-speaking population. (See entry 306 for complete annotation.)

JEWISH LITERATURE

154.   Davis, Enid. **A Comprehensive Guide to Children's Literature with a Jewish Theme.** New York: Schocken, 1987. 190p. indexes. ISBN 0-8052-3760-7.

Davis has developed a bibliography of 450 recommended children's books with well-organized and accurate plots and characterizations that reflect Jewish values and culture. The ages for which the fiction and nonfiction books are intended range from preschool to junior high/middle school. Although the content is slanted toward children of the Jewish faith, it is appropriate for children of all faiths. Entries are divided into twelve topics ranging from the Hebrew alphabet to biographies of people who are presently, or were in the past, prominent in the history of the Jewish faith. Entries comprise bibliographic information, an evaluative annotation, and a recommended age level. Chapters offer extensive lists of other recommended books not included with the annotated entries. Information on multimedia resources available is given in the concluding chapter.

Locating a guide to current children's literature with Jewish themes is difficult; therefore, in spite of the date of publication, this volume serves as a useful guide to the many books still available on library shelves. A more current bibliography of Judaica books for children has been produced by the Jewish Book Council (see entry 155), but it is more limited in scope and content.

155.   Jewish Book Council. **The Selected Children's Judaica Collection.** New York: Jewish Book Council, 1990. 77p. indexes.

This is an excellent referral source to Judaica books for children, most of which were published outside of Israel. Books in the catalog are arranged by age groups. The biblical entries are followed by legends and folklore. Other subjects under which titles are entered include "Exploring Jewish Identity," "Jewish Holidays," "History and Biography," "The Holocaust," and "Jewish History in Fiction." This book fills a major gap by bringing together children and recommended books relating to the Jewish culture.

156.   Sherman, Josepha. **A Sampler of Jewish American Folklore.** Little Rock, AR: August House, 1992. 215p. illus. ISBN 0-87483-193-8; 0-87483-194-6pa.

Sherman presents a well-documented compilation of 366 Jewish American folktales and customs. She has drawn her list from stories in oral, cultural, and religious traditions. Each entry is annotated and discusses the motif, as well as identifying the origin of the tale.

NATIVE AMERICAN LITERATURE

157.   Anderson, Vicki. **Native Americans in Fiction: A Guide to 765 Books for Librarians and Teachers, K-9.** Jefferson, NC: McFarland, 1994. 166p. indexes. ISBN 0-89950-907-X.

Anderson has selected fiction titles with main themes that reflect the lives and cultures of Native Americans. She lists 116 native tribes alphabetically within their geographical regions. Under the name of each designated tribe, books are entered alphabetically by author, using standard bibliographic format. Recommended grade levels and from one to three subject headings are included. The first appendix lists the major Native American tribes and their subtribes, each within geographical designations.

This book is a source of information that will be valuable for any library collection. Its approach is an interesting contrast to that used by Slapin and Seale (see entry 162).

158. de Usabel, Frances, and Jane A. Roeber. **American Indian Resource Manual.** Madison, WI: Wisconsin Department of Public Instruction, 1992. 147p. ISBN 1-57337-05-3.

The authors have designed a manual to provide practical assistance in the selection of Native American materials. It includes a checklist to be used as a guide for evaluating and recommending quality print and nonprint resources appropriate for all cultures. Although there is a Wisconsin emphasis, the list of recommended titles and suggestions for using them is appropriate throughout the United States. A human resources directory contains information on organizations, groups, and individuals who champion services to Native American populations.

159. Gilliland, Hap. **Indian Children's Books.** Billings, MT: Montana Council for Indian Education, 1980. 248p. maps. index. ISBN 0-89992-502-2.

The author advises the reader that the problem with books about Native Americans is not one of quantity but one of quality. A plethora of inaccurate, untrue, stereotypical portrayals of Native Americans are on bookshelves in homes and public libraries. It is difficult for the non-Indian to differentiate between portrayals that are accurate and those that are stereotypes. The Montana Council for Indian Education, using Native Americans to read and review most of the books, have developed an evaluative bibliography of children's books in which Native Americans are characters. In addition to the standard bibliographic information and a brief annotation, the following notations were used to indicate the extent to which each book portrays the Native American characters accurately: highly recommended, superior, questionable, and very questionable. A quick review of the bibliographic entries reveals that a great many of the books carry a "questionable" or "very questionable" notation. To assist in locating title entries, chapter 4 repeats the titles from the bibliography under one or more of these headings: tribe, region, interest area, and subject. Although the book is eighteen years old, many of the questionable titles are still available on library shelves.

160. Hirschfelder, Arlene B. **American Indian Stereotypes in the World of Children: A Reader and Bibliography.** Metuchen, NJ: Scarecrow, 1982. 296p. indexes. ISBN 0-8108-1494-3.

Hirschfelder discusses the all-to-often negative treatment of Native Americans in children's books. Seventy-five picture books are analyzed as examples of derogatory texts and illustrations to support her concern. Some of the titles she presents are still favorite children's books; some have received special recognition and awards. She also cites examples of uncomplimentary representations shown in other recreational reading books, textbooks, and even in children's toys.

This is an eye-opener! It raises the reader's consciousness about the negative impact that treatment of Native Americans in children's books has had over the years.

161.   Kuipers, Barbara J. **American Indian Reference Books for Children and Young Adults.** 2nd ed. Englewood, CO: Libraries Unlimited, 1991. 176p. indexes. ISBN 0-87287-745-0.

In her review of children's literature dealing with Native American culture, the author found, far too often, blatant stereotyping and misinformation. "Indians" were often depicted as apathetic and lacking in self-esteem. However, since the 1970s the demand for quality ethnic literature has increased, leading to a dramatic improvement in the way Native Americans are presented in fiction and nonfiction children's books. In spite of some improvements, the author expresses concern for the shortage of good nonfiction books for children on Native American culture. The author provides recommended criteria and guidelines for selecting high-quality and accurate representations. Annotated bibliographies of Native American reference books emphasizing an understanding and appreciation of the cultures make up a dominant portion of the text. The 200 entries are arranged by Dewey Decimal classification. Annotations are descriptive and evaluative and include relevant subject headings.

162.   Slapin, Beverly, and Doris Seale. **Through Indian Eyes: The Native Experience in Books for Children.** Philadelphia, PA: New Society, 1992. 312p. illus. index. ISBN 0-86571-212-3; 0-86571-213-1pa.

The authors have used an interesting and unusual approach in identifying children's books that present Native American cultures. They begin by providing a variety of approaches by which Native American cultures are reflected, including beautiful poetic expressions and spiritual contemplation. Materials included in the bibliography are a mixture of those highly recommended for their story content and portrayal of Native Americans, those identified as "acceptable," and those with which the authors find significant fault. It is surprising to observe that many titles identified in the latter category have received major awards or other special recognition. To be sure, the evaluations are quite subjective, but the reader's eyes are opened to stereotyping found in too many children's books considered "classics."

The bias of Slapin and Seale is quite evident, but their comments encourage the reader to look more critically at inaccuracies and stereotypes often found in literature for children.

163.   Stott, Jon C. **Native Americans in Children's Literature.** Phoenix, AZ: Oryx, 1995. 239p. indexes. ISBN 0-89774-782-8.

Recognizing that literature depicting Native American cultures has too often been replete with inaccuracies, misconceptions, and stereotypes, the author has made a sincere effort to examine literature for children in which Native American culture is an integral part and to identify books that are well crafted and faithful in their cultural representations. The introductory essay sets the tenor for the remainder of the book. The author analyzes five books in detail to illustrate how inaccurately they represent Native American peoples. Stott recognizes that often the misrepresentation is not intentional but rather a reflection of how society has historically viewed these native peoples. Each chapter focuses on one aspect of examining children's books for authentic cultural representation, such as reviewing major works by well-known authors to see how they present the Native American, examining a character in a well-known book to determine how well the cultural realities have been embodied in the text; and reviewing various genres of children's books in which Native Americans and their cultures are a major thrust of the text. Annotated reading lists and suggestions for incorporating Native American stories in language arts programs and in author and genre studies provide additional helpful guides.

This is a skillful, well-researched and well-presented source of valuable, thought-provoking information.

THE LITERATURE OF OTHER CULTURES

164. Beilke, Patricia, and Frank J. Sciara. **Selecting Materials for and About Hispanic and East Asian Children and Young People.** Hamden, CT: Shoestring, 1986. 178p. index. ISBN 0-208-01993-6.

Beilke and Sciara provide guidelines for in-service programs on using appropriate criteria for selecting multicultural literature for children. The emphasis is on identifying cultural relevance in books for children and young people. The first chapter is devoted to selection of Hispanic literature. The East Asian cultures about whom the authors did their research are Chinese, Japanese, Filipino, Korean, Vietnamese, Laotian, and Kampuchean (Cambodian). Each chapter includes a selective list of recommended books relating to each of the diverse cultures.

165. Blake, Barbara. **A Guide to Children's Books About Asian Americans.** Brookfield, VT: Scholar/Ashgate, 1995. 223p. index. ISBN: 1-85928-014-5.

Introductory chapters discuss the geographical areas, the culture, and the people of the three major Asian ethnic groups. East Asian cultures include China, Taiwan, Korea, Hong Kong, Southeast Asia, and South Asia; Southeast Asia includes the Philippines, Laos, Vietnam, Thailand, and Indonesia; and South Asia includes India, Pakistan, and Bangladesh. Fiction and nonfiction titles, published between 1970 and 1993, are first entered under their respective countries and then subdivided by category and recommended age level. In addition to the bibliographic information and a short synopsis, sources of reviews are presented. Indexes are by author, title, and culture.

This is an impressive source for locating recommended reading about countries from which many of our schoolchildren have emigrated; it also serves as a guide to collection building.

166. Jenkins, Esther C., and Mary C. Austin. **Literature for Children About Asians and Asian Americans: Analysis and Annotated Bibliography, with Additional Reading for Adults.** New York: Greenwood, 1987. 303p. indexes. ISBN 0-313-25970-4. ISSN 0742-6801.

Jenkins and Austin have provided approximately 575 titles of fiction and nonfiction books for children written by authors recognized as knowledgeable and perceptive about the cultures central to their stories. They selected literature mirroring the culture, history, physical setting, family, and social life of Asian people. Discussion of the native culture and their American counterparts are included for each of these cultures: Chinese, Japanese, Korean, and Southeast Asian. The bibliographic information is entered alphabetically by author within each racial group, and a descriptive and evaluative annotation is provided.

This information source makes locating references to literature on the cultures of Asia much easier.

167.   Khorana, Meena. **Africa in Literature for Children and Young Adults: An Annotated Bibliography of English-Language Books.** Westport, CT: Greenwood, 1994. 313p. indexes. ISBN 0-313-25488-5. ISSN 0742-6801.

This is a bibliography of African literature, consisting of stories and settings reflecting African cultures and religions and the diversity of tribal beliefs and customs. Annotations are provided for 697 books published between 1873 and 1994. Citations are provided for over 120 more books. Represented in the literature are the various African countries, their characteristic genres, authors, and literary trends. An overview of titles reveals an interesting multiplicity of viewpoints reflected in literature for children across this diverse continent. The introduction reflects on the historical development of African literature for children and analyzes the evolutionary steps that led to current standards. Entries are arranged according to regional locations and further subdivided into traditional literature, fiction, poetry, drama, biography and autobiography, and informational books. Bibliographic citations are followed by annotations that include thematic and literary analyses and a notation relating to the quality and appropriateness of the text. Author, title, and subject indexes are provided.

168.   Khorana, Meena. **The Indian Subcontinent in Literature for Children and Young Adults: An Annotated Bibliography of English-Language Books.** Westport, CT: Greenwood, 1991. 350p. indexes. ISBN 0-313-25489-3.

Khorana has prepared a generously annotated list of children's literature that reflects the culture, beliefs, and customs of five geographical areas on the subcontinent of India: Bangladesh; India; Pakistan; Sri Lanka; and the Himalayan kingdoms of Bhutan, Nepal, Sikkim, and Tibet. The author's purpose is to feature the unique qualities of each country's literature for children in order to promote a greater sense of national pride. More than 900 books written between 1940 and 1989 are entered under chapters with titles for the five geographical areas listed above. The selections, half of which were published outside the United States, focus on books for youth from preschool age to twelfth grade. Entries in each chapter are subdivided by the following genres: traditional literature, fiction, poetry, drama, biography and autobiography, and informational literature. Bibliographic citations are entered alphabetically by author and include a plot summary and thematic and literary evaluations. The indexes are by author/illustrator, title, and subject.

Khorana's publications are outstanding. They offer excellent guides for establishing diversified, multicultural library collections.

169. Makino, Yasuko, comp. **Japan Through Children's Literature: An Annotated Bibliography.** 2nd ed. Westport, CT: Greenwood, 1985. 144p. indexes. ISBN 0-313-24611-4.

The purpose of this publication is to help young Americans acquire an accurate image and understanding of Japanese people and their culture. Japanese Americans are not included; rather, the selection criteria is based on high-quality, authentic, and nonstereotypical presentations of people living in Japan. The books selected have been published in Japan and translated into English. The arrangement of entries is by subject, from "Art" to "Social Studies," and is further subdivided into more specific categories. Each entry, listed alphabetically by author, contains the bibliographic data, grade level, and annotation.

This is an interesting and useful source of information not easily located elsewhere.

170. Povsic, Frances F. **Eastern Europe in Children's Literature: An Annotated Bibliography of English-Language Books.** Westport, CT: Greenwood, 1986. 200p. ISBN 0-313-23777-8. ISSN 0742-6801.

Locating children's books with settings in Western Europe requires no special effort. Locating children's books set in the Eastern European countries is, however, a much more difficult task. Although many of U.S. citizens emigrated from countries in this geographical area, seldom do we find children's books that mirror these cultures and customs. The author points out the importance of identifying children's literature published in the United States and in other English-speaking countries that is set in Eastern European countries. She also strongly encourages more intercultural exchange with these countries. The 315 titles listed include traditional stories, fiction, collections of folk- and fairy tales, ballads, myths, legends, biographies, national proverbs, and collections of poetry. Countries in which the books have been set are Albania, Bulgaria, Czechoslovakia, Hungary, Poland, Rumania, and Yugoslavia.

Perhaps a greater recognition of the literature from and about Eastern European countries will result from the political changes this part of the world is currently undergoing.

171. Povsic, Frances F., comp. **The Soviet Union in Literature for Children and Young Adults.** Westport, CT: Greenwood, 1991. 284p. indexes. ISBN 0-313-25175-4. ISSN 0742-6801.

Povsic's bibliography provides a worthy reference source to Russian literature that offers a variety of worthwhile experiences for young readers. Included are 536 books published between 1900 and 1990 and written or translated into English. Entries are first grouped by major geographical and political regions of the Soviet Union and further subdivided by genre. The author introduces each geographical division with a discussion of the cultures of that region and their literary history. Within each group the titles are listed under one of the following headings: folklore, biography of Soviets and Soviet Americans, and historical and contemporary fiction about Soviets and Soviet Americans. The annotations include a plot summary, a literary analysis, awards received, and an evaluation of the illustrations. The indexes are easy to use and provide numerous cross-references.

Chapter 4

Subject Bibliographies

GENERAL SUBJECT BIBLIOGRAPHIES

172.   Barron, Neil, ed. **Anatomy of Wonder 4: A Critical Guide to Science Fiction.** 4th ed. New Providence, NJ: R. R. Bowker, 1995. 850p. 912p. ISBN 0-8352-3288-3; 0-8352-3684-6pa..

This fully revised and updated edition provides critical guidance to approximately 3,000 science fiction titles for adults and juveniles. It constitutes a historical survey of science fiction, including not only the most recent publications in this popular reading category but also the early books that introduced the science fiction genre to the world. The guide consists of short stories; poetry; comic books and comic strips; and nonprint media such as films, audiocassettes, and videocassettes. The contents are divided into two sections; section 1 contains primary source literature, and section 2 has secondary source literature. The annotations combine plot summaries and evaluative comments. A comprehensive theme index, excellent cross-references, and series information are useful features.

Because science fiction is currently one of the most popular recreational reading choices of readers young and old, no library serving the general public should be without this extensive guide.

173.   Brazouski, Antoinette, and Mary J. Klatt, comp. **Children's Books on Ancient Greek and Roman Mythology: An Annotated Bibliography.** Westport, CT: Greenwood Press, 1994. 185p. indexes. ISBN 0-313-28973-5.

The authors have compiled an excellent guide for teachers, librarians, and parents to use to introduce mythology to children. The introduction discusses the influence of classical mythology on the historical development of children's literature in the United States. Interesting commentaries on the sources from which each myth was drawn accompany the 381 books reviewed. References are made where significant deviations from the original ancient story lines have been found. Each entry contains the bibliographic information, an annotation that includes comments on the relevance of the illustrations to the theme of the myth, and recommended grade levels. Indexes include introductory materials, titles, illustrations, periods, and myths. This is an easy-to-use, detailed guide to mythology presented at children's level of understanding.

174. Carroll, Frances Laverne, and Mary Meacham, eds. **Exciting, Funny, Scary, Short, Different, and Sad Books Kids Like About Animals, Science, Sports, Families, Songs, and Other Things.** Chicago: American Library Association, 1984. 192p. indexes. ISBN 0-8389-0423-8.

A creative approach was used by the authors to determine what kinds of information children most often request when they come to the library. To make appropriate conclusions, over a considerable period of time the authors recorded and compiled the children's requests. They organized their findings under topics that reflect answers to questions such as "I want a book about [monsters]" or "I'd like to read a book by [Judy Blume]." The books are organized by age levels, then arranged alphabetically by author. Short annotations that accompany the entries are written to appeal to the interests of children. The authors' goal to be responsive to what children really want when they ask for a "book about . . ." has been more than adequately fulfilled.

175. Carroll, Frances Laverne, and Mary Meacham, eds. **More Exciting, Funny, Scary, Short, Different, and Sad Books Kids Like About Animals, Science, Sports, Families, Songs, and Other Things.** Chicago: American Library Association, 1992. 192p. indexes. ISBN 0-8389-0585-4.

The popularity of the first edition of this compendium of answers to the "I want a book about/by" questions of children paved the way for this most welcome update. It is not intended to replace the 1983 edition but rather to be used as a companion volume. New fiction and nonfiction titles have been added, and about seventy-five new topics are included: for example, "I want a twisted folktale," or "Do you have any books about aliens?" The brief annotations are written to pique the interest of the young reader.

What more can be said? It's a joy just to scan the entries and the time saved seeking answers is a godsend.

176. Cecil, Nancy L., and Patricia L. Roberts. **Developing Resiliency Through Children's Literature: A Guide for Teachers and Librarians, K-8.** Jefferson, NC: McFarland, 1992. 207p. index. ISBN 0-89950-707-7.

In their introduction the authors define the term "resiliency" as related to children; it is an interesting concept and worthy of the research involved in the preparation of this book. Some children are able to face squarely what may seem to be overwhelming odds. They are able to surmount the unpleasant experiences and ridicule associated with physical, emotional, and intellectual abuse and become stable and healthy adults. These children possess attributes that researchers identify as "resilience," or the ability to adapt to stressful environments or adjust to abusive situations. Cecil and Roberts, using this definition, ask the question, "Where are these traits of resiliency found in children's literature?" To answer the question, they sought models of resilience in children's books. They looked for characters who exhibited positive characteristics with which children can relate;

they pursued story lines in which characters were able to overcome their personal problems and take control of their lives. Section 1 identifies ninety-eight books written for children from kindergarten to grade three that reflect resiliency, as defined by the authors. Section 2 is a list of 139 books for grades four through eight that meet the resiliency criteria. Titles in each section are under one of four genres: contemporary fiction, folk literature, historical fiction, and geography. Each entry contains a bibliographic citation, with a brief annotation identifying traits of resiliency as presented in the story line. Also provided are suggested target activities. In-depth review and evaluation of each title is evidenced in this impressive, well-developed bibliography.

177.   Egoff, Sheila A. **Worlds Within: Children's Fantasy from the Middle Ages to Today.** Chicago: American Library Association, 1988. 339p. index. ISBN 0-8389-0494-7.

In her introduction, Egoff addresses emerging trends and patterns in fantasy literature significantly different from fantasy written before the 1960s. Current fantasy literature deviates from established conventions and, as a result, alters its purposes and values. Writers are now exploring new territories and incorporating new perspectives in their approaches to the world of fantasy. Chapter 1 is a discussion of the roots, substance, type, and value of fantasy. The author organizes titles chronologically, starting from the seventeenth century and continuing into the world of fantasy as mirrored in today's literature for children. Chapter headings lead the reader from the fantasy of the Middle Ages through Victorian times, the Edwardian age, and into the twentieth century. Following entries for the first quarter of the twentieth century, time segments no longer cover large blocks of time; from the 1940s forward each chapter covers a ten-year period, ending with the 1980s. Discussions of fantasy trends and patterns within each time segment are followed by bibliographies of books reflective of the trends and writing themes of that period.

Fantasy continues to be a popular genre for readers of all ages. The discussion of how it has altered in purpose, process, and content over the centuries is a fascinating topic for study and discussion.

178.   Fakih, Kimberly Olson. **The Literature of Delight: A Critical Guide to Humorous Books for Children.** New Providence, NJ: R. R. Bowker, 1993. 269p. indexes. ISBN 0-8352-3029-9.

Humor is a "natural" for children. They love the chuckle books, elephant books, and just plain silly books. Fakih's research brings together the books most representative of good humor in children's books. The 785 titles range from the most recently published books to those that have been around for a while and those that have stood the test of time (including many that perhaps even grandma and grandpa laughed at as kids). The list includes fables, jokes, poems, and short stories. Each entry is organized under one of seventeen specific humor categories, each of which has been given a clever title, such as: "Cautionary Tales," "Corrective Humor," " 's Not Fair!," and "Just Plain Silly." Entries include bibliographic information, a descriptive and evaluative annotation, format (such as novel, picture book, or chapter book), and grade level. *The Literature of Delight* is now available on the Bowker CD-ROM, *Children's Reference PLUS*.

This delightful compendium of interesting and witty literature, which takes the reader from *Curious George* to *Mary Poppins*, will delight children of all ages (and no doubt some parents as well). What fun!

179.   Horner, Catherine Townsend. **The Aging Adult in Children's Books and Nonprint Media: An Annotated Bibliography.** Metuchen, NJ: Scarecrow, 1982. 242p. index. ISBN 0-8108-1475-7.

In her introduction Horner discusses ageism as it appears in children's books. As more people live to an older age, concern about their portrayal in children's books becomes more significant. The author researched children's books to identify titles that present aging adults as stimulating and active, as opposed to the too-often depicted "rocking chair" sitters. She seeks to provide the reader with a bibliography of children's books that are more realistic in their depiction of the aging process and death. Each entry, arranged according to recommended age levels, includes a bibliographic citation and a descriptive paragraph. Horner's personal comments allude to misrepresentations or negative portrayals of senior citizens and the aging process. A multimedia section includes filmstrips, videotapes, and slides of books of which senior citizens are an integral part. A bibliography of topical magazine articles is also included.

180.   Horner, Catherine Townsend. **The Single-Parent Family in Children's Books: An Annotated Bibliography.** 2nd ed. Metuchen, NJ: Scarecrow, 1988. 339p. indexes. ISBN 0-8108-2065-X.

Horner's introduction implies that the loss of a parent to death or divorce too often is a child's first and most traumatic devastating experience. The child is faced with the realization that life, in the cycle of human experience, is a dynamic process of change and adaptation, of loss as well as gratification. Although single-parent homes are not a new phenomenon, seldom was reference made to them in children's books until recently. The sexual revolution of the 1960s opened doors to less stereotyping of single-parent families and more openness and realism in books for children and young adults; thus the problem novel became a popular genre. By the 1980s the single-parent home had come into its own as an acceptable family unit, and today it is a common theme in youth literature. Divorce, death, separation, desertion, remarriage, unwed mothers—all are life experiences that are no longer taboo to discuss. The 600 books selected for inclusion, most of which are fiction titles, are organized under one of the causes of single parenthood. More than 250 of the single-parent books fall into the categories of divorce, separation, and desertion; more than 230 identify the cause of the single-parent home as loss by death of a spouse. The annotations, which provide a good synopsis, are expository only. Included with each title index entry is a brief plot synopsis; this provides an excellent ready-reference source.

The author's interesting approach to identifying single-family themes in realistic fiction is worthy of consideration for purchase; this genre is quite reflective of today's more permissive society.

181.   Kilpatrick, William, Gregory Wolfe, and Suzanne M. Wolfe. **Books That Build Character: A Guide to Teaching Your Child Moral Values Through Stories.** New York: Simon & Schuster, 1994. 332p. index. ISBN 0-671-88423-9.

The authors' objective is to introduce children to books that will help them grow in virtue, understanding, and empathy toward others. They direct the reader to the many well-crafted stories that display honesty, responsibility, and compassion as valid attributes to possess. They identify book characters who exhibit acceptable codes of conduct in their ideals and actions. These characters are referred to as examples for children to emulate in their own lives. The first five chapters provide discussions of moral values, challenges for parents, and guides for selecting books that reflect positive values. These chapters are followed by bibliographies of children's books in which acceptable moral values are presented. The books are organized under nine subjects, which include sacred texts and books for holy days in addition to the standard subjects such as fables, contemporary fiction, and biography. Bibliographic citations are followed by a summary identifying one or more moral values reflected in the text. A brief list of recommended films available on videocassette, listed by title, concludes the textual materials.

Books selected for this bibliography reflect the authors' personal interpretations of "moral imagination." Examples of books discussed are Tomie dePaola's *The Clown of God* (Harcourt Brace Jovanovich, 1978); Katherine Paterson's *Jacob Have I Loved* (Harper, 1990); and Robert Cormier's *The Chocolate War* (Dell, 1974;1986).

182.   Lynn, Ruth Nadelman. **Fantasy Literature for Children and Young Adults: An Annotated Bibliography.** 4th ed. New Providence, NJ: R. R. Bowker, 1995. 1092p. indexes. ISBN 0-8352-3456-8.

The fourth edition of Lynn's annotated bibliography of fantasy maintains the quality and comprehensive coverage of her previous editions. Fantasy is an especially interesting literary genre because it cuts across all age levels and tends to be either "loved" or "hated." It seems to mean one thing to one reader and something quite different to another. Lynn recognizes this dichotomous response to the genre and has been able to provide answers to whatever questing mode the reader selects. Her primary criteria for selection is stated as "outstanding contemporary fantasy." She has also included science fiction and horror novels in which fantasy plays a dominant role.

Part 1 is an annotated bibliography of 3,150 numbered fantasy novels and story collections for children grades three to twelve; 1,500 have been added since the last edition. It also includes 1,650 sequels or related works by authors. Part 2 is a research guide to more than 10,000 articles, books, and doctoral dissertations related to fantasy literature, 4,000 of which have been added since the last edition. It includes books published in English in the United States between 1900 and 1994, plus a few classic titles written before 1900. The entries are arranged in ten topical chapters with excellent cross-references. Each entry includes an annotation, a grade-level designation, and citations to reviews from at least one of twenty-nine professional reviewing sources. Recommendation symbols are used, and references to awards and honors are included. *Fantasy Literature for Children and Young Adults* is now available on the Bowker CD-ROM, *Children's Reference PLUS.*

183.   MacDonald, Margaret Read. **Celebrate the World: Twenty Tellable Folktales for Multicultural Festivals.** New York: H. W. Wilson, 1994. 225p. index. ISBN 0-8242-0862-5.

The author, believing that folktales serve as a means of building bridges between cultures, has selected twenty folktales from various ethnic groups to illustrate how to use folk literature to encourage better understanding of diverse cultures. Special festivals in which folktales play a part are identified and described; they are accompanied by guidelines for using the tales as informational literature. Festivals chosen are those in which children play an integral part of the celebration. Also listed are titles of folktales that integrate into the text a description of the ethnic festivals celebrated. They are accompanied by suggested crafts, music, food, and games. Notes on reading and telling folktales provide additional suggestions for use.

184.   Miles, Susan G. **Adoption Literature for Children and Young Adults: An Annotated Bibliography.** Westport, CT: Greenwood, 1991. 201p. indexes. ISBN 0-313-27606-4. ISSN 0742-6895.

Miles has provided an extensive bibliography of literature for young people in which the issue of adoption is an integral part of the story. The 500 titles selected are arranged in four major sections by age levels, then alphabetically by author. Brief bibliographic information for each title is followed by a lengthy annotation that reviews each book's strengths and weaknesses as they relate to adoption. The topics used include the age of arrival; sibling adoptions; single-parent adoptions; adoptions by foster parents; and adoptions of transitional, minority, and special needs children. Appendixes and three indexes, which include many cross-references, complete the publication. The coverage is wide, and the critical comments help the reader make appropriate selections.

185.   Newman, Joan E. **Girls Are People Too! A Bibliography of Nontraditional Female Roles in Children's Books.** Metuchen, NJ: Scarecrow, 1982. 195p. index. ISBN 0-8108-1500-1.

Despite the fact that this book was published more than ten years ago, many of the titles cited are still popular with children. Although the double standard based on gender is not as prevalent in recently published children's books, it is still a topic that deserves attention. The author identifies books in which the female character does not reflect in her actions and attitudes the traditional passive roles so often found in children's books. Newman specifically looks for female role models who display, among other attributes, dignity, intelligence, a spirit of adventure, and self-confidence. The age levels for which these fiction and nonfiction books are intended range from preschool to the ninth grade. The books, with fiction and nonfiction entered separately, are organized under the following headings: "General," "Black," "Native American," "Handicapped," and "Other Minorities." Each entry provides bibliographic information, a brief plot summary, and a rating for positive female characterizations, using the terms excellent, good, or fair. The appendix offers an extensive chronological listing of notable events and personalities in the history of women.

186. Pearl, Patricia. **Children's Religious Books: An Annotated Bibliography.** New York: Garland, 1988. 316p. indexes. ISBN 0-8240-8531-0.

The purpose of this bibliography is to provide a comprehensive overview of fiction and nonfiction books with overt religious themes for children from preschool to sixth grade. All major religions are represented in the more than 1,000 titles listed in the bibliography. Books are arranged first by theme, then alphabetically by author. Bibliographic citations are followed by brief, critical annotations and age level designations. Although there is a chapter on Judaism and another on other religions of the world, the largest number of entries are for books with themes related to Christianity.

187. Pyles, Marian S. **Death and Dying in Children's and Young People's Literature: A Survey and Bibliography.** Jefferson, NC: McFarland, 1988. 173p. index. ISBN 0-89950-335-7.

Pyles indicates in the introduction that in recent years references to death and dying are seen more frequently in literature for children. The subject is common in folklore and often alluded to in classic literature, but it is only recently that authors have felt at ease with the topic in children's books. Death is no longer a taboo subject, only to be hinted at but never mentioned. Pyles's introduction provides an excellent essay about society's attitudes toward death and dying. She notes that no child is exempt from the possibility of being exposed to death and dying. Books can open doors for children, all of whom must personally deal with death and dying; they can help children come to a better understanding of the grieving process and can offer appropriate ways to cope with it. The author believes that reading about a character with similar problems or similar reactions to death and dying helps children articulate and accept what they cannot change. Chapter 1 discusses how well the topic has always been dealt with in folklore, and it includes references to well-known folk literature. Subsequent chapters survey the literature dealing with the death of a pet, the death of a friend, the death of relatives, and finally with one's own impending death. Pyles concludes her publication with two more bibliographies related to the topic, one for parents and one for children.

188. Roberts, Patricia L. **Alphabet: A Handbook of ABC Books and Book Extensions for the Elementary Classroom.** 2nd ed. Metuchen, NJ: Scarecrow, 1994. 264p. index. ISBN 0-8108-2823-5.

This is a revised and extended edition of Roberts's 1987 alphabet book (see entry 189). It is not intended to replace the earlier edition but rather to build upon it. The reader will need some knowledge of language development in young children in order to fully understand the terminology of some of the language patterns under which the nearly 500 books are entered. Within the variety of language patterns identified, books are grouped alphabetically by themes, such as animals, city life, history, games, and so on. Titles selected for inclusion are annotated and analyzed to identify specific language patterns and how they influence a child's language development.

189.   Roberts, Patricia L. **Alphabet Books as a Key to Language Patterns: An Annotated Action Bibliography.** Hamden, CT: Library Professional Publications, 1987. 263p. ISBN 0-208-02151-5.

The author discusses research on the role of patterns in supporting a young child's developing language, literacy, and learning skills. The bibliography of alphabet books that she has selected reflects the role alphabet books play in the early development of language skills. The alphabet books are arranged by the features they contain that can be presented as models of language patterns. Each of the approximately 500 books listed contains bibliographic information, an annotation, and recommended age levels. This is an interesting concept, and the alphabet books selected serve to provide a learning experience as well as a recreational activity.

190.   Roberts, Patricia L. **Counting Books Are More Than Numbers: An Annotated Action Bibliography.** Hamden, CT: Shoestring Press, 1990. 270p. index. ISBN 0-208-02216-3; 0-208-02217-1pa.

Counting books, if introduced in early childhood, can prepare children for an understanding of mathematical concepts, thus making the move toward higher-level concepts involving logic easier. Roberts's introduction discusses the difficulties some children have with math concepts, the varieties of approaches used in math books for children, and how simple primary math helps stimulate creative problem solving. The core content is an annotated action bibliography of 350 counting books, organized under four categories: "ABC and 1-2-3," "Rhymes," "Collection of Related Objects and Stories," and "Collection of Unrelated Objects." Emphasis is placed on the principle of combining counting aloud with a physical activity. The approach is especially useful for children in kindergarten to grade two. Each bibliographic entry provides a good content annotation and a description of the principles of mathematical concepts within the book.

This should be a valuable resource for parents and teachers working with children on the development of approaches to problem solving.

191.   Roberts, Patricia L., Nancy L. Cecil, and Sharon Alexander. **Gender Positive! A Teachers' and Librarians' Guide to Nonstereotyped Children's Literature, K-8.** Jefferson, NC: McFarland, 1993. 192p. index. ISBN 0-89950-816-2.

The authors have selected four genres of children's books to illustrate and promote positive, nonstereotypical images. Their goal is to communicate the message that behaviors do not have to be based on gender, that most activities and attitudes are appropriate for either sex. Two hundred and fifteen books have been selected in which the main character or characters have attributes and attitudes that discourage the sexual stereotyping too often found in children's books. Genres in which positive gender attitudes and actions are found tend to be contemporary realistic fiction, folk literature, historical fiction, and biography. Many of the books listed are popular favorites, especially with girls; two examples are Beverly Cleary's Ramona series and Elizabeth George Spear's *Witch of Blackbird Pond*.

Gender Positive! is a good guide to books that reflect positive gender experiences. It is well researched and easy to use.

192.　Sadler, Judith DeBoard. **Families in Transition: An Annotated Bibliography.** Hamden, NJ: Archon Books, 1988. 251p. ISBN 0-208-02180-9.

Although the first thirteen chapters of this book have adult-oriented entries, the author has devoted one chapter to books for children and young adults. She has identified more than 300 children's and young adult books relating to transitional families. Among the topics addressed in the books in the bibliography are the following: single parents, stepfamilies, adoptions, divorce, remarriage, parental kidnapping, and foster families. Despite the fact that only a portion of this publication relates to children, the topic is essentially appropriate in this bibliography of information sources for children's literature.

193.　Storey, Dee. **Twins in Children's and Adolescent Literature: An Annotated Bibliography.** Metuchen, NJ: Scarecrow, 1993. 410p. indexes. ISBN 0-8108-2641-0.

Storey has made an interesting choice of topics for her research. Of universal interest is the phenomenon of multiple births; the author's purpose is to identify children's books in which twins are an integral part of the story. Her research spans eighty-eight years of children's books, beginning with 1904 and continuing through 1992. She found that the profile of the average "twin" book reflects middle-class white families with some kind of family problem, and, strange as it may seem, she found that some mystery to be solved was usually an element of the plot. Each entry contains bibliographic information and an annotation that describes the family situation and identifies any special "twin" issue. Entries are either placed under the heading "twins" or a general topic that encompasses a variety of approaches to being a twin, such as facsimiles, clones, robots, or mistaken twins. The multidirectional indexes are entitled "Twins as the Main Characters," "Twins as Secondary Characters," and "Twins as Minor Characters." The findings are intriguing, and the format is easy to use.

194.　Strickland, Charlene. **Dogs, Cats, and Horses: A Resource Guide to the Literature for Young People.** Englewood, CO: Libraries Unlimited, 1990. 225p. indexes. ISBN 0-87287-719-1.

Children have a natural love for domesticated animals. The popularity of books in which dogs, cats, and horses play a major role attests to this fact. The bibliography includes fiction and nonfiction titles with underlying themes reflecting courage, compassion, fair play, and devotion. This genre attracts the reluctant reader as readily as it does the gifted child. The bibliography represents a core collection of 630 children's books for elementary to high school ages published within the last twenty years. Selections are made using literary quality as an important criterion, but at the same time appealing to children is equally significant. Each entry contains bibliographic information, a plot or content summary, the intended audience, and the theme. Entries are arranged under one of three subject categories: dogs, cats, or horses.

Young readers will delight in this reference source; it is a valuable tool for finding answers to questions such as, "How do I find another book about [dogs, cats, horses]?"

195.   Thomas, Virginia Coffin, and Betty Davis Miller. **Children's Literature for All God's Children.** Atlanta: John Knox Press, 1986. 107p. indexes. ISBN 0-8042-1690-8.

Thomas and Miller have developed an annotated list of children's stories, poems, folk tales, and fiction that express Christian principles. They describe their bibliography as a bridge between the Bible and contemporary life. The first half of the text contains selection guides and suggestions for using the recommended books in an effective way. Enduring children's favorites and other well-known books are cited in the discussions. Basic bibliographic information is provided for the 194 recommended titles, and comments on themes and values in the books are reflected in the annotations. Indexes are guides to themes and subjects, genre, and children's book awards.

This should be especially useful to the anyone seeking books whose contents reflect Christian principles.

196.   Ward, Martha E., and Dorothy Marquardt. **Photography in Books for Young People.** Metuchen, NJ: Scarecrow, 1985. 93p. indexes. ISBN 0-8108-1854-X.

The authors have prepared a representative sample of the use of photography in books for children and young adults, with emphasis on informational literature and using photography for illustrative purposes. Although the approach is biographical in nature (see entry 311 for complete annotation), explanations of each photographer's specialties, with a listing of the books in which the photographs are found, provide a useful tool for locating examples of the photographers' photos.

197.   Wear, Terri A. **Horse Stories: An Annotated Bibliography of Books for All Ages.** Metuchen, NJ: Scarecrow, 1987. 277p. indexes. ISBN 0-8108-1998-8.

It has been said that horse stories continue to have more universal appeal over the years than any other genre of children's books. In order to make it easier for children to locate a variety of books in which horses have an important role in the story, Wear has researched a wide variety of print resources to bring together this annotated bibliography of more than 1,500 fictional titles. The bibliography is composed of a broad range of horse stories, including, of course, the equine familiar to all, also ponies, donkeys, mules, merry-go-round horses, rocking horses, and toy horses (but no unicorns). The following are the categories in which the books are entered: picture books; easy readers; and juniors, young adult, and adult books. In each category the titles are arranged alphabetically by author and include brief bibliographic information with a two-sentence plot description. The most interesting index is the one identifying the many kinds and breeds of horses, accompanied by references to books in which they can be found. In relation to the recommended interest levels, it is clear that many horse stories written for adults are also read enthusiastically by younger children.

As evidence of the lasting value of horse stories, it is interesting to note that many of the horse storybooks published years ago are still on the popular/favorite reading lists of children today.

198. Wilkin, Binnie Tate. **Survival Themes in Fiction for Children and Young People.** 2nd ed. Metuchen, NJ: Scarecrow, 1993. 200p. indexes. ISBN 0-8108-2676-3.

This text is an examination of realistic children's books that explore the themes of human existence and survival. Wilkin uses the term "survival" to apply to the characters' struggles with matters of heart and to circumstances challenging the protagonist to question what is happening and to seek answers. Public awareness of and concern about issues such as AIDS, child abuse, incest, and other medical and social problems has been growing at a rapid pace. The author discusses the spirit of these often-controversial themes and identifies their presence in books for youth. Title entries are divided into the following broad sections: "The Individual," "Pairing and Grouping," and "Views of the World." Each of these sections is subdivided into chapters reflecting the section title. Standard bibliographic information, arranged alphabetically by title, includes broad age level categorization. The annotations are well written and include both descriptive and evaluative comments. Each section closes with programming suggestions and lists of selected audiovisuals available. Titles of articles, publications, and brochures relevant to the topic are supplied. The text concludes with separate author, title, and illustrator indexes. The selections included in this text reflect an intelligent approach to sensitive topics.

199. Wilms, Denise, and Ilene Cooper, eds. **A Guide to Non-Sexist Children's Books: Volume II: 1976-1985.** Chicago: Academy, 1987. 240p. indexes. ISBN 0-89733-161-3; 0-89733-162-1pa.

Literature for children mirrors the conventions of the times in which a book is written. Concern with the stereotypical models offered in books for children prior to the 1970s prompted this search by Wilms and Cooper for stronger, less subservient female characters. Picture books, novels, poetry, folklore, and nonfiction books included in this guide reflect a rich sampling of books that are nonsexist in attitude. More than 680 role-free recommended books for preschool through high school age children have been identified and annotated. Many of the books present strong female role models; others are about troubled young people, regardless of sex, who are working to establish their own identity, rise above difficult situations, and resolve their own problems. Fiction and nonfiction entries, listed separately, are entered under one of the three broad age groupings and then arranged alphabetically by author. They include a brief bibliographic citation and a short annotation with comments on the strengths of the protagonist.

THE SOCIAL SCIENCES

Geography

200. **Exploring the United States Through Literature Series.** 7 vols. Phoenix, AZ: Oryx Press, 1994.

This series updates a similar eleven-volume series of regional bibliographies published between 1979 and 1985 by the American Library Association, titled Reading for Young People. The purpose of the series is to provide assistance in locating quality literature set in seven geographical regions of the United States.

Each volume is put together by a different editor and within each state section, the information has been compiled by a resident of that state. References cited are appropriate for children from kindergarten to eighth grade. Each regional book is divided into state sections, and within each state section are annotated print and nonprint materials that relate to the history, culture, geography, resources, industry, literature, lore, and famous personages of that state.

Children will find this valuable information source easy to use independently to locate vital information about their own state, as well as to become familiar with a variety of useful and interesting information on other states in the United States.

200.1. Brodie, Carolyn S., ed. **Exploring the Plains States Through Literature.** Phoenix, AZ: Oryx Press, 1994. 124p. index. ISBN 0-89774-762-3.

200.2. Doll, Carol A., ed. **Exploring the Pacific States Through Literature.** Phoenix, AZ: Oryx Press, 1994. 131p. index. ISBN 0-89774-771-2.

200.3. Frey, O. Diane, ed. **Exploring the Northeast States Through Literature.** Phoenix, AZ: Oryx Press, 1994. 260p. index. ISBN 0-89774-779-8.

200.4. Latrobe, Kathy Howard, ed. **Exploring the Great Lakes States Through Literature.** Phoenix, AZ: Oryx Press, 1994. 149p. index. ISBN 0-89774-731-3.

200.5. Sharp, Pat Tipton, ed. **Exploring the Southwest States Through Literature.** Phoenix, AZ: Oryx Press, 1994. 107p. index. ISBN 0-89774-765-8.

200.6. Smith, Sharyl G., ed. **Exploring the Mountain States Through Literature.** Phoenix, AZ: Oryx Press, 1994. 157p. index. ISBN 0-89774-783-6.

200.7. Veltze, Linda, ed. **Exploring the Southeast States Through Literature.** Phoenix, AZ: Oryx Press, 1994. 205p. index. ISBN 0-89774-770-4.

History

201. Adamson, Lynda G. **Literature Connections to American History, K-6: Resources to Enhance and Entice.** Englewood, CO: Libraries Unlimited, 1998. 542p. indexes. ISBN 0-56308-502-X.

202. Adamson, Lynda G. **Literature Connections to American History, 7-12: Resources to Enhance and Entice.** Englewood, CO: Libraries Unlimited, 1998. 624p. indexes. ISBN 0-56308-503-8.

Adamson states as her goal a desire for "young readers to have emotional responses to the people who made history. . . ." Reading historical fiction can offer vicarious experiences with the times and places significant in the history of the United States. To achieve her goal, in each volume the author has divided more than 2,500 entries into thirteen chapters, each of which represents a historical period in U.S. history. The five age levels identified within each historical period are kindergarten through second grade and grades 3, 4, 5, and 6 for the first book, and grades 7, 8, 9, 10, and 11/12 for the second book. Within each grouping are sections for historical fiction, historical nonfiction, biography, CD-ROMs, and videotapes. Books are first entered alphabetically by the author's last name then by title. The last three chapters contain annotated bibliographies of the books, CD-ROMs, and videotapes. The indexes are by author and illustrator, title, and subject.

This masterful undertaking by the author has, indeed, fulfilled her stated goal. These bibliographies will serve as excellent guides for teachers, librarians, parents, and students. *Literature Connections to World History, K-6* and *Literature Connections to World History, 7-12* are also available.

203. Adamson, Lynda G. **Recreating the Past: A Guide to American and World Historical Fiction for Children and Young Adults.** Westport, CT: Greenwood Press, 1994. 494p. indexes. ISBN 0-313-29008-3.

Historical fiction can be used as a resourceful method of encouraging children to become interested in history and the historical events that shaped the world. Whether it's a "good read" about the century in which the pyramids were built, a look at the lives of the Pilgrims when they settled in the New World, or perhaps, even a view of the horrors of war during World War II, historical fiction can convey events of history in an insightful, discerning way. The book's introduction provides an interesting discussion of historical fiction as a genre that encourages children to read for instructional and recreational purposes. The author selected 970 historical fiction books notable for their readability and accuracy; of these, 200 have received awards or other recognition for their excellence. Seventeen chapters are arranged geographically and then, within each geographic unit, by historical time periods. Each entry contains bibliographic information and a brief annotation. The seven important appendixes cover readability level, interest levels, highlights in history, subject guides, famous persons, sequels, and works by countries. This guide is appropriately organized and easy to use, and the entries are current. It is a valuable addition to any library collection.

204. Adamson, Lynda G. **A Reference Guide to Historical Fiction for Children and Young Adults.** Westport, CT: Greenwood Press, 1987. 401p. index. ISBN 0-313-25002-2.

Adamson has produced a good reference guide to historical fiction written for youth by award-winning authors. She describes the works, written since 1940, of eighty historical fiction writers, all of whom are recognized for their meritorious writings and historical accuracy. The historical fiction bibliography, entered alphabetically by author, includes a bibliographic citation and lengthy annotation for each entry that includes the setting; historical dates; main characters; historical personages; and for some of the entries, important historical aspects. The four informational appendixes present works according to the date of the setting and locale, works according to readability and interest levels, a bibliography on writing about historical fiction by the authors, and a secondary bibliography about the authors and historical fiction included in the guide. Although the approach to presenting a guide to historical fiction in this publication is notably different from Adamson's more current book (see entry 203), both volumes provide well-selected, quality reading recommended for children and young adults.

205.   Cordier, Mary Hurlbut, and Maria A. Perez-Stable. **Peoples of the American West: Historical Perspectives Through Children's Literature.** Metuchen, NJ: Scarecrow, 1989. 230p. index. ISBN 0-8108-2240-7.

Far too often the history of the American West is presented in a fragmented, piecemeal manner. Historical literature written for children can remedy this failing. Cordier and Perez-Stable provide a broad examination of the people, settings, and historical events of the American West as presented in both fiction and nonfiction books for children. One hundred historical titles are carefully reviewed and selected for their ability to enrich children's concepts of the history of the West and to define the people who were instrumental in the Western expansion of the United States. Locating books with multicultural and nonsexist perspectives about the history of the American West were essential in the selection process. A wide range of settings, historical dates, characters, and writing styles are represented. Seven broad subject headings have been selected to reflect various aspects of the historical development of the West. Books are entered by title under the following subject headings: "Homesteading and Settling the West," "Overland Journey and Wagon Train Trips," "Immigration and the Immigrant Experiences," "Native Americans," "American Southwest," "West Coast," and "Non-fiction Enrichment." Titles are coordinated by grade level and include a bibliographic citation with an evaluative and descriptive annotation.

The intent and execution of this guide are creditable; it is a valuable addition to any library collection.

206.   MacDonald, Eleanor Kay. **A Window into History: Family Memory in Children's Literature.** Phoenix, AZ: Oryx, 1996. 227p. index. ISBN 0-89774-879-4pa.

A Window into History is a resource guide to 203 selected books and audiocassettes that connect readers to stories reflecting the universal experiences of family life. Selections range from picture books based on a single event to novels or series of novels that chronicle a family history. MacDonald calls attention to the fact that American history, such as how immigrants came to this land and how the United States evolved into the multiethnic, multicultural society of today, serves as background for many favorite children's books. To the extent possible, she has included fiction and nonfiction books based on direct, firsthand experiences or a recounting of stories passed down from generation to generation. The following chapter titles reflect the full range of historical experiences in America: "Coming to the New World"; "Opening the New Land"; "The Other Frontier Story" (Native American stories); "Growing Up in the Country"; "Growing Up in Cities and Suburbs"; and "Fear, Loss, and Courage" (World War II). The appendixes provide information on oral history, techniques for genealogical research, and recommended titles by ethnic origins.

MacDonald's bibliography reflects a remarkable degree of research and analysis. This book should be a valuable addition to all libraries serving children.

207. Perez-Stable, Maria A., and Mary Hurlbut Cordier. **Understanding American History Through Children's Literature: Instructional Units and Activities for Grades K-8.** Phoenix, AZ: Oryx, 1994. 312p. index. ISBN 0-89774-795-X.

Perez-Stable and Cordier work together once again (see entry 205) to bring us an excellent bibliography of American history for children. Their introduction suggests that the study of history is all too often lacking in continuity. The authors believe the best way to bring a conceptual view of history to children is through well-written historical fiction and nonfiction that mirror events in the founding and building of the United States and reflect its cultural diversity. Children are enabled to understand historical events in a chronological sequence, reflecting cause-and-effect relationships within history, politics, society, and the humanities. Although a focus of this book is the development of instructional units incorporating literature in learning activities, the annotated book lists accompanying every instructional plan are valuable guides to well-written, authentic historical fiction. Through use of this book, children can be encouraged to enjoy good historical literature,; but selecting the best from the plethora of books available is an overwhelming task. The books recommended in this publication, which include nonfiction, biographies, folklore, and historical fiction, have been critically reviewed for realism in setting, period, events, characters, and literary quality.

This is an invaluable reference source that can be used as a guide to recommended reading by teachers, librarians, and parents.

208. Stephens, Elaine C., Jean E. Brown, and Janet E. Rubin. **Learning About . . . the Holocaust: Literature and Other Resources for Young People.** New Haven, CT: Library Professional Publications, 1995. 198p. index. ISBN 0-208-02398-4.

The purpose of this bibliography is to assist adults in selecting and using literature about the Holocaust and its aftermath. The authors reviewed approximately 300 books written for young people from kindergarten through high school. Selection criteria include literary quality, historical authenticity, effectiveness in fostering connections with the subject, and appropriateness for each age group. Chapter 1 is a historical overview of the Holocaust. Chapters 2 through 6 contain a representative list of fiction and nonfiction titles on the Holocaust, divided into information books; photo essays and maps; personal narratives, biographies, and autobiographies; poetry; historical fiction; and plays. Entries provide bibliographic citations and annotated plot summaries, arranged first thematically by genre and then by grade levels, followed by abbreviated annotations of additional works. The concluding chapter provides information on additional resources for learning about the Holocaust, including films and video and audio recordings. The indexes are by author and title.

Holocaust literature is an expanding field; this publication provides an excellent selection of both recent publications and those now considered classics.

209.   Taylor, Desmond. **The Juvenile Novels of World War II: An Annotated Bibliography.** Westport, CT: Greenwood, 1994. 175p. indexes. ISBN 0-313-29194-2. ISSN 0742-6801.

During the process of selecting historical fiction books set during World War II, the author looked for plots and topics that provided a view of this time of conflict at a level youth could understand. The bibliography includes books with plots that reflect the events leading up to the outbreak of the war, wartime experiences, and the aftermath. Subjects dealt with in the 438 novels in Taylor's bibliography include the Holocaust and Japanese internment camps, as well as specific battles and the heroic efforts of soldiers involved in the conflicts. Entries are arranged first in chronological order then alphabetically by author. Age levels for whom the recommended titles are intended extend from upper elementary to high school. Although war itself is an unpleasant topic, the author carefully examined each novel for narrative that presents positive images, courage, and heroism.

210.   Van Meter, Vandelia. **American History for Children and Young Adults: An Annotated Bibliographic Index.** Englewood, CO: Libraries Unlimited, 1990. 324p. indexes. ISBN 0-87287-731-0.

Locating books on specific periods in American history can be a time-consuming task. Van Meter's annotated bibliography is an excellent guide to 2,901 fiction and nonfiction titles, including biography, which were published for children from kindergarten to twelfth grade. Most of the titles were published between 1980 and 1988 and include all aspects of American life from the very beginning of known history in this land to the present. In the selection process more than 6,000 reviews were read from nine reviewing periodicals. The entries are arranged chronologically under eleven time categories, then alphabetically by subject within each period. Each entry provides the bibliographic citation, citations to reviews, and a very brief annotation. Indexes are by author, title, subject, series title, and grade level.

211.   Van Meter, Vandelia. **World History for Children and Young Adults; An Annotated Bibliographic Index.** Englewood, CO: Libraries Unlimited, 1992. 266p. indexes. ISBN 0-87287-732-9.

The purpose of this publication is to provide an annotated bibliography of current fiction and nonfiction books relating to world history. Geographical designations are Africa, Asia and Oceania, Europe, North America, and South America. Historical designations are World War I and World War II, plus a general category. The 2,234 entries are arranged first by continent and then by nation. Each title, entered alphabetically by author, is followed by bibliographic information and a brief annotation. Entries also include citations to reviews from standard book reviewing sources. Indexes are by author, title, subject, series, and grade level.

This is a gold mine for teachers, librarians, and parents looking for the best way to get children turned on to historical fiction as a way of helping them understand the past and look to the future.

212. Walter, Virginia A. **War and Peace Literature for Children and Young Adults: A Resource Guide to Significant Issues.** Phoenix, AZ: Oryx Press, 1993. 171p. indexes. ISBN 0-89774-725-9.

Walter has prepared a bibliography of children's fiction and nonfiction books directed toward helping children understand the perplexities of war and peace, issues with which they are confronted daily on television and in newspapers. Books written at children's level can open their minds to a better understanding of the conflicts in history that have shaped the world. In schools and within family settings, curiosity about war and the peace process can be discussed and questions answered using appropriate children's books in historical settings as a bridge. In the first three chapters the author discusses elements related to finding the "right historically-oriented book for the right child at the right time," using specific book references to illustrate her points. This is followed by a classified bibliography of 480 titles divided into five major segments: real wars, imaginary wars, peace and conflict resolution, timeless truths, and visions for a better future. Each bibliographic entry is accompanied by a descriptive/evaluative annotation and recommended grade levels. The appendixes contain literature webs and activity webs that provide hands-on programs to extend an understanding of issues addressed in many of the books.

213. Welton, Ann. **Explorers and Exploration: The Best Resources from Grade 5 Through 9.** Phoenix, AZ: Oryx, 1993. 176p. index. ISBN 0-89774-799-2.

Welton's words may ring a bell for some readers when she suggests that perhaps the best reason to study explorers and exploration is that doing so provides a metaphor for our own inward dreams of travel and exploring new worlds. Although physical frontiers have diminished, the human urge to move outward and onward never disappears. The author brings us these worlds, as presented in literature for children. Chapters cover the last 1,000 years divided into ten decades. Each era is introduced with a brief narrative of the period, followed by an annotated bibliography of fiction and nonfiction books set in that period. Two hundred thirty titles, most of which have been published since 1986, have been selected to respond to the interests of students from fifth to ninth grade. The historical eras range from the days of Leif Eriksson and the Vikings to the present exploration of space. Each entry contains a bibliographic citation and a descriptive and evaluative annotation.

Students, researchers, teachers, librarians, and parents will enjoy using this excellent bibliography.

THE SCIENCES

214.   Gath, Tracy, and Marian Sosa. **Science Books and Films: Best Books for Children, 1992-95.** Washington, DC: American Association for the Advancement of Science, 1996. ca. 300p. index. ISBN 0-87168-586-8.

Based on reviews presented in the section "Science Books and Films" in the *AAAS Journal*, the editors have organized a bibliography of recommended science books and audiovisual materials appropriate to use with children from kindergarten age through the ninth grade. The entries are categorized into such topics as mathematics, ecology, animals, psychology, and ethics. Each critical annotation focuses on scientific accuracy. This publication from the highly respected AAAS is a valuable addition to any collection.

215.   Kennedy, Dayann M., Stella S. Spangler, and Mary Ann Vanderworf. **Science & Technology in Fact and Fiction: A Guide to Young Adult Books.** New York: R. R. Bowker, 1990. 363p. indexes. ISBN 0-8352-2710-3.

Too often the world of science and technology has been shunned by all but children identified as "gifted." The tide has turned. Today most elementary age children are familiar with terms such as lasers, rockets, satellite communications, genetic engineering, and artificial intelligence. The scientific world of fact and fiction is being woven into story plots in children's books with ease. Just as with adult novels, references to the technological world around us, its current status, and, even more often, future expectations serve as an adventure for the young reader. An interest in and an understanding of the world of science is being cultivated through the medium of reading. Interesting and adventurous new approaches to plot resolution are used more often. The authors indicate that although nonfiction books presenting the sciences once tended to use only the factual textbook approach, it is now more common to see these books replete with colorful pictures, interesting diagrams, and fun-filled ideas for experimentation. A wide variety of topics has been identified, and within each topic the authors have included both fiction and nonfiction book recommendations. Age levels range from upper elementary to high school. Reading levels are also broad, with some as low as third grade. Each entry provides a bibliographic citation, a plot/content summary, and an authoritative evaluation. The summary of each book is well written, and thought-provoking evaluations serve as good guides to recommended purchases. This publication is now available on the Bowker CD-ROM, *Children's Reference PLUS.*

216.   Lenz, Millicent. **Nuclear Age Literature for Youth: The Quest for a Life-Affirming Ethic.** Chicago: American Library Association, 1990. 315p. ISBN 0-8389-0535-8pa.

Using a consciousness-raising approach, Lenz introduces her book with a lengthy essay on concerns surrounding us as we see the effect of nuclear threats on the world and their potential future impact. The balance of the book, nine chapters, deals with different aspects of the nuclear age. Titles vary from "The Role of a

New Heroic Model" to "The Peace Pilgrim as Hero/Hera" to "The Quest for Wholeness in a Broken World." In each chapter Lenz cites books that refer in some way to what has happened, to what might happen, and to what is happening as result of the development of nuclear arms. The age levels of the books cited to illustrate and amplify the topic range from Dr. Seuss's *Butter Battle Book* to Pat Frank's *Alas Babylon*, and from Jean de Brunhof's *Babar* to Robert O'Brien's Newbery Medal–winning *Mrs. Frisby and the Rats of NIMH.*

Although this book is written on a scholarly level, the references to books written at all age levels identify it as a valuable reference source for children as young as elementary school age.

217.   Malinowsky, H. Robert. **Best Science and Technology Reference Books for Young People.** Phoenix, AZ: Oryx, 1991. 216p. indexes. ISBN 0-89774-580-9.

Malinowsky has provided a guide to 669 science and technology reference books for students from third grade through high school. The list is selected to ensure a good cross-section of subjects and includes both older, well-established titles and more recent publications. The chapters are organized under twelve science and technology-oriented subject headings, and within each chapter the books are entered according to format, such as bibliographies, manuals, encyclopedias, etc. Within each format, entries are arranged alphabetically by title with a bibliographic citation and brief annotation addressing special features. Appropriate grade levels and sources of book reviews also accompany each entry. Title, author, subject, and grade-level indexes provide quick access for the reader.

This is a very useful resource for all school and public library collections.

218.   Phelan, Carolyn. **Science Books for Young People.** Chicago: American Library Association, 1996. 80p. indexes. ISBN 0-8389-7837-1.

In her introduction, Phelan restates the truism that a good nonfiction book for children challenges minds with intriguing details about the complexity of the world without an overabundance of facts and details. She has selected a list of children's books that meet the criteria for the best in science for young people from kindergarten through eighth grade. Titles are entered under fourteen subject headings that reflect the pure sciences and range from astronomy to mammals. Included are such general science titles as Roy Gallant's *A Young Person's Guide to Science* (Macmillan, 1993) as well as Joanna Cole's *The Magic School Bus* series by McGraw-Hill Publishers and the Cousteau Society's *Seals* (Simon & Schuster, 1992). Bibliographies of science experiments are also provided. The annotations are based on reviews found in issues of the American Library Association's *Booklist* between 1990 and 1995. Bibliographic information, annotations, and suggested grade levels are provided for each recommended title.

This is a real bonanza for introducing science to children at a young age and continuing their interest and enthusiasm for science as they mature.

219.   Richter, Bernice, and Duane Wenzel, comps. **The Museum of Science and Industry Basic List of Children's Science Books, 1988.** Chicago: American Library Association, 1988. 80p. indexes. ISBN 0-8389-0499-8.

The authors have provided a comprehensive bibliography of science books for children. The following subjects are included: animals, astronomy, aviation and space, earth sciences, environment and conservation, life science, marine life, medical and health sciences, physics and chemistry, plant life, technology and engineering, and math and math concepts. Also included are biographical references and information about careers in the field of science and industry. Fiction and nonfiction books are included under the various subject categories. Appendixes provide indexes to publishers, science magazines and journals, and sourcebooks for adults.

220.   Sinclair, Patti K. **E for Environment.** New Providence, NJ: R. R. Bowker, 1992. 292p. indexes. ISBN 0-8352-3028-7.

This bibliography of children's books reflects current concerns about environmental issues. It is interdisciplinary in nature, involving science, art, literature, philosophy, technology, economics, sociology and politics. Apprehension about the environment and what is happening to the air, forests, wildlife, and streams has gained universal prominence during the last decade. Sinclair has researched current children's literature that addresses environmental issues and has located books that provide rich sources of both information and inspiration. With the goal of raising the consciousness of children from elementary to high school ages on environmental issues, many authors have chosen to focus on topics such as ecology, pollution, endangered animals, energy, and recycling. Five hundred and seventeen fiction and nonfiction books considered the best on environmental issues and themes have been selected for inclusion in this guide. Chapter bibliographies, each of which has a different environmental concentration, present a good balance of topics and age levels. Each entry is arranged alphabetically by author, with a bibliographic citation; where applicable, an indication of award-winning books; and interest level designations. Chapter focuses are books that help foster positive attitudes about nature; books about ecological communities; interrelationships between plants, animals and the environment; an extensive listing of selected books on current environmental concerns; and books to help children and adults become actively involved in learning more about nature and the environment through crafts and other activities. Appendixes provide a list of environmental classics and suggestions for further reading. *E for Environment* is now available on the Bowker CD-ROM, *Children's Reference PLUS.*

This is a very impressive compilation of books to help youth understand why we all must become more aware of what is happening environmentally and actively participate in activities such as recycling and Earth Day.

221.   Wilms, Denise Mureko. **Science Books for Children: Selections from *Booklist*.** Chicago: American Library Association, 1985. 183p. indexes. ISBN 0-8389-3312-2.

This is an earlier edition of the Phelan title (see entry 218) and has been included, in spite of the date, based on the number of books in this edition that are still located on library shelves and that, for the most part, are still appropriate for referral. In the introduction the author notes that young children love to explore the world around them. She states that books are an effective way to maintain that attraction and cultivate creative inquiry; they can "open new worlds." Her selections reflect the best of science trade books for children from preschool to junior high/middle school. She consulted the American Library Association's *Booklist* to locate most of the reviews. The Dewey Decimal Classification system is used as the access point for each title. Entries consist of bibliographic data, recommended grade levels, and a well-written descriptive and evaluative annotation.

This collection of recommended science books is a reliable resource to bring science and children together as early as possible.

222. Wolff, Kathryn, et al., comps. **The Best Science Books for Children: A Selected and Annotated List of Science Books for Children Age Five Through Twelve.** Washington, DC: American Association for the Advancement of Science, 1983. 271p. ISBN 0-87168-307-5.

To encourage children to learn about the wonders of life, earth, and the universe, the compilers have identified a representative list of recommended science books for children. They looked specifically for books that are scientifically accurate, that mirror science as a discovery process, whose writing style is clear and easy to understand, and that contain appropriate illustrative materials. The books, entered under the Dewey Decimal Classification format, include all aspects of science, for example, life sciences, medicine, engineering and technology, physics, mathematics, biology, geology, and family living.

Much has changed in the world of science since this was published, but many of the titles included are still appropriate for study and learning activities.

Chapter 5

Reference Books

GENERAL REFERENCE SOURCES

223.   Bingham, Jane M., and Grayce Scholt. **Fifteen Centuries of Children's Literature: An Annotated Chronology of British and American Works in Historical Context.** Westport, CT: Greenwood, 1980. 540p. indexed. ISBN 0-313-22164-2.

This outstanding reference source intended for scholars and serious researchers is a key to approximately 9,700 titles of book collections in Great Britain, Canada, and the United States. Each chapter matches a specific period of time, ranging from the Anglo-Saxon period (ca. 523-1099) to the twentieth century (1900-1945). Chapters begin with an introduction to the historical background of the period, a discussion of the development of books and writing during that period, and an overview of attitudes toward children and their place in the social customs of that era. An annotated bibliography of book collections, arranged chronologically, is provided in each chapter. The first two appendixes contain chronologically arranged checklists of U.S. and British periodicals for children. The third appendix lists facsimiles and reprints from the books included in the bibliography. Upon discovering this reference source, the historian and researcher of literature for children will find it hard to set aside.

224.   Dunhouse, Mary Beth, comp. **International Directory of Children's Literature.** New York: Facts on File, 1986. 128p. ISBN 0-8160-1411-6.

The author has compiled a resource guide to all aspects of information relating to the study of literature for children. The international scope, which includes eighty-four countries, provides access to data otherwise difficult to locate. Each directory item is entered first under the country of its origin, then organized under one of the following broad subject sections: book publishers; magazine publishers; magazine titles; organizations; fairs, seminars, and conferences; prizes; major library collections and special collections; and statistics on children's books. This is an interesting and informative reference source for locating a wide variety of information related to children's literature worldwide, in a one-volume publication.

225.   Horning Kathleen, ed. **Alternative Press Publishers of Children's Books: A Directory.** 3rd ed. Madison, WI: Cooperative Children's Book Center with the University of Wisconsin at Madison, 1988. 88p. ISBN 0-931641-02-4.

One hundred thirty-nine small, independently owned and operated presses in the United States and Canada that publish books for children are identified. Each entry contains a brief description of the press, the address and telephone number, the press's ISBN number, a contact person, the number of books in print, information on library holdings, and a description of the books published.

This is a small but important reference source for locating information about children's books published outside the mainstream publishing industry.

226.   Kastan, David Scott, and Emory Elliott, eds. **The Reader's Adviser: The Best in Reference Works, British Literature and American Literature.** 14th ed. Vol. 1 of 6. New Providence, NJ: R. R. Bowker, 1994. 1512p. indexes. ISBN 0-8352-3321-9.

This volume of *The Reader's Adviser* is designed for the nonspecialist as well as the professional researcher. The entire set is a survey of writers and writings that have made a significant impact on the world. Volume 1 is an introduction to general reference books and to British and American literature. It is organized into sixteen topics that vary from books about books to books on American literature and children's literature. Within each topic, where appropriate, references to literature for children are identified. Although the section devoted to children's literature provides many entries, readers are also advised to use the comprehensive index to locate entries in other sections. Each title entry contains extensive coverage, including critical and evaluative comments.

227.   Kohn, Rita, comp. **Once Upon . . . a Time for Young People and Their Books: An Annotated Resource Guide.** Metuchen, NJ: Scarecrow, 1986. 211p. index. ISBN 0-8108-1922-8.

The compiler's objective is to provide selective guides to locating materials on print and nonprint literature for children whose ages extend from infancy to young adult. Approximately 832 bibliographies of information sources to literature are recorded. To direct the user to the desired information, 220 subject headings have been selected. All genres of literature are represented in the guide. Entries are alphabetically listed by author and include bibliographic citations. The three appendixes list resource locations, review sources, and addresses of publishers. Title and subject indexes are included.

228.   Malinowsky, H. Robert. **Best Science and Technology Reference Books for Young People.** Phoenix, AZ: Oryx, 1991. 216p. indexes. ISBN 0-89774-580-9.

Malinowsky's guide to 669 science and technology reference books ensures a selective cross section of subjects in the sciences that are appropriate for children from grades three through high school. (See entry 217 for a complete annotation.)

229. Peterson, Carolyn Sue, and Ann D. Fenton. **Reference Books for Children.** 4th ed. Metuchen, NJ: Scarecrow, 1992. 399p. index. ISBN 0-8108-2543-0.

Reference Books for Children serves as a selection tool and a valuable informational guide to reference books on all subjects. The scope is broad, spanning many interests and providing entries at different levels of difficulty. The goal of the authors is to provide a bibliography of quality reference sources to be used with and by children. The introduction provides suggestions for the implementation of a variety of reference activities with children. An especially helpful chapter is that which provides guidelines for evaluating bibliographies, indexes, encyclopedias, dictionaries, almanacs, yearbooks, handbooks, directories, biographical sources, and atlases. Entries are arranged under five broad fields of knowledge: general reference, the humanities, recreation, science, and the social sciences; and within each field subdivisions have been established. Individual entries are arranged alphabetically by main entry and numbered consecutively. For each entry there is a complete bibliographic citation, followed by a descriptive annotation.

230. **Reference Books for Children's Collections.** 3rd ed. New York: New York Public Library, 1996. 97p. index. ISBN 0-87104-735-7.

This is an update of the New York Public Library's list of reference books of the highest quality, prepared by the Children's Reference Committee. The 399 titles are organized under nine topics: general reference; religion; folklore and mythology; the social sciences; language; science and technology; the arts; sports, games, and hobbies; and literature. Although most entries are either new titles or new editions of previous entries, some out-of-print titles of high quality are retained. They cover topics for which there are no current titles and they demonstrate continued relevance.

This inexpensive, excellent selection of reference sources should be a top-priority purchase for libraries serving children.

231. Rollins, Deborah, and Dona Helmer. **Reference Sources for Children's and Young Adult Literature.** Chicago: American Library Association, 1996. 56p. index. ISBN 0-8389-7838-X.

Two annotated bibliographies originally published in the "Reference Books Bulletin" section of ALA's reviewing periodical, *Booklist,* have been combined and updated with newly published titles. The result is this inexpensive, selective list of 150 titles of major reference sources to children's literature. Sources for children's literature and young adult literature are entered separately, with cross-references to titles appropriate for either age group.

This is a highly recommended, authoritative reference for school, public, and home libraries.

232.   Short, Kathy G., ed. **Research and Professional Resources in Children's Literature: Piecing a Patchwork Quilt.** Newark, DE: International Reading Association, 1995. 272p. indexes. ISBN 0-87207-126-X.

The need to review the knowledge base that supports the theory, research, and practice of using children's literature in school curricula was the impetus for the development of this research and professional resource guide, according to the editor. It was compiled by a group of fourteen professionals working together to search the literature and synthesize the body of research. The book is divided into three sections; the first section is an overview of research related to children's literature between 1985 and 1993, including analysis of trends and issues. Section 2 highlights professional journals used to locate reviews and provides lists of books and articles on specific topics. The last section contains annotations of professional books, theoretical foundations, literature discussions and response, cultural and genre studies, and more. Each section lists extensive bibliographic sources used or recommended.

233.   Siegel, Alice, and Margo McLoone Basta. **The Information Please Kids' Almanac.** Boston, Houghton Mifflin, 1992. 363p. illus. index. ISBN 0-395-64737-1; 0-395-58801-4pa.

Written in a manner similar to that of the world-renowned *Information Please Almanac* (McGraw-Hill), Siegel and Basta bring us an almanac that will tickle the fancies of kids of all ages. Children are just as fascinated with unusual facts and trivia as adults; and in this publication they have access to a wide variety of facts, offered at their level of interest and understanding. Fifteen topics are arranged alphabetically, and the informational entries are chosen to reflect the interests of children. For example, the first entry, "Animals," is followed by a list of subentries ranging from aardvark to zebra. The writing style is simple, and the line drawings and photographs enhance the articles. The book is replete with trivia, fascinating facts, and, to be sure, scholarly information, written to excite children's curiosity and at the same time provide for "just for fun" reading time. As is true of the adult version, browsing is ultimately the best way to really enjoy it; otherwise the reader is very likely to overlook some fascinating tidbit. (Did you know that an albatross can sleep while it is flying? Do you know when the yo-yo was first introduced as a toy?) Answers to these trivia questions and many more are easy to find in *The Information Please Kids' Almanac.*

Although the title identifies this as a reference source for children, adults will also be hooked as soon as they open the cover.

DICTIONARIES/ENCYCLOPEDIAS/GUIDES

234.   Carpenter, Humphrey, and Mari Prichard. **The Oxford Companion to Children's Literature.** New York: Oxford University Press, 1984. 587p. illus. ISBN 0-19-211582-0.

This reference book, modeled after the prestigious *Oxford Companion to English Literature* (Oxford University Press) covers both English and American books and authors of children's literature. The approximately 2,000 entries cover

traditional materials, along with less traditional formats such as cartoon characters, films, radio, and television related to children and reading. The wide variety
of topics range from early legends to current topics popular in children's literature.
Descriptive articles, including more than 900 biographical sketches, are entered in
dictionary format, moving from the beginning entry by Kate Greenaway, *A—Apple
Pie*, and closing with biographical information about the well-known author Charlotte Zolotow. Entries vary in length from multiple columns to only a portion of a
column. The carefully selected illustrations and the use of cross-references augment the quality and usefulness of this outstanding reference source. Another plus
is the coverage of literature from Canada, Australia, and New Zealand.

   The Oxford Companion is easy to use, the articles are well written, and the
coverage is noteworthy. This is the kind of publication that readers will want to
purchase for their personal library collections.

235.   Carruth, Gorton. **The Young Reader's Companion.** New Provi-
       dence, NJ: R. R. Bowker, 1993. 681p. illus. indexes. ISBN
       0-8352-2765-0.
       The Young Reader's Companion is an illustrated A-to-Z short-entry ency-
clopedia with the primary goal of promoting reading. Encyclopedic entries include
authors, book titles, and even characters from books. Classics, books that have
stood the test of time, and contemporary novels are selected for their appeal to
young people from grades five to high school. Genres include mystery, adventure,
fantasy, science fiction, problem novels, and nonfiction titles. Plot synopses are
written in direct, informal style. Entries are arranged alphabetically and range
from the article on the love story of Abelard and Heloise to the well-known author
Paul Zindel. The subject index is well organized and comprehensive.

   What a bonanza for eager readers of all ages! It will serve as a gold mine in
children and young adult collections in public libraries and school library media
centers.

236.   Garraty, John A., ed. **The Young Reader's Companion to Ameri-
       can History.** Boston: Houghton Mifflin, 1994. 964p. illus. indexes.
       ISBN 0-395-66920-0.
       Garraty has produced an excellent guide for youth to use to answer ques-
tions about the historical development of the United States, written at the interest
and readability level of children from fourth grade through middle school. Even high
school students and adult history buffs will revel in its simple, yet quality, coverage
of much of what made the United States what it is today. Articles, entered alphabetically, range from an excellent explanation of abolitionism to the impact of Flo Zieg-
feld on the world of entertainment during his years in Hollywood. Biographies of
presidents, writers, political leaders, and male and female shapers of history as well
as familiar personalities in the entertainment world are interesting and informative.
Topics cover the social, cultural, and political history of the United States. Young
readers are able to locate information on the history of the comic strip; on scouting;
and, yes, even on the history of children's literature in America. Entry articles do
more than just describe the significance of each topic/entry; they also define why
and how the topic is of historical significance. Articles were contributed by 150

persons, many of whom are writers of children's books. Appendixes include a map of the United States, a list of the states, a copy of the Declaration of Independence, and a copy of the Constitution of the United States. A general index follows credits for illustrations and contributor information.

The coverage, the philosophical approach to the historical information presented, and the readability of this publication distinguish it as an especially valuable book for the home library as well as school and public library collections.

237.　Sader, Marion, ed. **Reference Books for Young Readers: Authoritative Evaluation of Encyclopedias, Atlases, and Dictionaries.** New York: R. R. Bowker, 1988. 615p. illus. index. ISBN 0-8352-2366-3.

Selecting the best encyclopedia, atlas, or dictionary from the ever-increasing new publications of reference sources becomes a frustrating and overwhelming task. The editor has provided approximately 200 descriptive evaluations of encyclopedias, atlases, and dictionaries considered appropriate for young people from preschool through high school ages. The text is divided into five main sections. Part 1 includes the introduction, guidelines for selection, and useful comparison charts. Parts 2 through 4 cover, in this order, encyclopedias, atlases, dictionaries, and word books. The large print and easy-to-use format make this an information source children can use independently.

The update of this reference has been integrated into the adult edition and is now titled *Encyclopedias, Atlases & Dictionaries* (R. R. Bowker, 1995).

INDEXES

Fiction

238.　Anderson, Vicki. **Fiction Index for Readers 10 to 16: Subject Access to Over 8,200 Books (1960-1990).** Jefferson, NC: McFarland, 1992. 477p. index. ISBN 0-89950-703-4.

Librarians and library media specialists are approached on almost a daily basis with requests such as "Where can I find a book about [or by]. . . ." To facilitate answering questions like these, Anderson has provided subject access to more than 8,200 fiction books. She contends that her ultimate goal, "getting good books off the shelf," is more likely to be achieved through a subject-related index. The 225 topical headings under which the titles are entered represent a wide variety of subject and interest levels; they range from topics that are bound to attract the attention of even reluctant readers to topics that challenge the most competent readers. Criteria for selection are quality of writing, reader interest, and popularity. Broad subject headings, such as American history, are divided into more specific subheadings; it is possible for a book to be listed under as many as four subject headings. Interesting and somewhat unusual is the index to books with fewer than 100 pages (which will be popular with students trying to locate a book for a last-minute book report) and another for books with more than 300 pages. Also convenient is the index to books translated from a foreign language into English.

Fiction Index is a comprehensive, easy-to-use guide to fiction. It is a must-have for all libraries.

239. **Fiction, Folklore, Fantasy & Poetry for Children, 1876-1985.** 2 vols. New York: R. R. Bowker, 1986. 2562p. indexes. ISBN 0-8352-1831-7.

This comprehensive bibliography was begun in 1983 in response to the need for a single reference source to fiction literature for children. Critical guidelines were used in selecting the 133,000 entries provided in the text. The author and illustrator entries are located in volume 1; title entries and year-by-year winners of major awards for children's books are located in volume 2. The entry format mirrors that used in Bowker's *Books in Print.*

240. Lima, Carolyn, and John A. Lima. **A to Zoo: Subject Access to Children's Picture Books.** 4th ed. New Providence, NJ: R. R. Bowker, 1993. 1158p. illus. indexes. ISBN 0-8352-3201-8.

Selecting judiciously from the thousands of picture books available is made much easier as the result of this index to picture books for children. *A to Zoo* indexes more than 14,000 titles, recorded under nearly 800 subject headings. It is a pleasure to use; the design and illustrations are appealing. (See entry 72 for the complete annotation.)

241. Magill, Frank N., ed. **Masterplots II: Juvenile and Young Adult Fiction Series.** Vol. 3 of 4 vols. Pasadena, CA: Salem Press, 1993. index. ISBN 0-8935-6582-2.

Magill's Masterplots series has been considered a major literary reference source since it was first published in 1952. The newer series, Masterplots II, is a welcome addition to reference sources in literature for children and young adults. It focuses on literature that appeals to readers from ages ten to eighteen. Selection criteria are eclectic in nature, allowing for inclusion of children's classics, writers from the recent past, and contemporary writers. The more than 500 books discussed are arranged alphabetically by title. Included in each entry is the author's name, first publication date of the book, type of book, time of plot, locale, principal themes, recommended age levels, a brief plot summary, and major characters. The three-part essay detailing the story discusses themes, meanings, and context of the novel.

This set deserves to be a part of any library collection. Its contribution to children and young adult literature rivals the Masterplots series' contributions to adult literature. A supplement published in 1997 is now available from Salem Press (ISBN 0-8935-6916-X).

242. Pettus, Eloise S. **Master Index to Summaries of Children's Books.** 2 vols. Metuchen, NJ: Scarecrow Press, 1985. 1036p. indexes. ISBN 0-8108-1795-0.

Pettus's index to summaries of children's books, preschool to grade six, located in bibliographies, textbooks for teaching children's literature, and books of activities based on children's books, is unique. Reference sources cited are those published between 1974 and 1980. Volume 1 contains the introduction; a list of the eighty-six sources in which summaries are located, each with a unique key code; and the master index of 18,631 book summaries. Each book in the master index is entered alphabetically by author or editor with brief bibliographic information, followed by the key code and page numbers for locating the summary. Volume 2 contains a title index and a comprehensive subject index.

This was quite an undertaking on the part of the author. It is especially useful to the researcher seeking multiple summaries and reviews for a particular title.

243.   Pflieger, Pat. **A Reference Guide to Modern Fantasy for Children.** Westport, CT: Greenwood, l984. 690p. ISBN 0-313-22886-8.

This volume is a valuable guide to plot summaries for the avid fantasy reader and even for the lukewarm reader looking for "something different." The fantasy genre continues to grow in popularity; many well-known writers of adult fantasy have entered the field of writing for children, adding to the acceptability of fantasy as a literary form. The author makes no attempt to be comprehensive in coverage of fantasy literature; rather, she is selective. She identifies thirty-six nineteenth- and twentieth-century British and American writers who have written more than 100 works of fantasy recommended for children. The dictionary format is used, and entries for authors, titles, book characters, places, and magical objects are arranged alphabetically. Each entry includes a one- to two-paragraph commentary. The three appendixes list general reference sources that discuss fantasy as a genre, the chronology of fantasy as a form of literature, and illustrations in the books identified. A general subject index completes this well-organized, easy-to-use reference source.

244.   Sprug, Joseph W., comp. **Index to Fairy Tales, 1987-1992: Including 310 Collections of Fairy Tales, Folktales, Myths, and Legends with Significant Pre-1987 Titles Not Previously Indexed.** Metuchen, NJ: Scarecrow, 1994. 587p. index. ISBN 0-8108-2750-6.

Norma Ireland's *Index to Fairy Tales* (F. W. Faxon, 1973) is the standard reference source familiar to most librarians. The Sprug index is not as comprehensive in scope, but it is much easier to use and also more current. He analyzes twenty-five collections of tales and provides a location key to guide the user from the tale to the collection(s) in which it is found. Collections are entered by title, with a bibliographic citation, a list of reviews, and a reading level. Because the titles of many folktales, fairy tales, myths, and legends change over the years and because they usually have variant names in different cultures, the subject index is the appropriate index to use for most searches. This book is not intended to provide access to hard-to-find tales, but it does provide information for locating those most commonly known. It has been designed as a guide that children will be able to use with minimal help.

History

245. Fisher, Janet. **An Index to Historical Fiction for Children and Young People.** Brookfield, VT: Scholar/Ashgate, 1994. 192p. illus. indexes. ISBN 1-85928-078-1.

Recognizing that too often good historical novels for children and young people remain on the shelves unread, the author has developed this concise index to historical fiction to serve as an easy-to-use ready-reference tool. Each of the more than 460 books have been selected for quality and authenticity of historical perspective. They are entered alphabetically by author and include the bibliographic information, a brief plot summary, an evaluation of the work, and an indication of the age ranges for which the books are intended. Time frames vary from ancient history up to and including World War II. Line drawings, used to reflect historical events, add to the attractiveness of the text. A title index and a very detailed subject index are provided.

246. Van Meter, Vandelia. **American History for Children and Young Adults: An Annotated Bibliographic Index.** Englewood, CO: Libraries Unlimited, 1990. 324p. indexes. ISBN 0-87287-731-0.

Locating books on specific periods in our history can be a time-consuming task. Van Meter's annotated bibliography is an excellent guide to 2,901 fiction and nonfiction books, including biographies for children from kindergarten to twelfth grade. The list of titles, published between 1980 and 1988, includes all aspects of American life from the very beginning of known history in this land to present times. (See entry 210 for the complete annotation.)

247. Van Meter, Vandelia. **World History for Children and Young Adults: An Annotated Bibliographic Index.** Englewood, CO: Libraries Unlimited, 1992. 266p. indexes. ISBN 0-87287-732-9.

The purpose of this publication is to provide an annotated bibliographic index to current fiction and nonfiction books relating to world history. The geographical designations are Africa, Asia and Oceania, Europe, North America, and South America. Historical designations are World War I and World War II, plus a general category. (See entry 211 for the complete annotation.)

Plays/Poetry/Songs

248. Blackburn, G. Meredith. **Index to Poetry for Children and Young People 1988-1992: A Title, Subject, Author, and First Line Index to Poetry in Collections for Children and Young People.** Vol. 7. New York: H. W. Wilson, 1994. 358p. ISBN 0-8242-0851-7.

Locating a specific poem is often a difficult, frustrating task. To make the task much easier, Blackburn has analyzed and indexed 123 children's poetry collections. The primary selection criterion was that the poetry, regardless of type, must appeal to children and young adults. Poetry collections, listed alphabetically by title, are given an abbreviation symbol as a location key, and a complete bibliographic citation accompanies each collection entry. Individual poems may be located by using any of the following indexes: title, subject, author, or first line. Because the title entry contains the most complete information, it is the most convenient starting place to locate a particular poem. Readers familiar with *Granger's Index to Poetry* (Columbia University Press) will find this easy to use.

249.   Karp, Rashelle S., and June H. Schlessinger. **Plays for Children and Young Adults: An Evaluative Index and Guide.** New York: Garland, 1991. 580p. indexes. ISBN 0-8240-6112-8.

The authors intend this index to be a guide for locating plays for children ages five to eighteen. They have provided plot summaries and evaluations of plays published between 1973 and 1989 that are appropriate for production by or for children and young adults. The book indexes 3,500 plays, playlets, choral readings, scenes, monologues, musical reviews, readers' theater, and skits. Each entry includes the following: recommended grade levels; reviews, both positive or negative; the author's name; full title of the play; the cast analysis; playing time; a brief plot summary; an evaluation of the play; royalty information; a full bibliographic citation; a listing of the play's subjects; and an indication of the type of play. The five indexes cover original title, cast, grade level, subject, play type, and playing time. These indexes provide an excellent starting point for the user whose first access point is something other than a specific title.

This is quite an extensive list of plays, with brief but adequate information to guide the seeker to a variety of appropriate choices of plays for children and young adults.

250.   Karp, Rashelle S., June H. Schlessinger, and Bernard S. Schlessinger. **Plays for Children and Young Adults: An Evaluative Index and Guide, Supplement 1, 1989-1994.** Hamden, CT: Garland, 1996. 384p. indexes. ISBN 0-8153-1493-0.

This continues and updates the first play index by Karp and Schlessinger. The format and approach is the same as in the earlier edition. Play types, such as cantatas, Bible plays, Kabuki plays, television spots, and others are new in this supplement.

251.   Laughlin, Kay, Pollyanne Frantz, and Ann Branton, comps. **The Children's Song Index, 1978-1993.** Englewood, CO: Libraries Unlimited, 1996. 153p. ISBN 1-56308-332-9.

The Children's Song Index is a compilation of 2,654 songs derived from seventy-seven songbooks published between 1977 and 1994. Most of the songs are familiar to children and adults, are in the English language, and reflect Western culture. Each of the seventy-seven songbooks is given a unique number to serve as a location key. The first index lists the songs by title and the second index by first line. A thesaurus of broad subject headings helps in searching the extensive subject index. The subject index lists the songs by title, with keys to the volumes in which the song is located and the page numbers.

This current song index should be in every elementary school. It is comprehensive in coverage of songs familiar to children all over the United States.

252. **The Neal-Schuman Index to Finger-Plays.** Kay Cooper, comp. New York: Neal-Schuman, 1993. 319p. index. ISBN 1-55570-149-3.

Finger plays are used for explaining colors and numbers; for telling time; for learning cardinal directions; and for introducing abstract concepts, such as "up" and "down." The Neal-Schuman index is a guide to finger plays for use in preschools, kindergartens, and early elementary classrooms. The contents of sixty collections in which 1,600 finger plays are located have been analyzed. Part 1 is an index to the finger plays entered alphabetically by first line, with a key to the collection in which the finger play is located. Part 2 is a subject index, and part 3 lists finger plays for calendar days and for letter days.

Many good learning activities can be developed by consulting the collections analyzed in this reference source.

253. Olexer, Marycile E. **Poetry Anthologies for Children and Young People.** Chicago: American Library Association, 1985. 285p. indexes. ISBN 0-8389-0430-0.

Olexer seeks to encourage children to experience the joy of poetry, to hear it and to "see" the pictures the poet paints with words. She believes that good poetry can help young people come to terms with their environment, to live with life's ups and downs, and to find beauty in words. This index to anthologies of poetry analyzes approximately 300 volumes of children's poetry and also includes brief annotations for an additional 300 volumes to which reference is made in the text. The anthologies offer a variety of kinds of poetry, for example, haiku, ballads, lyric poetry, and nonsense rhymes. The first section of the text contains the analyses of about half of the 600 anthologies. They are entered under one of two divisions: "Anthology" or "Collection of Individual Poets." Each entry is arranged alphabetically by author or compiler under three age groups: preschool to grade three; grades four to six; and grades seven to nine. For each anthology, the bibliographic information and an evaluative statement is provided; purpose and scope of the poetry is examined; and references are made to similar collections. At least one poetry example from each anthology is provided to illustrate style, quality, vocabulary, imagery, tone, and use of language. Another bibliography contains the recommended poetry anthologies that are mentioned in the text but not analyzed.

The format and coverage of this reference source distinguish it as a valuable, easy-to-use reference to anthologies of poetry.

254. **Play Index.** New York: H. W. Wilson, 1947- .

Play Index is published at irregular intervals. The most recent volume is the 1983-1987 index, which contains 3,964 plays published during this five-year period, both individual plays and plays in collections. The symbol "*c*" is used for plays for children up through grade six. The symbol "*y*" is used for plays for young people from grades seven through ten. Collections of plays and individual plays are analyzed. The citation for each title entry includes a brief play theme, the number of actors required, the number of male and female parts, the number of acts, and information about the settings. Author and subject entries refer the user to the title entry for complete information.

Play Index, first published in 1947, continues to be the standard reference tool for professionals and the general public.

255.   Snow, Barbara. **Index to Songs on Children's Recordings.** Eugene, OR: Staccato Press, 1993. 210p. ISBN 0-9636149-0-8.

Snow's index is an interesting and somewhat unusual guide to children's recorded songs. She analyzes 674 recordings of children's songs on audiotape, records, and CDs from which she identifies more than 7,300 song titles. The book provides an alphabetical recording with an entry number, names of performers, recording label information and date, a song title index, performer index, producer/distributor index, and a list of awards for children's recordings. This much-expanded second edition provides a useful guide to anyone working with children.

256.   Trefny, Beverly Robin, and Eileen C. Palmer. **Index to Children's Plays in Collections: 1975-1984.** 3rd ed. Metuchen, NJ: Scarecrow, 1986. 108p. ISBN 0-8108-1893-0.

This third edition updates and expands previous editions of *Index to Children's Plays in Collections* by Trefny. It comprises 540 plays in various formats, including skits, monologues, and one-act plays, from forty-eight collections of plays. New in this edition are pantomimes and puppetry. The index to authors, titles, and subjects is entered as a single alphabetical list, with the author entry being the most complete. An extensive subject heading list establishes the basis for the index's continuing popularity as a reference source for those working with children. The list of subject headings includes themes, types of plays, occasions for use, holidays, historical periods, geographical settings, famous or legendary personalities, special cast requirements, and genre.

Book Reviews

257.   **Book Review Digest.** Bronx, NY: H. W. Wilson, 1906- . Supplements issued 10/yr.

Book Review Digest indexes and excerpts book reviews of current United States and Canadian fiction and nonfiction books. Reviews given in digest form include children's books, books about children, and children's literature, along with the adult book digests.

258.   **Book Review Index.** Detroit, MI: Gale Research, 1965- .

Book Review Index is a master key representing reviews of popular, academic, professional and children's books and periodicals, books on tape, and electronic media.

259. **Children's Book Review Index.** Detroit, MI: Gale Research, 1975- .

The intent of Gale's annual publication, *Children's Book Review Index*, is to provide a comprehensive index to reviews of children's books in an easy-to-use format. More than 25,000 review citations of more than 10,000 books, periodicals, books on tape, and electronic media are provided. Appropriate citations are selected from *Book Review Index*. Entries are arranged alphabetically by author and contain a complete bibliographic citation of recently published books, a brief content description, and a list of sources in which the book has been reviewed. Ages for whom the books are intended range from early childhood through age ten. Title and illustrator indexes expedite the search process.

> 259.1. **Children's Book Review Index, Master Cumulation, 1985-1994.** 4 vols. Detroit, MI: Gale Research, 1996. indexes. ISBN 0-8103-5457-8.

260. Day, Serenna F., ed. ***Horn Book* Index.** Phoenix, AZ: Oryx Press, 1990. 534p. ISBN 0-89774-156-0.

The author's cumulation of the annual indexes to *Horn Book Magazine* from 1924 through 1989 contains a record of more than 80,000 articles and book reviews appearing in issues of *Horn Book* over the sixty-five year period covered. The single index contains author's names, book titles, and article titles arranged alphabetically. Entries provide data necessary to locate books by title, author, and book reviews.

This publication is especially appropriate for libraries with access to the sixty-five-year accumulation of issues of *Horn Book*. It is also an excellent tool for the serious researcher.

SERIES AND SEQUELS

261. Anderson, Vicki. **Fiction Sequels for Readers 10 to 16: An Annotated Bibliography of Books in Succession.** Jefferson, NC: McFarland, 1990. 150p. index. ISBN 0-89950-519-8.

Since the late 1970s, fiction sequels have become phenomenally popular. Young readers are more apt now than ever to come back for more when they especially like an author, genre, or character in a book. Anderson warns the reader that sequels are not to be confused with series books. Sequel books can stand alone, but they are, at the same time, related to other books with the same characters and the same or similar themes. The author's choices are eclectic; she includes sequels of high literary quality as well as easy readers and those that are of mediocre literary quality but are popular with children in grades three and higher. The bibliography consists of 1,500 titles written by 350 authors. The sequels represent a broad spectrum of topics, from families to sports to humor to ethnicity. A bibliographic citation, brief annotation, and an explanation of the title placement within the sequence are included in each entry. It is interesting to review the authors included in this guide; they range from classic writers, such as Louisa May Alcott to the fantasy writer and Newbery Medal–winner Robin McKinley. Because entries are by author, the index is by title only.

This index serves primarily as a ready-reference rather than as an evaluative, critical reference to sequels. It provides an important service to the professional and to the young reader.

A second edition by Anderson is now available: *Fiction Sequels for Readers 10 to 16: An Annotated Bibliography of Books in Succession.* Jefferson, NC: McFarland, 1997. 192p. index. ISBN 0-7864-0185-0. This fully expanded and updated edition presents more than 2,500 titles.

262.   Roman, Susan. **Sequences: An Annotated Guide to Children's Fiction in Series.** Chicago: American Library Association, 1985. 134p. index. ISBN 0-8389-0428-9.

This is a guide to children's fiction written in series format, an approach that has proved to be popular with children. The books come from a wide variety of genres, including realistic fiction, historical fiction, science fiction, and fantasy. The ages for which series books are written extend from ages three to middle school. Each series title is prefaced by a short introduction, followed by titles within the series listed in their suggested reading order. Indexes are to book titles, series titles, and main characters. To provide guidance for readers who don't want to miss any books in a series, this guide is a gold mine.

263.   Rosenberg, Judith K. **Young People's Books in Series: Fiction and Non-Fiction, 1975-1991.** Englewood, CO: Libraries Unlimited, 1992. 424p. indexes. ISBN 0-87287-882-1.

The author explains that in her publication the term "series" includes both sequel and series titles. Each notation is entered alphabetically by author, followed by a chronological listing of the titles in each series/sequel. Entries include paperback as well as hardcover editions. Every title in a series/sequel is included, even if it is considered mediocre. The fiction series/sequels are listed first, and each series author is entered alphabetically with the series title. Under each series heading, titles are entered by date of publication. A brief annotation and a suggested grade level accompany entries. Because it is not unusual for separate entries in a nonfiction series to have been written by different authors, the nonfiction series are entered first by series title and then by author and title. Entries also have brief annotations and suggested grade levels. In addition to the combined author and title index, a fiction series title index and a nonfiction series title index are provided.

Although this book includes both sequels and series entries, it does not replace the Anderson book (see entry 261); rather, the two can be used well together.

COMMERCIAL BIBLIOGRAPHIES

264.   **Children's Books in Print: An Author, Title, and Illustrator Index to Books for Children and Young Adults.** 27th ed. 2 vols. New Providence, NJ: R. R. Bowker, 1996. 1855p. ISBN 0-8352-3687-0.

Children's Books in Print, an annual bibliography of children's books, is the most complete list of currently available books for children published in the United States. The age levels for which the books are written range from three to eighteen. The current edition lists approximately 100,875 books, recorded from the more comprehensive *Books in Print* by Bowker. Entries are by author, title, and illustrator. Each entry contains a complete bibliographic citation.

265.   **Children's Catalog.** 17th ed. Anne Price and Juliette Yaakon, eds. New York: H. W. Wilson, 1996. 1373p. indexes. ISBN 0-8242-0893-5.

Children's Catalog is considered the definitive selection tool for children's literature, curricular books, and magazines for children. It is a classified catalog to nonfiction, fiction, story collections, and easy books. Fiction titles are entered alphabetically by author, and nonfiction entries are arranged under the Dewey Decimal Classification system. Each bibliographic entry includes a brief annotation and subject headings using *Sears List of Subject Headings* (H. W. Wilson). The indexes are by author, title, and subject. An extensive analytical index and a directory of publishers and distributors are also provided. A new and important feature is the selected list of recommended reference works on CD-ROM. Annual supplements maintain currency of the catalog entries.

This authoritative, accurate, and reliable publication serves as a cataloging tool, a reference guide, and an aid to selecting recommended books for children and to use with children.

266.   **El-Hi Textbooks and Serials in Print, 1995.** New Providence, NJ: R. R. Bowker, 1970- . index.

This is an annual, nonselective guide to textbooks, periodicals, maps, test series, workbooks, programmed learning materials, teaching aids, professional and reference books, audiovisual materials, posters, and more. The subject index provides grade and reading level. Author, title and series, and serials indexes are also included.

267.   **The Elementary School Library Collection: A Guide to Books and Other Media. 20th ed. Phases 1-2-3.** Linda L. Homa, ed. Williamsport, PA: Brodart, 1996. 1157p. indexes. ISBN 0-87272-105-1.

The Elementary School Library Collection is a biannual bibliography of more than 78,000 trade books published for children from preschool through sixth grade. The collection includes fiction, nonfiction, reference materials, and professional publications. Entries are keyed using a recommendation scale that identifies them as a first, second, or third choice for purchase. Nonfiction entries are arranged using the Dewey Decimal Classification system. The bibliographic information is followed by a brief annotation, a reading level, and suggested subject headings. Indexes are by author, title, and subject. The appendixes cover media for preschool children, books for independent reading, and a directory of publishers and producers.

268.   **Middle and Junior High School Library Catalog.** 7th ed. Anne Price and Juliette Yaakon, eds. New York: H. W. Wilson, 1995. 988p. indexes. ISBN 0-8242-0880-3.

Middle and Junior High School Library Catalog is organized in the same format as Wilson's elementary school catalog. Some overlap with *Children's Catalog* (entry 265) exists because most school districts now use the middle school concept, that is, sixth graders and sometimes fifth graders are taught at the middle school level.

269. **Subject Guide to Children's Books in Print: 1995.** 2 vols. New Providence, NJ: R. R. Bowker, 1995. 1100p. ISBN 0-8352-3596-3.

This is a subject guide to children's nonfiction and fiction books currently in print. It is arranged alphabetically by broad subject headings, which are then subdivided into more specific aspects of each subject. Within each subject, the entries are listed by author and provide the complete bibliographic information. Also included in this publication are listings of the major awards and prizes for children's books awarded in the United States and the United Kingdom as well as Canada, Australia, and New Zealand.

GUIDES TO ISSUES

270. Field, Carolyn, and Jaqueline Shachter Weiss. **Values in Selected Children's Books of Fiction and Fantasy.** Hamden, CT: Library Professional Publications, 1987. 298p. indexes. ISBN 0-208-02100-0.

The goal of Field and Weiss is to heighten awareness of children's books that highlight positive values and help children cope with stress and other problems in their complex world. The authors define the term "values" as beliefs that reflect ethical ideals and that motivate personal effectiveness and social commitment. Seven hundred and thirteen books of fiction and fantasy that realistically mirror positive values in their story lines were selected. Titles are divided into three age categories from preschool to eighth grade. The ten reference areas of values include cooperation, courage, friendship, humanness, loyalty, and self-respect. The authors' research found that courage and friendship are the two most prevalent values found in children's books. Annotations for each book are entered in a discussion format, identifying values and how they are presented through the actions of the major characters in the book. Supplementary bibliographies are provided at the end of each chapter.

The topic, contents, and procedures used by Field and Weiss in presenting research have produced a reference source that is of significant value to all who work with children.

271. Kilpatrick, William, Gregory Wolfe, and Suzanne M. Wolfe. **Books That Build Character: A Guide to Teaching Your Child Moral Values Through Stories.** New York: Simon & Schuster, 1994. 332p. index. ISBN 0-671-88423-9.

The authors' objective is to introduce children to books that will help them grow in virtue, understanding, and empathy toward others. They direct the reader to the many well-crafted stories that display honesty, responsibility, and compassion as valid attributes to possess. They identify book characters who exhibit acceptable codes of conduct in their ideals and actions. (See entry 181 for a complete annotation.)

272.   Rasinski, Timothy V., and Cindy S. Gillespie. **Sensitive Issues: An Annotated Guide to Children's Literature K-6.** Phoenix: Oryx, 1992. 277p. index. ISBN 0-89774-777-1.

The authors believe that children must be exposed to meaningful literature in order to become lifelong readers. Reading about sensitive issues can help children deal with many of the problems that may confront them in their own lives such as divorce, death and dying, substance abuse, nontraditional home environments, child abuse, prejudice and cultural differences, moving, and illness and disability. (See entry 109 for a complete annotation.)

273.   Rudman, Masha Kabakow. **Children's Literature: An Issues Approach.** 3rd ed. White Plains, NY: Longman, 1995. 497p. indexes. ISBN 0-8013-0537-3.

Rudman has designed her book as a reference, a text, and a guide. Using an issues approach to literature, she presents a resource guide for the study and selection of books for children that deal with sensitive issues. She examines how the literature treats many important and often controversial issues. Practical suggestions are provided for using books to help children confront concerns with which they often must deal, such as sexuality, divorce, death, and abuse. The topically organized contents are entered under part 1, "Family," which is a four-chapter section; part 2, "Life Cycle," which is a three-chapter section; and part 3, "Society," which is a five-chapter section. Each chapter opens with an introduction to and an exploration of a personal or social issue. Bibliographic information, an annotation, and meaningful activities are given for a selective list of recommended books relevant to the topic. Appendixes contain lists of activities for extending literature, selected children's book awards, and publishers' addresses.

This issues approach to children's literature is replete with ideas, activities, and recommendations for reading that address concerns with which society is struggling today.

REVIEWS OF CHILDREN'S LITERATURE

274.   **Children's Literature: Annual of the Modern Language Association Division of Children's Literature and the Children's Literature Association.** New Haven, CT: Yale University Press, 1972- . Annual.

This is a scholarly annual review containing critical and historical essays on nineteenth- and twentieth-century children's books. It represents serious analysis and interpretation of books and authors, who were selected for their contributions to making the study and investigation of children's literature a recognized literary pursuit. It covers all aspects of literature for children and young adults and represents a wide range of choices.

275.   **Children's Literature Abstracts.** Austin, TX: Federation of Library Associations, 1973- . Quarterly. ISSN 0306-2015.

Children's Literature Abstracts provides access to more than 400 articles in British, American, Russian, and Australian journals. Entries are arranged by subject within the fields of children's fiction and nonfiction. Subjects include illustrators, awards, prizes, and many other related topics. A bibliographic citation and short descriptive annotation accompany each entry.

276.   **Children's Literature Review: Excerpts from Reviews, Criticisms, and Commentary on Books for Children and Young People.** Detroit: Gale Research, 1976- . 2/yr. illus. portraits. ISSN 0362-4145.

In the preface, the editors address the importance of criticism of juvenile literature in recognition of artistic creation. Critical reviews of literature for and about children and youth reveal new trends as well as controversies appearing in the ever-changing worlds of children and children's literature. The expressed purpose of the *Children's Literature Review* is to help readers make informed reading choices by introducing them to a representative group of authors. Entries range from James M. Barrie's *Peter Pan* to the books of Betsy Byars. Presented in the series are lengthy excerpts from books, essays, and reviews of more than 500 writers and illustrators. A typical entry consists of four principal elements: a list of major works by the author/illustrator, a critical introduction placing the author/illustrator in historical and literary or artistic perspective, a commentary by the author/illustrator on the development of his or her own work, and excerpts from significant reviews and commentaries. The author, title, and nationality indexes are all cumulative.

Teachers, librarians, and researchers will appreciate the scholarly yet highly readable quality of this critical series.

277.   Hendrickson, Linnea. **Children's Literature: A Guide to the Criticism.** Boston: G. K. Hall, 1987. 664p. indexes. ISBN 0-8161-8670-7.

The author's expressed purpose is to draw together significant articles, books, unpublished dissertations, and ERIC documents relating to critical reviews of children's literature. Sources of the reviews and criticisms are from diverse disciplines and represent popular as well as scholarly publications. Books, articles, and dissertations, listed in part A under "Authors and Their Works: An Annotated Listing of Criticism," are entered alphabetically by author. Part B, "Subjects, Themes, and Genre: An Annotated Listing of Criticism," provides a diversified list of themes that range from topics such as "Adaptations" to "Yugoslavia." A six-page appendix offers a resource bibliography, and the indexes include a guide to critics, along with the traditional author, illustrator, title, and subject indexes.

The extent to which Hendrickson has researched her topic is commendable. Her publication is a scholarly resource to critical reviews of literature for children.

278.   **The *Horn Book* Guide to Children's and Young Adult Books.**
Boston: Horn Book, 1989- . 2/yr. ISSN 1044-405X.

The Horn Book *Guide* provides short, critical annotations of all hardcover books for children and young adults published in the United States within the previous six months. Fiction is arranged by grade level, and nonfiction is entered using the Dewey Decimal Classification system. Entries are subarranged by an evaluation rating scale that ranges from outstanding (1) to unacceptable (6). A full bibliographic citation accompanies each entry, arranged alphabetically by author. When a book has previously been reviewed in *Horn Book*, reference is made to location of the review. Indexes are by author/illustrator, title, subject, series, new editions, and reissues.

279.   Lukins, Rebecca J. **A Critical Handbook for Children's Literature.** 4th ed. Glenview, IL: Scott, Foresman/Little, Brown Higher Education, 1990. 309p. indexes. ISBN 0-673-38773-9.

Lukins's critical commentaries continue to fulfill a valuable role in the review and evaluation of literature for children. The following chapter titles reflect her analysis of literature from a critical point of view: "Literature, What Is It?"; "Genre in Children's Literature"; "Point of View"; "Tone: From Rhyme to Poetry"; "Picture Books"; and "Nonfiction." To enhance the usefulness and clarity of content, Lukins includes examples to illustrate each of the points of reference.

280.   Moir, Hughes, Melissa Cain, and Leslie Prosak-Beres, eds. **Collected Perspectives: Choosing and Using Books for the Classroom.** Boston: Christopher-Gordon, 1990. 280p. indexes. ISBN 0-926842-03X.

The authors have collected 500 book reviews from five years of the reviewing journal, *Perspectives*, published by Cooperative Services for Children's Literature at the University of Toledo, in Ohio. The reviews, written by practitioners in the field, address ways in which books can be integrated into learning programs for children. Selections include picture books, fiction, nonfiction, and poetry for youth from kindergarten to twelfth grade. Each book review is two paragraphs in length and includes the bibliographic citation, a brief summary, evaluative comments, and ideas for activities. Where appropriate, companion books are listed. A list of publishers' addresses and indexes by author, title, and subject are included.

This is an impressive publication and contains many ideas for helping bring children and books together, with the goal of encouraging children to become lifetime readers.

TEXTBOOKS

Textbooks are often-overlooked referral sources for locating recommended books for children by title, author, subject, and genre. Because they are used in the preparation of elementary school teachers whose challenge will be to encourage their students to become lifetime readers, they are an outstanding source of information on authors and illustrators recognized for their excellence in writing and illustrating books for children. Their bibliographies are extensive and their indexes easy to use. Although the Sutherland textbook is the only one annotated here as a representative of the content of the other textbooks, all of the texts listed below are recognized for their excellent presentations of literature for children.

281. Cullinan, Bernice E. **Literature and the Child.** 3rd ed. San Diego: Harcourt Brace Jovanovich, 1994. 546p. illus. index. ISBN 0-15-5009-85-0.

282. Huck, Charlotte, and Barbara Kiefer. **Children's Literature in the Elementary School.** 6th ed. Burr Ridge, IL: McGraw-Hill, 1997. 800p. indexes. illus. ISBN 0-697-3414-3.

283. Norton, Donna E. **Through the Eyes of a Child: An Introduction to Children's Literature.** 4th ed. Englewood Cliffs, NJ: Merrill, 1995. 713p. illus. indexes. ISBN 0-01388-313-8.

284. Sutherland, Zena. **Children and Books.** 9th ed. New York: Harper-Collins, 1997. 720p. illus. indexes. ISBN 0-673-99733-2.

Children and Books, begun fifty years ago, continues as a major text for teachers and librarians seeking to bring books and children together. Appreciation of the role that children's literature plays in reflecting society's values and in instilling those values in children is a major tenet of this text. This edition is divided into four broad topics. Part 1, "Knowing Children and Books," includes chapters 1 through 5. Part 2, "Exploring the Types of Literature," a genre approach, includes chapters 6 through 13. Part 3, "Bringing Children and Books Together," includes chapters 14 through 16. Part 4, "Areas and Issues," discusses the impact of books and reading on children. The appendixes include book selection aids, children's book awards, and publishers' addresses. Indexes include an integrated author, illustrator, and title index and a separate subject index. This thorough study of literature for children embraces all the elements for developing a successful literature program for children.

Chapter 6

Biographies

285. Bingham, Jane M., ed. **Writers for Children: Critical Studies of Major Authors Since the Seventeenth Century.** New York: Charles Scribner's Sons, 1988. 661p. index. ISBN 0-684-18165-7.

This major reference work serves as a critical guide to authors of classic literature for children. It includes important writers from the seventeenth century to the first part of the twentieth century. This single-volume collection surveys eighty-four writers whose works have endured through the years and who have gained acclaim for their writings. Included in each entry is a lengthy biographical sketch, an evaluation of the author's writings, and a selected bibliography of original works. Entries range from Charles Perrault, to whom the Mother Goose tales have been attributed, to Carol Ryrie Brink, who wrote *Caddie Woodlawn*. Although none of the authors are living, the books are still read eagerly by children.

This is a well-prepared publication and can be used as a supplement to *Twentieth-Century Children's Writers* (see entry 310) and Anne Commire's *Yesterday's Authors of Books for Children* (see entry 288).

286. Breen, Karen. **Index to Collective Biographies for Young Readers.** 4th ed. New York: R. R. Bowker, 1988. 494p. ISBN 0-8352-2348-5.

This much-needed update of the 1979 edition of *Index to Collective Biographies for Young Readers* profiles 9,773 notable people whose lives have made a difference, including presidents, writers, authors, sports figures, and other superstars. Its purpose is to be inclusive rather than selective. The biographical citations come from 1,129 collective biographical sources. The preliminary section, "Key to Indexed Books," provides symbols as keys to identify the collective biography in which the biographical entry is found. The same symbols are used in the two main sections, the author and subject listings. The alphabetical listing of the biographee contains the key symbol(s) and pertinent data, such as birth, death, nationality, and field of activity. The subject listing is a guide to nationalities and fields of activity/occupation of the biographees. The listings of fields of activity are eclectic and thorough. This index is now available on the Bowker CD-ROM, *Children's Reference PLUS*.

This is an impressive and useful reference guide for children seeking biographical information about people who have made noteworthy contributions in the history of our country.

287. **Children's Authors and Illustrators: An Index to Biographical Dictionaries.** Joyce Nakamura, ed. 5th ed. Detroit: Gale Research, 1995. 811p. ISBN 0-8103-2899-2.

This all-new edition of the highly regarded biographical index to authors of children's books contains more than 200,000 citations to biographical information on about 30,000 authors and illustrators. Included are writers and illustrators, both prominent and lesser known, who have produced books for preschool through middle school readers. Each entry provides the name; birth and death dates; and an alphabetically arranged list of reference sources, including a location key. This index is quite expensive for a school library or small public library, but it is worth the cost if it can be worked into the budget.

288. Commire, Anne, ed. **Yesterday's Authors of Books for Children: Facts & Pictures About Authors and Illustrators of Books for Young People, from Early Times to 1960.** 2 vols. Detroit: Gale Research, 1977. 275p. illus. ISBN 0-8103-0073-7 (Vol. 1); Detroit: Gale Research, 1978. 335p. illus. ISBN 0-8103-0090-7 (Vol. 2).

This two-volume set, abundantly illustrated, contains biographical sketches of major children's authors and illustrators from the 1800s through 1960. The sketches range from one page in length to more than sixteen pages. Each entry lists a chronology of the author's personal and professional background and references to other sources of information. Portraits of each author and illustrations from their books enhance the sketches. When used with Gale's Something About the Author series (see entry 309), the reader has access to the biographical world of authors and illustrators of children's books.

For anyone, child or adult, fascinated by the classic writers of children's literature, this is a marvelous find. Learning more about writer and illustrator Beatrix Potter or finding how Pooh Bear came into being through the pen of A. A. Milne will keep the reader entranced.

289. Cummins, Julie, ed. **Children's Book Illustration and Design.** New York: PBC International, 1992. 240p. illus. index. ISBN 0-86636-147-2.

290. Cummins, Julie, ed. **Children's Book Illustration and Design.** Vol. 2. New York: PBC International, 1997. 240p. illus. index. ISBN 0-86636-393-9.

As the editor says, this is "a showcase of outstanding contemporary children's book illustration." Although it is not a biographical reference in the truest sense, the biographical approach is used to highlight illustration in books for children. The more than eighty illustrators selected are given a two- to three-page entry that includes a photograph of the artist, biographical information, and selections of works. Often it is through knowing something about the life of the artist that a reader can understand and appreciate his or her "message in artistic form."

291. Day, Frances Ann. **Latina and Latino Voices in Literature for Children and Teenagers.** Portsmouth, NH: Heinemann, 1997. 228p. indexes. ISBN 0-435-07202-1.

To fill the gap in biographical information about Latina and Latino writers of children's books, the author presents highlights in the lives and careers of twenty-three established and emerging writers. Their writings reflect the racial, ethnic, and religious traditions of Latino communities. In addition to the biographical profiles, with pictures, of the major authors, an introduction to fifteen more emerging authors with promise are introduced. Six appendixes extend the information, and four indexes provide easy-to-use guides to the contents.

292. Day, Frances Ann. **Multicultural Voices in Contemporary Literature: A Resource for Teachers.** Portsmouth, NH: Heinemann, 1994. 244p. photos. ISBN 0-435-08826-2pa.

Day celebrates the lives and works of thirty-nine highly regarded authors and illustrators from twenty different cultures. She feels that when students know more about the authors and illustrators whose works they are reading, they will more easily identify with them. Bringing children and authors together stimulates excitement, deepens personal interaction with the story and its characters, and encourages cultural sensitivity. The introduction provides eleven well-developed guidelines for evaluating and selecting children's multicultural books. The selection of thirty-nine individuals for recognition as outstanding writers/illustrators of children's books achieved a representative balance of the major cultures prevalent in our country. Each entry contains a photograph of the author/illustrator, the address of a publisher to contact for more information about the entrant, a listing of works completed, and an interesting, easy-to-read biographical sketch. Selected books are annotated and reflectively evaluated. Awards and honors received and suggested classroom activities are provided. Appendixes include a long list of additional multicultural authors and illustrators, arranged by culture; an assessment plan; optional activities; author/illustrator birthdays; a calendar of dates of multicultural activities and festivals; and a list of resources.

293. **Dictionary of Literary Biography: Children's Writers Series.** Detroit: Gale Research.

The multivolume *Dictionary of Literary Biography (DLB)*, each of which is freestanding, is a biographical/bibliographic appraisal of the accomplishments of significant figures in literary history. This series combines literary criticism, biographic sketches, illustrations, and photographs of outstanding writers of children's literature. The author of volumes 52 and 61, Glenn Estes, points out that the 1960s through the 1980s represented a particularly creative and innovative period in the publishing of literature for children; it was a time of transformation in style and content in children's books. The inclusion of realism in texts and illustrations in children's books and the portrayal of problems, such as divorce and death, in contemporary society opened doors to the "real" world and, at the same time, generated unprecedented censorship and controversy. The forty-four writers presented in volume 52, many of whom are award-winning authors, are known primarily for their realistic novels, historical fiction, and fantasy novels. Experts in the field of children's literature were selected to edit each entry. A lengthy article, with basic biographical information, provides an interesting discussion of each author's contributions to the world of children's literature and includes a bibliography of the author's publications. Analysis of some of the major works of the writer helps the reader understand how the writer's life influenced his or her writings. Copies of dust jackets, notes, and rough drafts of popular books create an even more personal contact with each author. Location of manuscripts and checklists for further reading accompany each entry. The index is cumulative for all of Gale Research's biographical references on authors.

Historical Volumes

293.1.   Cech, John, ed. **American Writers for Children: 1900-1960.** Vol. 22. Detroit: Gale Research, 1983. 442p. illus. index. ISBN 0-8103-1146-1.

293.2.   Estes, Glenn E., ed. **American Writers for Children Before 1900.** Vol. 42. Detroit: Gale Research, 1985. 441p. illus. index. ISBN 0-8103-1720-6.

Current Writers

293.3.   Estes, Glenn E., ed. **American Writers for Children Since 1960: Fiction.** Vol. 52. Detroit: Gale Research, 1986. 488p. illus. index. ISBN 0-8103-1730-3.

293.4.   Estes, Glenn E., ed. **American Writers for Children Since 1960: Poets, Illustrators, and Non-Fiction Authors.** Vol. 61. Detroit: Gale Research, 1987. 430p. illus. index. ISBN 0-8103-1739-7.

294.   Fisher, Margery. **Who's Who in Children's Books.** New York: Holt Rinehart and Winston, 1975. 399p. illus. ISBN 0-03-015091-4.

The Fisher biography is a historical approach to characters in children's literature. Although the copyright date is 1975, the reader will find reference to book characters in books that are still very popular with boys and girls. This is a good quick reference to use when a child asks about book characters such as Peter Rabbit, Anne of Green Gables, or even Harriet the Spy. Entries are alphabetical by the characters' names, and the articles give readers information to jog their memories or just for reminiscing. It is easy to use and a good reference source to just sit back and enjoy.

295.   Hopkins, Lee Bennett. **Pauses: Autobiographical Reflections of 101 Creators of Children's Books.** New York: HarperCollins, 1995. 233p. index. ISBN 0-06-024748-7.

Hopkins produced his autobiographical reflections in response to the numerous questions received about favorite children's writers. His selective group of "creators" ranges from those born in the 1880s, such as the beloved Marguerite de Angeli, to very current writers, such as Robin McKinley, born in 1957.

Biographical information is enhanced by the writers' reminiscences and personal thoughts, making the reflections more intimate than merely factual. The contents are divided into four sections: authors, author/illustrators, illustrators, and poets. The arrangement within each section is first chronological, then alphabetical by author.

This is a fascinating reference source; the reader will find it hard to put aside. It is recommended for personal collections as well as school and public library collections.

296. **The Junior Book of Authors and Illustrators Series.** New York: H. W. Wilson.

The H. W. Wilson Company began its series on authors of children's books in 1934 and has continued to update the series periodically. These early efforts have resulted in seven volumes that offer a total of 1,750 sketches with cumulative indexes in each volume. It is, effectively, the "Who's Who" of authors and illustrators of books for children and young adults.

296.1. **The Seventh Book of Junior Authors and Illustrators.** Sally Holmes Holtze, ed. New York: H. W. Wilson, 1996. 356p. photos. index. ISBN 0-8242-0874-9.

This is the latest in the acclaimed H. W. Wilson series on authors, revised in 1978 to include illustrators. This edition contains 250 sketches of authors and illustrators who have come into prominence since the sixth edition. Selection for inclusion is based on reviews, recommended lists, awards, honors, and popularity. The photographs of each entrant and interesting anecdotes written by the author help to personalize the biographical entry. Selected works are listed, and citations to biographical entries in Gale Research's series Contemporary Authors and Something About the Author (see entry 309) are included.

The following are titles of the earlier guides:

296.2. **The Junior Book of Authors.** Stanley J. Kunitz, ed. New York: H. W. Wilson, 1934.

296.3. **The Junior Book of Authors.** 2nd rev. ed. Stanley J. Kunitz and Howard Haycraft, eds. New York: H. W. Wilson, 1951. 309p. ISBN 0-8242-0028-4.

296.4. **More Junior Authors.** Muriel Fuller, ed. New York: H. W. Wilson, 1963. 235p. ISBN 0-8242-0036-5.

296.5. **The Third Book of Junior Authors.** Doris De Montreville and Donna Hill, eds. New York: H. W. Wilson, 1972. 320p. ISBN 0-8242-0408-5.

296.6. **The Fourth Book of Junior Authors and Illustrators.** Doris De Montreville and Elizabeth D. Crawford, eds. New York: H. W. Wilson, 1978. 370p. ISBN 0-8242-0568-5.

296.7.   **The Fifth Book of Junior Authors and Illustrators.** Sally
Holmes Holtze, ed. New York: H. W. Wilson, 1983. 355p. ISBN
0-8242-0694-0.

296.8.   **The Sixth Book of Junior Authors and Illustrators.** Sally
Holmes Holtze, ed. New York: H. W. Wilson, 1989. 345p. ISBN
0-8242-0777-7.

297.   Kovacs, Deborah, and James Preller. **Meet the Authors and Illustrators: 60 Creators of Favorite Children's Books Talk About
Their Work.** Vol. 2. New York: Scholastic Professional Books,
1993. 143p. illus. portraits. ISBN 0-590-49237-3.

The sixty individuals selected for inclusion in this update of volume 1
come from a variety of geographical locations and represent a diversity of talents.
Their books are very popular with children, and many are award-winning con-
tributors to children's literature. Each entry includes a checklist of the author or illustrator's books for children, a portrait, and a two-page biographical sketch
written to encourage personal reader interaction with the biographee. Each author
and illustrator has provided at least one simple "do-it-yourself" activity idea to use
in conjunction with one or more of his or her books. The writing style, vocabulary,
visuals, and format of this book are at a reading and understanding level that will
enable elementary children to use it independently. Because all entries are arranged in alphabetical order, there is no index. This work complements other biographical sources.

298.   Magill, Frank N., ed. **Masterplots II: Juvenile and Young Adult
Biography Series.** 4 vols. Pasadena, CA: Salem Press, 1993. index.
ISBN 0-8935-6700-0.

Masterplots II introduces us to another outstanding contribution to the
Masterplots series. Magill's Juvenile and Young Adult Biography Series is a welcome addition to biographical sources in literature for children and young adults. It focuses on biographees who appeal to readers from ages ten to eighteen. Five hundred
and twenty-one individual and collective biographies are analyzed and reviewed. The
selection of entrants is eclectic in nature; however, a preponderance of the entries are
for writers of children's literature. Biographies are analyzed in a two- to three-page essay discussing the approach used by the author of the biography in presenting the biographee (or biographees in collective biographies), and the content is critically
analyzed. Another interesting informational section is the sixty-four-item annotated
bibliography of works on children's literature and the art of biography.

299.   **Major Authors and Illustrators for Children and Young Adults:
A Selection of Sketches from *Something About the Author*.** Laurie
Collier and Joyce Nakamura, eds. 6 vols. Detroit: Gale Research,
1993. 2700p. photos. portraits. indexes. ISBN 0-8103-7702-0.

The editors selected 800 of the most popular and widely read authors and illustrators from Something About the Author (SATA) to create this separate biographical and bibliographic publication. Entries have been revised and updated to

ensure the currency of the information. Arrangement follows the format of SATA, including portraits and illustrations. The publication is designed to meet the budget constraints of smaller libraries that are not able to purchase the ever-growing multivolume series from which the entries come.

300. Marantz, Sylvia, and Kenneth Marantz. **Artists of the Page: Interviews with Children's Book Illustrators.** Jefferson, NC: McFarland, 1992. 255p. portraits. index. ISBN 0-89950-701-8.

The Marantzes' interviews are much more than just biographical entries; they are written to give the reader the feeling that he or she is actually in the room as an observer while the interview with each illustrator is taking place. The questions presented and the answers given create a feeling that, when the interview is over, you know the illustrator personally. Many highly recognized illustrators, as well as some fairly new to the picture book world, have been included. The authors have purposely chosen artists whose biographical information is not included as readily in other biographical sources. In addition to recording responses on a two- to three-page spread, samplings of the artists' works in print are provided. The initial interview is with Janet and Allan Ahlberg, the husband and wife team known for their delightful *The Jolly Postman* books (Little, Brown, 1986), and the book ends with Paul Zelinsky, whose illustrations for *Rapunzel* (Dutton, 1997) earned him a Caldecott Medal.

301. McElmeel, Sharron L. **Bookpeople: A First Album.** Englewood, CO: Libraries Unlimited, 1990. 176p. illus. photos. ISBN 0-87287-720-5.

McElmeel's goal is to encourage the enjoyment of literature as an everyday activity for all children. She is well known for her interesting ideas for turning kids on to books and reading; for example, her Author a Month series (Libraries Unlimited) abounds with interesting ideas and activities for classroom and library programs. The focus of *Bookpeople: A First Album* is on authors and illustrators who create picture books. It answers questions children often ask, such as "Where do you get your ideas?" Each author/illustrator entry presents brief biographical information, a photograph, and a selective list of publications. Where appropriate, line drawings related to popular books or characters are included. The authors/illustrators have provided many interesting approaches for stimulating reading as a lifetime activity. Indexes are cross-referenced with McElmeel's *Bookpeople: A Second Album.*

302. McElmeel, Sharron L. **Bookpeople: A Second Album.** Englewood, CO: Libraries Unlimited, 1990. 200p. illus. photos. ISBN 0-87287-721-3.

Bookpeople: A Second Album focuses on forty-seven authors for upper elementary and middle school grades. It adds new dimensions to the study of authors and illustrators; it takes you deep into each author's philosophy. Entries close with a list of "Response Ideas" as follow-ups to author studies. Volumes 1 and 2 contain cumulative and cross-referenced indexes.

303.   Munroe, Mary Hovas, and Judith Rogers Banja. **The Birthday Book: Birthdates, Birthplaces and Biographical Sources for American Authors and Illustrators of Children's Books.** New York: Neal-Schuman, 1991. 499p. indexes. ISBN 1-55570-051-9.

The Birthday Book is an index to published collective biographical information on more than 7,000 American authors of children's books. Each entry includes the birth date, death date, birthplace, and reference sources to use to locate additional information on the author. The index is cross referenced to serve as an aid for the user to locate information. This biographical source is equally useful for teacher, librarian, and student.

304.   Roginski, Jim. **Behind the Covers: Interviews with Authors and Illustrators of Books for Children and Young Adults.** 2 vols. Englewood, CO: Libraries Unlimited, 1985. 249p. ISBN 0-87287-506-7 (Vol. 1.); Englewood, CO: Libraries Unlimited, 1989. 261p. ISBN 0-87287-627-6 (Vol. 2.).

This publication is a welcome supplement to the series by H. W. Wilson (The Junior Book of Authors and Illustrators Series—see entry 296) and Gale (Something About the Author—see entry 308). Roginski's interview format provides an interesting, noncritical, and personal view of each of the authors and illustrators selected. He records the responses of the writer/artist verbatim to achieve authenticity, allowing the reader to experience a fresh, candid interaction with the twenty-two authors and illustrators. His selection of entrants is broad and interesting; he has included novelists, nonfiction writers, poets, folklorists, biographers, and artists—certainly a sampling of diversity. He succeeds in creating a balance in the entries between well-known authors and illustrators and those new to the profession. Entries contain biographical information; a bibliography of books, awards, and honors; and any other significant information related to the biographee. An appendix lists the location of libraries owning or housing original manuscripts and artwork of those interviewed.

Roginski's use of the question-and-answer approach to introduce children and young people to biographical information about authors and illustrators recognized for their works will generate enthusiasm in readers to look for more of the biographee's books.

305.   Rollock, Barbara. **Black Authors and Illustrators of Children's Books: A Biographical Dictionary.** 2nd ed. New York: Garland, 1992. 234p. illus. index. ISBN 0-8240-7078-X.

This edition serves as an update and extension of Rollock's 1988 edition. She continues to strive to acquaint all children, regardless of color, with the black creative presence in children's literature. Acknowledgment of the contributions of black writers and artists to the world of literature for children is gaining momentum, as reflected in the increase in national awards for excellence they are receiving. One hundred and fifteen biographical sketches, arranged alphabetically by author, are provided for black authors and illustrators whose works were published in the United States. Some of the sketches are an update of entries in the first edition; others are new to this edition. They are accompanied by a selective list of each individual's works, and, in some cases, photographs are included. Appendixes provide award and publisher information.

306.　Schon, Isabel, ed. **Contemporary Spanish-Speaking Writers and Illustrators for Children and Young Adults: A Biographical Dictionary.** Westport, CT: Greenwood, 1994. 248p. index. ISBN 0-313-29027-X.

Schon's biographical dictionary provides accurate biographical and bibliographic information on more than 200 contemporary Spanish-speaking writers and illustrators of books for children and young adults. Included are writers from Mexico, Spain, the United States, and Spanish-speaking countries in Central and South America. The dictionary format provides personal data for entrants, including awards and honors received; their writings or illustrations; interesting sidelights about their lives; and sources of book reviews. An appendix lists individual names alphabetically by country of birth or citizenship or both.

This is an impressive and useful tool for a library. The editor has made available important reference information to enhance a library's ability to respond to the reading/library needs of the Hispanic population.

307.　Silvey, Anita, ed. **Children's Books and Their Creators.** Boston: Houghton Mifflin, 1995. 800p. ISBN 0-395-65380-0.

Silvey remarks that few readers have time to experience the full intensity of children's literature. The richly illustrated *Children's Books and Their Creators* is her attempt to "bring the banquet to everyone." It is both biographical and encyclopedic in content and arrangement. The criteria for selection include historical importance, popularity, interest in current books, and overall contributions to children's literature. In addition to the biographical sketches, which include the full scope of the author's writings, the book offers an overview of the history, issues, and genre of children's literature and a section entitled "Voices of the Creators," in which seventy-five of the creators offer personal reflections on their lives and their works.

Children and adults alike will enjoy reading this book. It is not only a source of important and interesting information but also a pleasant read.

308.　**Something About the Author: Autobiographical Series.** Vol. 20. Joyce Nakamura and Gerard J. Senick, eds. Detroit: Gale, 1995. 355p. illus. portraits. index. ISBN 0-8103-4469-6. ISSN 0885-6842.

This volume is representative of all of the volumes of the autobiographical series Something About the Author. The autobiographical essays are written especially for the series. Distinguished authors and illustrators of fiction, nonfiction, and poetry for children and young adults are presented in one of twenty-three volumes. The artists write about their lives in personalized, brief autobiographical sketches. They reveal to the readers their sources of inspiration and methods they have used in their writing or drawing. The indexes are cumulative for all volumes of the series.

This series is another example of the highly regarded Gale Research series on authors and illustrators. Its value in a library serving children and young people is inestimable.

309.   **Something About the Author: Facts and Pictures About Contemporary Authors and Illustrators of Books for Young People.** Anne Commire, ed. Detroit: Gale Research, 1971- . illus. portraits. index.

This highly regarded biographical series is an appealing resource that will be used enthusiastically by children and young people as well as by adults. It allows readers to learn more about their favorite authors and illustrators. The series covers more than 7,000 authors and illustrators, ranging from very well known artists to those who are in the early stages of their careers. Author sketches span a broad spectrum of years. One can read about L. Frank Baum, author of the children's classic *The Wizard of Oz*, or about Cynthia Rylant, whose book *Missing May* won the Newbery Medal and who is also the author of the delightful *Mudge* stories loved by the younger set. Each volume provides biographical information on between 100 and 140 authors and illustrators. The arrangement is alphabetical by author's name, or pseudonym if appropriate. Lengthy biographical sketches cover personal information, careers, works in progress, and author sidelights, as well as a portrait and sometimes illustrations from their works. Entries are updated periodically; obituaries include references to the original entry. Each newly added volume contains a cumulative index to previous volumes. An added feature, begun with volume 36, is the cross-reference to author references found in *Children's Literature Review* (see entry 276). Volumes 85 to 95 are now available for purchase.

This outstanding publication continues to be recommended for its high standards and for the quality of its content. It is worth being on the must-buy list for every library serving children and young people.

310.   **Twentieth-Century Children's Writers.** Laura Standley Berger, ed. 4th ed. Chicago: St. James, 1995. 1288p. index. ISBN 1-558-62177-6.

This bio-critical guide includes more than 800 twentieth-century authors of fiction, nonfiction, poetry, and drama for children. It is arranged alphabetically by biographee, and each entry consists of a biography, a bibliography of published books, the location of manuscript collections, and a signed critical essay. Appendixes include short entries for nineteenth-century writers for children and writers in languages other than English. A lengthy title index provides easy location of fiction, poetry, and drama in the main entries.

Although, in some ways, this volume is similar to Something About the Author (see entry 309), its one-volume format makes it more cost-effective for small library collections.

311. Ward, Martha E., and Dorothy A. Marquardt. **Photography in Books for Young People.** Metuchen, NJ: Scarecrow, 1985. 93p. indexes. ISBN 0-8108-1854-X.

Recognizing the importance of photographs in informational literature for children, Ward and Marquardt have compiled data to introduce the readers to 270 photographers whose photographs are used extensively in books for children. Each entry, listed alphabetically by the photographer's last name, provides biographical information and identifies any particular subject for which he or she is known, such as scientific photos. A list of the books in which the photographer's pictures are found is also provided in each entry. The author index includes brief title information for each of the books cited.

This is a one-of-a-kind guide to photographers whose works have enhanced many of our children's books. It offers information not easily found elsewhere.

312. Ward, Martha E., Dorothy A. Marquardt, Nancy Dolan, and Dawn Eaton. **Authors of Books for Young People.** 3rd ed. Metuchen, NJ: Scarecrow, 1990. 780p. ISBN 0-8108-2293-8.

This is a revision and update of the authors' 1980 edition. Their goal continues to be to provide comprehensive yet brief biographical sketches of authors and illustrators of children's books. This edition contains biographical entries for 3,708 authors and illustrators, more than any other one-volume source, and 297 of the entries are new to this edition. Gale Research's Contemporary Authors series is used as the source for the biographical information. Although the biographical information in this book is primarily factual, without the photographs or sidelights provided in some of the other biographical sources, it is recommended for its comprehensive coverage in a one-volume format.

Chapter 7

Core Periodicals/Multimedia Reviews

PERIODICAL GUIDES

313. **Children's Magazine Guide.** New Providence, NJ: R. R. Bowker, 1948- . 9/yr. ISSN 0743-9873.

Children's Magazine Guide, a subject index to the most popular children's magazines, indexes forty-five magazines for children ages eight to twelve and eleven professional journals. Titles are arranged alphabetically by subject, and entries provide the title, author, dates, and number of pages. The section on professional magazines includes reviews of audiocassettes, computer software, and videocassettes. This is valuable as a guide for professionals seeking to keep up-to-date on new journal publications.

314. Katz, Bill, and Linda Steinberg Katz. **Magazines for Young People.** 2nd ed. New Providence, NJ: R. R. Bowker, 1991. 361p. indexes. ISBN 0-8352-3009. ISSN 0000-1368.

This reference source, formerly *Magazines for School Libraries*, is a reliable, critical guide to the selection of magazines for children and young adults. Statistics indicate that the number of children's magazines has increased significantly in the last ten years and continues to grow. Approximately 1,000 titles were reviewed and evaluated in the preparation of the guide. Titles are arranged alphabetically by subject within the following age designations: magazines for children ages four to fourteen, magazines for young adults ages fourteen to eighteen, and professional education and library journals. Consultants have identified titles they recommend as "first choice." Each entry contains bibliographic information, location of reviews, and a descriptive and evaluative annotation. The indexes are guides to titles, major subjects, and titles by age groups.

This should be a first-priority purchase for public and school libraries. It is a comprehensive search tool and an excellent subscription guide.

315. Richardson, Selma K. **Magazines for Children: A Guide for Parents, Teachers, and Librarians.** 2nd ed. Chicago, IL: American Library Association, 1991. 139p. index. ISBN 0-8389-0552-8pa.

The focus of Richardson's guide is to help in the process of evaluating magazines for placing a subscription. Referring to the importance of children's magazines, she states that they furnish valuable information for children and, at the same time, provide pleasurable experiences. Each of the more than 100 annotated entries is comprehensive in scope and contains a content description and

119

entries is comprehensive in scope and contains a content description and evaluation. Identification of special features, graphics, and guides for placing a subscription accompany each entry. The following five appendixes provide additional vital and helpful information: "Magazines of Religious Publishing Houses," "Editions for the Visually Impaired," "Age and Grade Levels Suggested by Publisher," "Year of First Publication," and "Circulation Figures." The subject index concludes this useful selection tool.

316.   Stoll, Donald R. **Magazines for Kids and Teens: A Resource for Parents, Teachers, Librarians, and Kids!** Glassboro, NJ: Educational Press Association of America with the International Reading Association, 1994. 101p. indexes. ISBN 0-87207-397-1.

Stoll's publication began as an update of the American Library Association's *Magazines for Children* (see entry 315) but evolved as a new publication that includes more than twice as many entries. Changes in language arts curricula, such as the whole language approach to instruction, have created a demand for more curricular resources. Suggestions for using magazines in lesson planning and implementation are an integral part of many of the entries in Stoll's bibliography. Annotations for each of the 249 entries give the goals and philosophy of the magazine, as well as the publisher, intended audience, circulation figures, cost, and number of issues. The author also includes titles of special-subject magazines that have particular interest to children and young adults, such as hobbies, foreign cultures, music, chess, and crafts. Exceptionally readable comments provide information useful in the decision-making process for all who are considering subscribing to the magazines indexed.

PROFESSIONAL JOURNALS

317.   **Book Links: Connecting Books, Libraries and Classrooms.** Chicago: American Library Association, 1991- . bimonthly. ISSN 1055-4742.

This bimonthly periodical, published by the American Library Association, is designed as a guide for connecting children, preschool through grade eight, with books. The primary users are teachers, librarians, and booksellers. Provided are annotated bibliographies on a variety of topics and themes, essays linking books and themes, retrospective reviews, as well as other specialized features.

318.   **Bookbird: World of Children's Books.** Aurora, IL (subscription): International Board on Books for Young People, 1963- . quarterly.

Bookbird, an international periodical on literature for children and young adults, contains articles about books and authors from all over the world. It also announces award-winning books and lists books recommended for translation.

319.   **CBC Features: Containing News of the Children's Book World.**
New York: Children's Book Council, 1963- . quarterly. ISSN
0006-7377.
The Children's Book Council (CBC) newsletter is "devoted to a topic of
interest to people working with books and children." Provided are a variety of
thought-provoking data and information on publishers; trends; inexpensive and
free materials, such as posters, bookmarks, author brochures; and more.

320.   **Childhood Education: Infancy Through Early Adolescence.**
Wheaton, MD: Association for Childhood Education International
(ACEI), 1924- . 5/yr. ISSN 0009-4056.
The ACEI journal focuses on information appropriate for classroom teachers and others who work with children. Each issue includes annotations of recommended children's books; a bibliography of audiovisual materials; and reviews of
computer software, films, and professional books.

321.   **Children's Literature.** New Haven, CT: Yale University Press. annual. ISSN 0092-8208.
This scholarly periodical devoted to studies of children's literature contains reviews of children's books and media.

322.   **Children's Literature Association Quarterly.** Battle Creek, MI:
Children's Literature Association, 1976- . quarterly. ISSN
0885-0429.
The Children's Literature Association, a nonprofit association, encourages
scholarship and research in children's literature. Issues of its quarterly journal focus on special topics such as "mothers and daughters in children's literature." The
contents are diverse, including bibliographies, literary theory, historical studies,
minority literature, and other significant issues in children's literature.

323.   **Children's Literature in Education.** New York: Human Sciences
Press, 1970- . quarterly. ISSN 0045-6713.
This scholarly publication focuses primarily on the use of children's literature by educators. Articles, written by experts from around the world, discuss content analysis, social issues in children's books, textual analyses, literary criticism,
and historical studies. The magazine contains interviews with noted children's
authors and illustrators.

324.   **The Five Owls: A Publication for Readers Personally and Professionally Involved in Children's Literature.** Minneapolis, MN:
The Five Owls, 1986- . bimonthly. ISSN 0892-6735.
The focus of this journal is to encourage reading by children and youth
through promoting quality children's books. Articles are useful in curriculum
planning and as guides to what is currently happening in the world of children's
books. Each issue contains bibliographies of recommended books, thematic bibliographies, extensive book reviews, and interviews with authors.

325.   **Journal of Youth Services in Libraries.** Chicago: American Library Association for the Association of Library Services to Children (ALSC) and Young Adult Library Services Association (YALSA), 1942- . quarterly. ISSN 0894-2498.

This is the official journal of ALSC and YALSA, divisions of the American Library Association. Issues cover information related to children's literature, library services to children, international publishing news, the May Hill Arbuthnot honor lecture, and the Caldecott and Newbery awards speeches.

326.   **Language Arts.** Urbana, IL: National Council of Teachers of English, 1924- . 8/yr. ISSN 0360-9170.

This peer-reviewed journal covers language arts learning and teaching for educators working with preschool to middle school age children. Theme-oriented articles and articles on a particular aspect of children's literature are the major format used. Reviews and profiles of authors and illustrators are in each issue. The October issue lists notable children's books for language arts.

327.   **Library Talk: The Magazine for Elementary School Librarians.** Worthington, OH: Linworth Publishing. bimonthly. ISSN 1043-237X.

This issues-oriented publication offers articles for elementary school librarians on such subjects as selecting books on cultural diversity and multiculturalism. Book reviews and media reviews are numerous and of good quality.

328.   **The Lion and the Unicorn: A Critical Journal of Children's Literature.** Baltimore, MD: Johns Hopkins University Press, 1977- . annual. ISSN 0147-2593.

The subtitle, *A Critical Journal*, reflects the intent of this publication. It is a genre- and theme-centered journal. It offers critical analyses of children's literature and other aspects of literature for children. It includes articles, interviews, and book reviews on the designated topic.

329.   **Media & Methods: Educational Products, Technologies & Programs for Schools and Universities.** Philadelphia: American Society of Educators, 1964- . 5/yr. ISSN 0024-6897.

Each issue presents articles applicable to recent technological advances for use in schools. Reviews of children's, professional, and audiovisual materials related to the newer technologies, such as interactive video, computers, and CD-ROMs are provided. (See entry 375 for complete annotation.)

330.   **The New Advocate.** Boston, MA: Christopher-Gordon. 1998- . quarterly. ISSN 0895-1381.

Each issue presents articles by authors, illustrators, scholars, and educators who share their personal views on the creative process, its concepts and themes. Recent research, critical studies, practical reflections, and appraisals of books and nonprint media are also included.

331. **The Reading Teacher: A Journal of the International Reading Association.** Newark, DE: International Reading Association, 1947- . ISSN 0034-0561.

This peer-reviewed journal serves as an open forum on new trends in reading research for reading and classroom teachers, primarily at the elementary level. Each issue contains reviews of current children's literature and often includes articles on the use of children's literature in the classroom. Reviews of audiovisual materials, computer software, and educational software are integral to the publication. The October issue features the annual bibliography of books chosen by children as their favorites and announces the winners of the "Children's Choices" awards.

332. **School Library Journal: The Magazine of Children's, Young Adult, & School Librarians.** Marion, OH: School Library Journal, 1954- . monthly. ISSN 0362-8930.

School Library Journal reviews annually more than 3,000 books and audiovisual materials, including video recordings, computer software, and CD-ROMs. Articles in each issue are timely and relevant to the profession. Reviews for current publications are written by practitioners in the field and are both descriptive and evaluative. Special monthly features, for example, a checklist of inexpensive pamphlets, serve as excellent selection guides. The annual "SLJ Reference Books Roundup" is especially beneficial in locating the best in current reference sources. A subscription to the *School Library Journal* is a must for school and public libraries.

333. **School Library Media Activities Monthly.** Baltimore, MD: LMS Associates, 1984. monthly. ISSN 0889-9371.

This magazine provides many creative ideas and activities for promoting books and reading with children. A regular feature is the review of new books, computer software, and other media formats. School library media specialists are encouraged to share successful ideas and activities with others. Its practicality and nominal cost has made it a highly appreciated journal for school libraries and teachers.

334. **Signals: Approaches to Children's Books.** South Woodchester, England: Thimble Press, 1970- . 3/yr. ISSN 0037-4954.

Although this professional journal is primarily written for British readers, the articles and book reviews will be useful to readers in other English-speaking countries. Articles are on children's poetry, picture books, popular science fiction, and other genres of children's literature. Features on teaching children's literature and on guiding children in learning to read are representative of the content.

335. **Young Children.** Washington, DC: National Association for the Education of Young Children, 1944- . bimonthly. ISSN 0044-0728.

The goal of this journal is to keep early childhood educators current on new developments in the profession. Articles on children's literature and reviews of children's books, audiovisual materials, and professional books are incorporated into each issue.

BOOK-REVIEWING JOURNALS

336.   **Appraisal: Science Books for Young People.** Boston: Children's Science Book Review Committee, Boston University, 1967- . quarterly. ISSN 0003-7052.

The goal of the Children's Science Book Review Committee, composed of librarians and subject specialists, is to identify quality science books written for children and young adults. Monographs are arranged alphabetically by author; reviews of science book series are entered by series titles, followed by individual titles. Reviews are lengthy and critically evaluate science books, using a rating scale from one to five.

337.   **Booklist.** Chicago: American Library Association, 1905- . 22/yr. ISSN 0006-7355.

Booklist is published twice a month from September through June and monthly during July and August. It is a reviewing guide to print and nonprint media recommended for purchase in school and public libraries. Only media recommended for purchase are included. Stars are used to denote titles that are "highly recommended" by the reviewers. Excellent additional features are the special bibliographies on selected topics, which vary with each issue.

338.   **Braille Book Review.** Washington, DC: National Library Service for the Blind and Physically Disabled, 1932- . bimonthly. Free to qualified individuals.

Information on Braille books and magazines available through the National Library Service for the Blind and Physically Disabled is provided by this reviewing source. The reviews are available in both large print and Braille. Entries are limited to recent acquisitions, and each review includes a short annotation and ordering information. *Braille Book Review* is an excellent source of information for the visually impaired.

339.   **Bulletin of the Center for Children's Books.** Champaign, IL: University of Illinois Press, 1947- . monthly (except August). ISSN 0008-9036.

A publication of the Graduate School of Library and Information Science at the University of Illinois, this bulletin is a critical and analytical reviewing journal for children's and young adult literature and professional books related to literature for children. Each issue reviews approximately seventy fiction and nonfiction titles. *Bulletin of the Center for Children's Books* is highly selective in choosing the books for inclusion in each issue. The reviews are lengthy and critical; recommendation symbols accompany each review.

340. **Children's Book Review Service.** Brooklyn, NY: Children's Book Review Service, 1972- . monthly plus 2 supplements. ISSN 0090-7987.

This service reviews between sixty and eighty children's books in each monthly issue. The goal is to provide concise reviews of children's books that reflect the reading interests of children. The coverage of picture books and books for younger children is especially commendable.

341. **Children's Folklore Review.** Greenville, NC: East Carolina University, 1979- . ISSN 0739-5558.

The journal of the Children's Folklore section of the American Folklore Society covers all aspects of children's literature as it relates to folklore, folktales, and the study of storytelling activities for children.

342. **The *Horn Book* Guide to Children's & Young Adult Books.** Boston: Horn Book, 1989- . 2/yr. ISSN 1044-405X.

The guide contains critical annotations on all hardcover children's and young adult trade books, fiction and nonfiction, published in the United States during the previous six months. Each book is reviewed and evaluated on a six-point scale, with the number one indicating the highest quality and the number six indicating "not recommended." The arrangement of entries by subject, grade level, genre, and quality recommendation level makes it a valuable guide to children's literature.

343. **The Horn Book Magazine.** Boston: Horn Book, 1924- . bimonthly. ISSN 0018-5078.

The Horn Book Magazine is considered one of the most reputable among many reviewing sources for children's literature; it strives to uphold standards of excellence for children's books. Reviews of current books and articles on award-winning books are among the journal's regular features. Interviews with authors and illustrators, which include personal essays and reminiscences, are major features. Often included are reviews for books in Spanish, books that have been reissued, and books published in paperback form. A list of the most outstanding books at each age level appears annually.

344. **Kirkus Reviews: A Pre-publication Review Service.** New York: Kirkus Association, 1933- . twice monthly. ISSN 0042-2598.

Kirkus Reviews is the most comprehensive and current book review publication available; often reviews appear before the book is available for purchase. The fiction and nonfiction reviews encompass adult, young adult, and children's books. The judgments expressed by the reviewers often pull no punches, a practice that may affect decisions of potential purchasers. Subscription costs may prohibit all but large library systems from subscribing to this reviewing source.

345. **Science and Children.** Washington, DC: National Science Teachers Association, 1963- . 8/yr. ISSN 0036-8148.

Science and Children is a peer-reviewed journal devoted to preschool through middle school science teaching. Each issue contains reviews of recent science books, and audiovisual materials are included in each issue. Every spring a notable science books list is published.

346. **Science Books and Films.** (Formerly **AAAS Science Books and Films**). Washington, DC: American Association for the Advancement of Science, 1965- . 9/yr. ISSN 0098-342 X.

Science Books and Films serves as a guide for purchasing scientific and technological books and nonprint media for elementary school children through college level students. It serves as a valuable guide for general readers as well. A major focus is evaluation of appeal and accuracy in books and films written and produced for children. Reviews are rated using four evaluation definitions, ranging from "highly recommended" to "not recommended." The November-December issue provides an annual list of the best science books and audiovisual science materials.

347. **Social Education: The Official Journal of the National Council for the Social Studies.** Washington, DC: National Council for the Social Studies, 1937- . 7/yr. ISSN 0037-7724.

The focus of this journal is on teaching social studies curricula. Bibliographies highlighting special themes and book reviews appear monthly. The April-May issue features a list of notable books in the social studies.

348. **The WEB: Wonderfully Exciting Books.** Columbus, OH: The WEB, Center for Language, Literature and Reading, Ohio State University. 3/yr.

Each issue of *The WEB* features a specific genre, author, or theme. Reviews of books for children, written by teachers and librarians, incorporate children's responses to the books. Also included in each issue are "webs of possibilities" for integrating the "wonderfully exciting books" into the classroom. This is an excellent reviewing tool.

CHILDREN'S BOOK REVIEWS IN MAJOR NEWSPAPERS

349. **Book World.** Washington, DC: The Washington Post, 1877- . weekly.

In the Sunday issue of *The Washington Post*, in the "Book World" section, reviews for hardcover and paperback children's books and children's books on tape are found. Approximately 120 books a year are reviewed, and the fall and spring issues highlight a "Best Books" list.

350. **Los Angeles Times Book Review.** Los Angeles: Los Angeles Times, 1881- . weekly.
A special feature of the Sunday issue is the review of children's books.

351. **New York Times Book Review.** New York: The New York Times, 1896- . weekly. ISSN 0028-7806.
The *New York Times* reviews children's books weekly in the "For Younger Readers" column. Each November and December selected lists of outstanding children's books are provided.

352. **San Francisco Chronicle Review.** San Francisco: San Francisco Chronicle. weekly.
The book review section includes approximately 200 children's book reviews annually. Special issues highlighting children's books are published at Christmas time and in the spring.

353. **Tribune Books.** Chicago: Chicago Tribune, 1847- . weekly.
Monthly reviews of recently published books for children are featured. Special articles on books and authors are also provided.

Chapter 8

Nonprint Media

GENERAL REFERENCE SOURCES

354. Association for Library Services to Children (ALSC). **Notable Children's Films and Videos, Filmstrips, and Recordings, 1973-1986.** Chicago: American Library Association for the Association for Library Services to Children, 1987. 118p. indexes. ISBN 0-8389-3342-4.

During the 1970s ALSC, a division of the American Library Association, established three nonprint media evaluation committees on films and videos, filmstrips, and recordings; their goal is to identify high-quality nonprint titles designated for children. A list of recommended new titles is released annually and published in professional journals for school library media specialists. In 1987, the lists were cumulated into one volume to provide quick access to titles released between 1973 and 1986. Recommended media titles are entered alphabetically under one of the three media formats. Pertinent bibliographic information and a brief annotation accompany each title. Four indexes provide easy-to-use location information. The index to the performers, an often-sought-after source of information, is especially useful.

This inexpensive guide to nonbook sources is an asset to anyone working with children. An update that includes the newest technology, the CD-ROM, is needed.

355. **AV Market Place: The Complete Directory of Audio, Audio Visual, Computer Systems, Film, Video, Programming, with Industry Yellow Pages.** New Providence, NJ: R. R. Bowker, 1995. 1,500p. indexes. ISBN 0-8352-3579-3.

This annual publication is a comprehensive, cross-referenced directory to nonprint products and services. Information is provided on more than 8,750 companies that create, supply, and distribute audiovisual equipment and services to schools, businesses, and government agencies. It is indexed for ease of use, with cross-references to the main entries. A new edition is scheduled for publication in 1999: *AV Market Place: The Complete Directory of Audio, Audio Visual, Computer Systems, Film, Video, Programming, with Industry Yellow Pages.* New Providence, NJ: R. R. Bowker, 1999. ISBN 0-8352-4098-3.

356. **Bowker's Complete Video Directory, 1995.** New Providence, NJ: R. R. Bowker, 1995. 3 vols. 3976p. index. ISBN 0-8352-3586-6.

This publication covers a full range of videos. Volume 1 provides entertainment videos; volumes 2 and 3 contain educational and special interest videos, including children's videos. The extensive indexes provide title, genre, cast/director information, and more.

357. **Children's Media Market Place.** 4th ed. Barbara Stein, ed. New York: Neal-Schuman, 1995. 400p. indexes. ISBN 1-55570-190-6. ISSN 0734-8169.

The fourth edition of *Children's Media Market Place*, a ready-reference directory to multimedia materials, has been completely revised and expanded. It is designed as an index to media and services for people working with children from preschool age through grade twelve. Twenty-one resource sections provide directory information to the marketplace of resources and services available. Data include software producers and distributors; audiovisual producers and distributors; publishers; periodicals for children; periodicals for professionals and parents; resources related to cultural diversity; professional associations; a listing of awards for children's media; grants for children's programs; and more. Reference information includes data for the largest publishing houses in the field of children's literature. The index provides information to use in making direct contact with any of the agencies listed.

This comprehensive, easy-to-use reference source is a warehouse of vital information. The format and extensive coverage distinguish it as an invaluable publication for libraries serving children, for authors and illustrators, for teachers and parents, for the publishing industry—for anyone providing services to children.

358. Donavin, Denise Perry, ed. **Best of the Best for Children: Books, Magazines, Videos, Audio, Software, Toys, Travel.** New York: Random House, 1992. 366p. indexes. ISBN 0-679-40450-3; 0-679-74250-6pa.

Children need to read, see, hear, and interact with books and reading in order to grow intellectually as well as creatively. Emerging technologies are increasingly having an effect on children's interests and tastes; therefore, it is imperative that parents have access to a source of evaluations to help in the selection of quality media. Donavin has organized her chapters by type of medium. In conjunction with Donavin's well-presented section on books are sections in which she identifies recommended titles and sources of children's magazines, videos, computer software, and toys; an excellent listing of audio titles and sources; and finally, an unusual but interesting section on guides for family travel. With the ever-increasing number of children's books available on video, current bibliographies of this nature will continue to serve as good guides for selecting and evaluating quality items. (See entry 27 for the complete annotation.)

359. Gallant, Jennifer Jung. **Best Videos for Children and Young Adults: A Core Collection for Libraries.** Santa Barbara, CA: ABC-CLIO, 1990. 185p. indexes. ISBN 0-87436-561-9.

The recent increase in the production of videos prepared specifically for children and young adults has created a need for guides to locate the best. The author, using recommended selection guides, has produced an annotated core collection of approximately 350 highly recommended half-inch VHS videos considered appropriate for use in schools, public libraries, and private homes. In order to ensure the availability of video titles, Gallant limits her list to those produced between 1975 and 1990. Except for series videos, entries are listed alphabetically by title. Each entry includes an age level designation, usage data, format, showing time, and cost. The names of the director and distributor are also provided. A brief annotation concludes each entry. Appendixes are titled "List of Video Distributors," "Keeping Up with Videos," and "Sources of Other Video Titles for Children and Young Adults." Indexes are to audience/usage designations; age groupings; and to subjects and titles.

This is a well-organized guide to good video selections appropriate for school and public libraries.

360. Green, Diana Huss, ed. **Parents' Choice: A Sourcebook of the Very Best Products to Educate, Inform, and Entertain Children of All Ages.** Kansas City, MO: Andrews and McMeel, 1993. 173p. illus. indexes. ISBN 0-8362-8036-9.

The goal of this sourcebook is to provide a compilation of a variety of media to help children learn and develop self-esteem. Information on products parents can locate in local bookstores and through family-oriented magazines, such as the publisher's *Parents' Choice Magazine,* is supplied. Entries are arranged by chapters under the following media formats: toys, books, videos, audiotapes, computer programs, and magazines. Each entry contains brief bibliographic information, an annotation, recommended age levels, and a purchase price. Selection guidelines are given for each of the media formats. Addenda include a bibliography of suggestions for further reading and a list of catalogs to use in placing orders. The extensive indexes are as follows: titles by category and recommended age levels; authors, editors, and illustrators; composers and studio and recording artists; and media producers.

Green's sourcebook is organized so that parents, as well as professionals working with children, can use it with ease. The information provided makes it a worthy volume to be placed in all libraries serving children.

361. **High/Scope Buyer's Guide to Children's Software.** 11th ed. Charles Hohmann, Barbara Carmody, and Chica McCabe-Bran, eds. Ypsilanti, MN: High/Scope Press, 1995. 175p. index. ISBN 0-929816-96-x. ISSN 1060-9504.

The *High/Scope Buyer's Guide to Children's Software* is designed to help the user make good choices when purchasing software to use to enhance learning opportunities for children. Recommended guidelines for use during the selection process are provided. Entries contain information related to educational content and technical features and an evaluation of the degree to which the software is user-friendly. In-depth reviews and ratings are provided for forty-eight of the selected software titles. Titles are entered alphabetically and range from *A to Zapp* to *Zurk's Learning Safari*. The first appendix contains approximately 515 additional entries with brief bibliographic information accompanying each entry. The second appendix provides a list of software publishers, and the third identifies software programs by concept areas.

362.   Levine, Evan. **Kids Pick the Best Videos.** New York: Citadel, 1994. 306p. index. ISBN 0-8065-1498-1.

Video entertainment for children has proliferated to the extent that selection of high-quality productions is virtually a nightmare. *Kids Pick the Best Videos* is a guide to help professionals and nonprofessionals working with children from ages three to fourteen make intelligent selections of well-produced video productions. To ensure that the videos selected for inclusion reflect the interests of children and meet the criteria expected by parents, the author involved children in the selection and review process. The selected video titles are entered under one of twenty categories, first by age group and then alphabetically by title. Each entry includes the title, producer, approximate running time, and a one-to-ten rating scale to signify appropriateness for the intended audience in each of the following five categories: visual quality, humor, fun facts, social value, and appropriateness for children. The author admits that the list is subjective; however, a quick review of the entries confirms the quality of the titles selected for inclusion.

This extends and updates the Association for Library Services to Children's videocassette bibliography (see entry 354). The comprehensive coverage and the guides to evaluating each entry help the reader make appropriate selections with confidence.

363.   Miranker, Cathy, and Alison Elliott. **The Computer Museum Guide to the Best Software for Kids: More Than 200 Reviews for Windows, Macintosh, and DOS Computers, Including the Best CD-ROMs.** New York: HarperPerennial, 1995. 282p. illus. indexes. ISBN 0-06-273376-1pa.

The authors open their guide with two brief "Bests Lists." The first list is organized into five age groups ranging from three to twelve; the second list is a "best of the 'New and Notable Titles.'" Nine "Best Title" groupings have broad subject headings: "Playing to Learn," "Creative Pursuits," "Reading," "Math," "Explorations for Curious Kids," "Fun and Games," "Information, Please!" "Productivity," and "New and Notable." "More Best Lists" provide other recommendations for selecting quality software. Topics under which recommendations are located include "Best Simulation Programs," "Most Challenging Programs," "Best Videos," "Best Homework Helpers," and more.

This highly selective, easy-to-use guide is perfect for parents seeking advice for purchasing software for their children. It should also be a top-priority purchase for schools and public libraries. The following address can be used to access the Computer Museum on the World Wide Web: http://www.tcm.org.

364. Moss, Joyce, and George Wilson, eds. **From Page to Screen: Children's and Young Adult Books on Film and Video.** Detroit: Gale Research, 1992. 443p. indexes. ISBN 0-8103-7893-0.

Moss and Wilson state that adapting books to film and video formats allows the user to explore the relationship between a printed story and its screen adaptation. With this in mind, they have identified more than 750 literary works for youth, with ages ranging from kindergarten to twelfth grade, adapted to 16mm film, videocassette, and laser disc formats. Literary formats include novels, some nonfiction, short stories, plays, songs, poems, and folklore. Entries, organized alphabetically by title, contain a synopsis, an identification of genre, an evaluative listing of the cinematic adaptations, the awards received, and the location of reviews. Quality ratings are indicated by a series of icons. Appendix A lists films for the hearing impaired, and appendix B lists film and video distributors. The four indexes categorize by age level (with appropriate titles entered alphabetically); awards; subject; and author/film title.

This comprehensive, well-researched, and annotated bibliography is impressive. It will be a useful addition to any library collection.

365. Reid, Rob. **Children's Jukebox: A Subject Guide to Musical Recordings and Programming Ideas for Songsters Ages One to Twelve.** Chicago: American Library Association, 1995. 225p. index. ISBN 0-8389-0650-8.

The author admitted that working on this manuscript proved to be a "fun project"; this is apparent in the format he uses to present the information, as well as in his criteria for selection. He looked for ease of availability, subject matter that fell into the thirty-five subject categories identified as child-oriented, and musical recordings that "kids will really like." The opening section of his book contains a discography of the featured records listed alphabetically by artist, a listing of the Robbie Award Hall of Fame recipients, a section designated "Hello Songs," and the twenty top-selling children's recordings. The most comprehensive section contains approximately 300 analyzed and evaluated musical recordings, entered first by subject headings that range from "anatomy" to "weather" and then alphabetically by title. In addition to bibliographic information, a brief annotation, a recommended age level, and a programming idea are given for each entry. In another section, entitled "Short Takes," he enters subjects that don't quite fit into the other categories but are popular with children, for example, cowboys/girls, goodbye, and toy songs. A third section lists songs by special type, for example, cumulative songs. Appendixes provide a selected list of children's musical videos and a listing of resources to be used for locating musical recording. The index is a song titles index.

Children's Jukebox is attractively presented and as much fun to review as it must have been for the author to write. It will be a popular reference source in any library serving children.

366.   Sharkey, Paulette Bochnig. **Newbery and Caldecott Medal and Honor Books in Other Media.** Jim Roginski, ed. New York: Neal-Schuman, 1992. 160p. indexes. ISBN 1-55570-119-1.

In response to interest in finding alternative ways for children to enjoy the award-winning Newbery and Caldecott books, many of their texts and illustrations have been converted to different media formats, including video and audiocassettes, filmstrips, large print books, Braille, posters, postcards, television programs, and even bookmarks. Information on available taped interviews with the award-winning authors and illustrators is also included.

Because computers have virtually become standard equipment in schools and homes, a list of CD-ROMs related to children's books, authors, and illustrators is recommended for inclusion in any planned update. (See entry 14 for the complete annotation.)

REFERENCE SOURCES ON CD-ROM

Because this technology has recently "come into its own," a bibliography of titles currently available will quickly become outdated. The following citations are only a representative list intended to illustrate the types of information available in the CD-ROM format.

367.   **Bookbrain*Bookwhiz.** Boca Raton, FL: Sirs, Inc.

This interactive CD-ROM is a database developed to assist children and young adult readers in locating informational and entertaining reviews of more than 3,200 books identified as "best books." Ages for which it is intended range from grades one through twelve. The reviews may be accessed by title, author, and subject. Information provided includes the review, reading level, main characters, type of story, and paging. As a result of its ease of access, the database is especially appropriate for the reluctant reader, yet it serves as a motivational tool for all children. It is also available in an English/Spanish format. The price is right for this storehouse of book reviews.

368.   **Children's Reference PLUS.** New Providence, NJ: R. R. Bowker. annual.

Children's Reference PLUS provides fast, easy-to-use access to more than forty children's and young adult references on one innovative CD-ROM. It covers reference books published by R. R. Bowker and cited in *Children's Books in Print* and *Subject Guide to Children's Books in Print.* Citations and full-text searching are available for diverse formats, such as books, serials, audio, and videocassettes. The CD-ROM, updated annually, is expensive, but where the budget allows, it should be a priority item. The large number of reference sources the CD-ROM provides makes it more cost-effective than purchasing each reference separately.

369.   **Junior DISCovering Authors.** Detroit: Gale Research, 1994.

Gale Research has selected 300 authors from the Something About the Author series and presents them on CD-ROM. Detailed biographical information, a portrait, and bibliographies are provided for each of the author entries. Book plots, characters, time lines, and settings as well as media adaptations provide multiple access to information about each author. The concentration is on well-known, contemporary American writers whose books are recommended for children grades five to nine. The format allows for a wide variety of search options.

370.   **Multimedia CD-ROM Reviews on the World Wide Web**
       URL: http://volvo.gslis.utexas.edu/~reviews
       A collection of detailed reviews of multimedia CD-ROM products for children and young adults is now available on the World Wide Web. Information provided in the Website includes descriptions of the contents of the CD-ROM, the interface design, and usability factors. Recommendations for use and intended audience are also noted. Where available, reviews are cited. This is an excellent site for the Web user to consult when seeking current recommendations and reviews of multimedia sources.

371.   *Variety's* **Video Directory PLUS.** New Providence, NJ: R. R. Bowker. quarterly.
       This video directory on CD-ROM provides access to virtually every video-cassette available, including children's videos. Entries provide complete and reliable bibliographic information and ordering information. The easy-to-use indexes provide information from a wide variety of access points. Included in the guide are full-text entries and critical reviews from *Variety* magazine. The database is kept current quarterly through cumulative updates.
       This basically provides the "ultimate world of videos," but the cost will be prohibitive for smaller library systems.

REVIEWING SOURCES FOR NONPRINT MEDIA

372.   **AV Guide: The Learning Media Newsletter.** Des Plaines, IL: Scranton Gillette Communications, 1922- . monthly. ISSN 0091-360X.
       AV Guide is an informational guide and selection tool featuring new products and services, audiovisual equipment, and computer software and hardware. Product announcements include purchasing information as well as product descriptions.

373.   **CD-ROMs for Kids:** *Booklist's* **Best Bets.** Irene Wood, ed. Chicago: American Library Association, 1997. 48p. ISBN 0-8389-7838-X.
       More than 100 CD-ROMs for children ages three to ten are arranged by age groupings. The annotations reflect content ranging from that appropriate for young children to that which can be used for curricular applications. This very current, inexpensive bibliography is a valuable resource.

374.   **Children's Video Report.** New York: Children's Video Report, 1985- . 8/yr. ISSN 0883-6922.
       This excellent tool for schools, public libraries, and parents provides guides for the selection of quality video productions for children. Each issue highlights a particular theme or genre. Each title includes a lengthy, easy-to-read, evaluative annotation and a quality rating. Approximately six major reviews are included in each issue.

375.   **Media & Methods: Educational Products, Technologies & Programs for Schools and Universities.** Philadelphia: American Society of Educators, 1964- . 5/yr. ISSN 0024-6897.

The focus of *Media & Methods* is on using technology in the classroom to increase learning opportunities. Each issue consists of three to six articles dealing with recent technological advances available for use in the classroom at all educational levels. Media discussed include interactive video, computers, and CD-ROMs. Reviews of children's and professional audiovisual materials provide valuable selection guides for libraries. Annually the publication announces the year's best educational media.

376.   **Parents' Choice: A Review of Children's Media.** Waban, MA: Parents' Choice Foundation: 1978- . quarterly.

This journal provides a well-balanced selection of reviews of children's media. The entries are annotated by highly qualified personnel and include books, television programs, movies, videos, computer software, music, toys, and games. Approximately 350 reviews a year are provided.

377.   **School Library Journal: The Magazine of Children's, Young Adult, & School Librarians.** Marion, OH: School Library Journal, 1954- . monthly. ISSN 0362-8930.

This is perhaps the most often used journal for locating reviews of literature for children. Each issue contains extensive reviews of the newest in audiovisual materials, including video recordings, computer software and CD-ROMs. (See entry 332 for complete annotation.)

Chapter 9

Special Collections
of Children's Literature

DIRECTORIES

378. Ash, Lee, and William G. Miller. **Subject Collections: A Guide to Special Book Collections and Subject Emphases as Reported by University, College, Public, and Special Libraries and Museums in the United States and Canada.** 7th ed. 2 vols. New Providence, NJ: R. R. Bowker, 1993. 2466p. indexes. ISBN 0-8352-3141-0.

Ash and Miller's guide to subject collections is more extensive than the Jones guide (see entry 379); they have extended their coverage to include many less expansive collections as well as the more comprehensive special collections in larger institutions. This publication has been referred to as the "cornerstone resource" for thousands of special collections. Subject headings, using the Library of Congress subject heading list, are entered alphabetically. Under each subject heading, states and then cities are entered alphabetically, followed by names of libraries housing subject collections. Each entry contains the library or museum address, telephone number, fax number, and an explanation of the subject collection, including the number of items in the collection.

As reflected by the size of this publication, virtually every imaginable subject collection in the United States and Canada can be located using this volume.

379. Jones, Dolores Blythe, ed. **Special Collections in Children's Literature: An International Directory.** 3rd ed. Chicago: American Library Association for the Association for Library Service to Children, 1995. 235p. illus. index. ISBN 0-8389-3454-4.

The Committee on National Planning for Special Collections of Children's Books was formed in 1964. Initially their activities and research were limited to collections located in the United States and Canada. The coverage has been extended and now includes international collections of stature. Their goal is to identify and coordinate special collections of children's literature for purposes of research and preservation. The directory's third edition, building upon the first two editions, identifies 300 collections in the United States, eighty-two of which are new to this edition. The segment of the directory addressing international collections describes the holdings of 119 institutions in forty countries. Only institutional collections are included; no private collections are presented. The directory of collections in the United States is arranged alphabetically by state, city, and institution. Within each institution, collections are arranged alphabetically, followed

137

by descriptive information about the institution and the collection. International collections are entered alphabetically by country and followed by geographical divisions within the country. Indexes provide guidance to collections by subject and location.

This is a uniquely valuable resource for the serious researcher. The collections described include holdings of original manuscripts of children's authors and illustrators; original research of literature for children; and often items associated with a particular book, such as dolls or stuffed animals. Most of the cited institutions welcome all visitors, the interested layperson as well as the researcher, to their special collection(s) of children's literature.

A SELECTIVE LIST OF RESEARCH COLLECTIONS

380. **Cooperative Children's Book Center (CCBC)**
      Helen C. White Hall
      University of Wisconsin
      600 North Park Street
      Madison, WI 53706
      Telephone: 608-263-3720
      E-mail: CCBC-net@ccbc.soemadison.wisc.edu

The CCBC is located in the School of Education at the University of Wisconsin at Madison. A noncirculating examination, study, and research collection of children's and young adult literature is housed in the center. The purpose of the CCBC is to make available to students and researchers a significant collection of current, retrospective, and historical children's books. Special emphasis is placed on multicultural literature, small press publishing, and Wisconsin authors and illustrators. The director and staff encourage the study and teaching of children's literature through outreach programs, seminars, and workshops. The center is open to teachers, scholars and researchers. Access to lively and informative book discussions of children's literature is available through the center's Internet site. To join send a "subscribe" request to listserv@ccbc.soemadison.wisc.edu.

381. **The de Grummond Children's Literature Collection**
      McCain Library and Archives
      University of Southern Mississippi
      Hattiesburg, MS 39406-5053
      Telephone: 601-266-4349
      World Wide Web site: http//www.lib.usm.edu/~degrumm

The de Grummond collection, one of the largest research collections of its kind in the United States, is housed at the University of Southern Mississippi. The goal of the collection is to provide access to materials related to historical stages in the development of literature for children in the United States and to illustrate formative stages of manuscript development and artwork in children's literature. The holdings consist of 52,000 published volumes dating from the 1530s to contemporary literature for children. It encompasses original manuscripts and illustrative materials from more than 1,200 authors and illustrators. Represented are a wide range of materials extending from the best to mediocre and even some items of poor quality. All types of literature are located in the collection, including alphabet books, chapbooks, series books, fables, folk- and fairy tales, nursery rhymes, classics, children's magazines, reference books, and textbooks. Its archival materials include original books and illustrations of Kate Greenaway. The manuscripts of Ezra Jack Keats, Trina Shart Hyman, Scott O'Dell, Ernest Shepard, and Charlotte Zolotow are among the many author/illustrator collections. The exhibition catalog, "The Image of the Child," with illustrations from the Greenaway collection and other exhibits, is available for purchase. A special trip to visit the collection is well worth the time.

382. **The Kerlan Collection**
The Walter Library
University of Minnesota
117 Pleasant Street SE
Minneapolis, MN 55455
Telephone: 612-624-4576
The Kerlan collection, begun in the 1940s, is housed in the University of Minnesota library. The collection includes more than 60,000 children's books, dating from the 1700s to the present. More than sixty-eight languages are represented in the collection. It contains manuscript materials for more than 3,900 titles, illustrative materials for more than 4,090 children's books, and 226 periodical titles. The collection's resources for the study of children's literature are prodigious; they include audiovisual materials, figurines, photographs, posters, toys, and more. *The Kerlan Collection Manuscripts and Illustrations for Children's Books: A Checklist,* compiled by Karen Nelson Hoyle and published by the University of Minnesota in 1985, is an outstanding guide to the collection's contents. The Kerlan Award, established in 1975, is given in recognition of singular attainments in the creation of children's literature and in appreciation for donations of unique resources to the Kerlan Collection.

383. **Schomburg Center for Research in Black Culture**
New York Public Library
515 Lenox Avenue
New York, NY 10037-1801
Telephone: 212-491-2200
World Wide Web site: http://www.nypl.org/research/sc/sc.html
The Schomburg Center houses an outstanding research collection on African American culture. Within the holdings is an exceptionally fine collection of children's books relating to African American culture. The collection contains children's books about African Americans and books written and/or illustrated by African Americans.

A REPRESENTATIVE LIST OF CENTERS

384. **Arthur Rackham Collection**
Columbia University
Butler Library
535 West 114th Street
New York, NY 10027
Telephone: 212-854-2231
The Rackham collection, located in the Rare Book and Manuscript Library of Columbia University, is a collection housing more than 400 English and American first editions and printed ephemera of Arthur Rackham. Original letters from the author/illustrator, letters relating to him, manuscript documents, and notebooks are all a part of the collection. Outstanding features of the collection are Rackham's original sketchbooks and more than 500 original drawings, watercolors, and oil paintings. Located in the collection are the proofs of Derek Hudson's book, *Arthur Rackham: His Life and Work* (New York: Scribner's, 1960).

385. **Children's Literature Center**
Center for the Book
Library of Congress
Washington, DC 20540-5510
Telephone: 205-707-5535
World Wide Web site: http://lcweb.loc.gov/loc/cfbook
Founded in 1963 as an information center, the Children's Literature Center is mandated to serve organizations and individuals who study, produce, collect, interpret, and disseminate children's books, films, television programs, and other literature-related materials for children's recreational and informational use. The center houses approximately 180,000 children's books and related items. An annual annotated bibliography, *Books for Children,* which identified and annotated 100 significant American children's books published the previous year, was in publication until 1995. The center offers lectures, tours, and symposia and supports celebrations of children's literature, such as Children's Book Week. Reviving *Books for Children* would be welcomed by teachers and librarians.

386. **The Elizabeth Nesbitt Room**
University of Pittsburgh Library
University of Pittsburgh
Pittsburgh, PA 15260
Telephone: 412-624-4710
World Wide Web site: http://www.pitt.edu/~enroom
The Elizabeth Nesbitt Room is a depository of books that reflect the history of children and books from the 1600s through today. The collection houses an excellent collection of chapbooks, a significant step in the development of children's literature in this country, and also an extensive collection of historical pop-up books and toy books. Many of the outstanding illustrations from books published during the Golden Age of Children's Literature, the 1890s and early 1900s,

are in the collection. It also houses the Clifton Fadiman Book Collection and archives. The manuscripts and archives of E. L. Konigsburg, the Newbery Medal winner for 1968 and 1996, are located here.

387. **Historical Children's Collection**
Ward Edwards Library
The Ophelia Gilbert Center
Central Missouri State University
Warrensburg, MO 64093
Telephone: 816-543-8850
E-mail: ogilbert@cmsuvmb.cmsu.edu
The children's historical literature collection in the Ward Edwards Library of Central Missouri State University contains a general collection of about 12,000 volumes of children's books written and illustrated by authors and illustrators who have gained recognition for their outstanding contributions to children's literature. Collection titles date from 1799 to the present. The several thousand first editions and autographed books are a showcase of the collection. Personal correspondence, photographs, and original interviews with 200 contemporary writers are included in the collection. Although emphasis is on Missouri authors and illustrators, the collection contains a wide variety of adolescent novels, Mother Goose books, alphabet and counting books, toy and movable books, foreign language books, and Victorian series books. Housed in the center is a complete collection of the Mark Twain Reading Award books, an annual award selected by elementary schoolchildren of Missouri. Most of the books have been personally autographed for center staff members. It is a well-rounded, well-organized, and eclectic collection of children's books.

Chapter 10

Professional Associations

388. **American Association of School Librarians (AASL)**
Division of the American Library Association
50 East Huron Street
Chicago, IL 60611
Telephone: 1-800- 545-2433
World Wide Web site: http://www.ala.org/aasl.html
The membership of AASL is made up of school librarians, library media specialists, library educators, and others concerned with the improvement and extension of library services for schoolchildren, from preschool through high school.
Journal: *School Library Media Quarterly* (SLMQ)
Publications: books, pamphlets, and other items related to school libraries

389. **American Library Association (ALA)**
50 East Huron Street
Chicago, IL 60611
Telephone: 1-800-545-2433
World Wide Web site: http://www.ala.org
Membership in the American Library Association is required in order to become a member of any of its divisions, including the American Association of School Librarians, Association for Library Service to Children, Public Library Association, and Young Adult Library Services Association. The goal of the library association is serve as a leader in the development, promotion, and improvement of library and information services. It supports and promotes programs providing educational training for the library professional. The objective is to ensure access to information for all people.
Journals: *American Libraries, Choice,* and *Booklist*
Publications: books for library professionals

390. **Association for Childhood Education International (ACEI)**
11501 Georgia Avenue, Suite 315
Wheaton, MD 20902
Telephone: 1-800-423-3563
World Wide Web site: http://www.udel.edu/bateman/acei
Teachers, librarians, and parents are members of ACEI. The association's focus is on working toward the establishment of a favorable environment in which children can learn and on ensuring that high standards are required for the preparation of classroom teachers. Workshops and seminars are offered through the association.

Journals: *Childhood Education* and *Journal of Research in Childhood Education*

Publications: books, booklets, and nonprint media

391. **Association for Library Service to Children (ALSC)**
Division of the American Library Association
50 East Huron Street
Chicago, IL 60611
Telephone: 1-800-545-2433
World Wide Web site: http://www.ala.org/alsc.html
Membership is composed of librarians, library media specialists, library educators, and others interested in library services to children. The ALSC is dedicated to the improvement and extension of library services to children in all types of libraries. It provides guidelines for the evaluation and selection of library materials for children, conducts research, and helps libraries meet the requirement of quality services to children.
Journal: *Journal of Youth Services in Libraries*
Publications: books, pamphlets, and other publications related to library services to children
Awards and honors: sponsors the annual Arbuthnot Lecture program; presents annually the Caldecott Medal and Honor Books awards, the Newbery Medal and Honor Books awards with the Young Adult Library Services Association, and the Mildred L. Batchelder award; presents the Laura Ingalls Wilder Award every five years

392. **Association of Jewish Libraries (AJL)**
15 East 26th Street, Room 1034
New York, NY 10010-1599
Telephone: 212-678-8092
E-mail: carolynhessel@jewishbooks.org
The purpose of AJL is to foster Judaica literature and librarianship and to promote awareness of Judaica literature among children and adults.

393. **Catholic Library Association**
22 Maplewood Avenue
Pittsfield, MA 01201-4780
The purpose of CLA is to promote Catholic principles through quality library services to children and adults. The Regina Medal is awarded annually by the Catholic Library Association for dedication to literature for children.
Journal: *Catholic Library World*

394.   **The Children's Book Council (CBC)**
568 Broadway
New York, NY 10012
Telephone: 212-966-1990
World Wide Web site: http://www.CBCBooks.org
The membership consists of sixty publishers of children's trade books. Their goal is the promotion of reading and enjoyment of children's books through workshops, posters, pamphlets, and many other items to encourage love of reading.
Journal: *CBC Features*
Publications: *Children's Books: Awards and Prizes* and reading promotion materials
Sponsors National Children's Book Week

395.   **Children's Literature Assembly of NCTE**
c/o Marjorie R. Hancock
1037 Plymouth Road
Manhattan, KS 66502
This division of the National Council of Teachers of English focuses on all aspects of literature for children.

396.   **Children's Literature Association (CLA)**
P.O. Box 138
Battle Creek, MI 49016
Telephone: 616-965-8180/3568
E-mail: chla@mlc.lib.mi.us
The membership consists of librarians, library media specialists, scholars, teachers, professors, and graduate students. The purpose is to encourage research and high standards in literature for children and to enhance the professional stature of the teaching of children's literature in institutions of higher education. They sponsor awards for research and literary criticism of literature for children. They are affiliated with the Modern Language Association of America.
Journal: *Children's Literature: An International Journal*
Publications: books and pamphlets for teachers and librarians

397.   **Children's Reading Round Table of Chicago (CRRT)**
2045 North Seminary Avenue
Chicago, IL 60631
Telephone: 312-525-7257
Membership in this nonprofit organization consists of authors, illustrators, librarians, library media specialists, educators, publishers and booksellers. They support activities for children and young adults that foster interest in and enjoyment of books and reading. They promote interaction among persons who are involved in juvenile literature.
Journal: *CRRT Bulletin*

398. **Children's Television Workshop (CTW)**
       1 Lincoln Plaza
       New York, NY 10023
       Telephone: 212-595-3456
       World Wide Web site: http://www.ctw.org
       Children's Television Workshop explores new uses of television and re-
lated communication media for educational and informational purposes. They create
and produce *Sesame Street, Big Bag,* and *The New Ghostwriter Mysteries.*

399. **Council on Interracial Books for Children**
       1841 Broadway, Room 608
       New York, NY 10023
       Telephone: 212-757-5339
       Persons interested in eliminating racism and sexism in children's literature
may become members of this group. Children's books, textbooks, and other learning materials are reviewed and evaluated for evidence of sexism and racism in content and intent. The council publishes books, pamphlets, and other media formats
as a means of informing the public of their findings.
       Journal: *Interracial Books for Children Bulletin*
       Publications: informational media for the general public as well as profes-
sionals working with children

400. **Great Books Foundation**
       35 West Wacker Drive, Suite 2300
       Chicago, IL 60601-2298
       Telephone: 312-332-5870; 802-222-5870
       World Wide Web site: http://www.greatbooks.org
       The Great Books Foundation provides a lifelong program of liberal educa-
tion through reading and discussion of great works of literature, philosophy, psychology, and history for all ages. They publish a Great Books Reading Aloud
Program series for three separate age groups: K-1, 2-9, and 10-12.

401. **International Reading Association (IRA)**
       800 Barksdale Road, Box 8139
       Newark, DE 19714-8139
       Telephone: 302-731-1600
       World Wide Web site: http://www.reading.org
       The membership is made up of reading specialists at all levels, including
classroom teachers. The IRA's goals are improving the quality of reading instruction, encouraging research, improving teacher education, and working toward
making reading a lifetime habit for children.
       Journal: *The Reading Teacher: The Journal of the International Reading
Association*
       Publications: books and recommended reading lists for children and young
adults

402. **Jewish Book Council**
     15 East 26th Street
     New York, NY 10010
     Telephone: 212-532-4949
     World Wide Web site: http://www.avotaynu.com/jbc.html
     The council promotes and disseminates Jewish books for adults and children. The Jewish Book Award recognizes authors of adult and children's books who combine literary merit with an affirmative expression of Jewish values.
     Publications: pamphlets, posters, and bibliographies of children's books
     Awards and honors: The Jewish National Book Awards

403. **National Braille Association, Inc.**
     3 Townline Circle
     Rochester, NY 14623-2513
     Telephone: 717-427-8260
     The goal of the National Braille Association is the development and distribution of materials for the visually impaired. Materials in all three media (Braille, large print, and tape) are available. The association maintains a depository of Braille books that are made available to the visually impaired.

404. **National Council of Teachers of English (NCTE)**
     1111 West Kenyon Road
     Urbana, IL 61801-1096
     Telephone: 217-328-3870
     World Wide Web site: http://www.ncte.org
     Membership consists of teachers and librarians at all grade levels. The NCTE's purpose is to promote literacy and high-quality literature through recognition of outstanding books and writers and through workshops and seminars. They also recognize outstanding student contributions.
     Journals: *Language Arts, Primary Voices K-6, The English Journal* for secondary schools
     Publications: books and pamphlets related to the teaching of language arts and English

405. **Parents' Choice Foundation**
     P.O. Box 185
     Newton, MA 02168-0185
     Telephone: 617-965-5913
     This is a nonprofit service group organized to encourage parents to work toward establishing an environment that encourages lifetime learning for children. The foundation's publications and awards identify the year's best in all media for children.
     Journal: *Parents' Choice*
     Publications: bibliographies and other pamphlets related to children and learning

406.   **Public Library Association (PLA)**
Division of the American Library Association
50 East Huron Street
Chicago, IL 60611
Telephone: 1-800- 545-2433
World Wide Web site: http://www.ala.org/pla.html
The membership of PLA is made up of public librarians, library educators, and others concerned with the improvement and extension of library services in the public sector. Their focus is on services to the adult clientele, young adults, children, and special services endemic to the public whom they serve.
Journal: *Public Libraries*
Publications: books and pamphlets related to public library services for all ages of library users

407.   **Reading Is Fundamental, Inc. (RIF)**
Smithsonian Institution
RIF-Department WB
P.O. Box 23444
Washington, DC 20626
Telephone: 202-287-3220
World Wide Web site: http://www.si.edu/ref/start.htm
The goals of RIF are to help young people discover the joy of reading and to become lifetime readers. The foundation provides book sharing guides to promote motivational programs that bring books and children together. It is a nonprofit organization whose members are primarily volunteer workers.
Publication: *RIF Newsletter*

408.   **U.S. Board on Books for Young People (USBBY)**
c/o International Reading Association
800 Barksdale Road, Box 8139
Newark, DE 19714
Telephone: 302-731-1600
The membership is made up of authors, illustrators, librarians, publishers, and teachers. Their goal is to promote the development of quality reading materials for youth around the world, and they facilitate the exchange of information on reading programs and children's media throughout the world. This board is an affiliate of the International Board on Books for Young People.
Journal: *USBBY Newsletter*
Award: Bridge to Understanding, to build bridges between children of the United States and children around the world

409. **Young Adult Library Services Association (YALSA)**
Division of the American Library Association
50 East Huron Street
Chicago, IL 60611
Telephone: 1-800-545-2433
World Wide Web site: http://www.ala.org/yalsa.html

Membership is composed of librarians, library media specialists, library educators, and others interested in library services to young adults. The association is dedicated to the improvement and extension of library services to young adults ages twelve to eighteen. They provide guidelines for the evaluation and selection of materials for young people, conduct research, and help libraries meet the requirement of quality services to young adults.

Journal: *Journal of Youth Services in Libraries*

Publications: books, pamphlets, and other publications related to library services to young adults; "Best Books for Young Adults"; "Selected Films and Videos for Young Adults"

Awards and honors: presents annually the Newbery Medal and Honor Books awards with Association for Library Service to Children

Chapter 11

The Information Superhighway via the Internet

PRINT REFERENCE SOURCES

410. Hahn, Harley. **Harley Hahn's Internet and Web Yellow Pages: 1998.** 5th ed. Berkeley, CA: Osborne/McGraw Hill, 1998. 914p. ISBN 0-07-882-387-0.

In the yellow pages format of a telephone book, Hahn's guide appears to cover the waterfront of the Internet world.

411. Miller, Elizabeth B., ed. **The Internet Resource Directory for K-12 Teachers and Librarians, 97/98.** Englewood, CO: Libraries Unlimited, 1997. 319p. indexes. ISBN 1-56308-617-4. ISSN 1084-5798.

This latest edition of the *Internet Resource Directory* contains approximately 400 new entries and 200 entries that have been updated. Designed primarily for educators, it organizes data into curriculum categories for ease of use. Each entry furnishes the name of the resource and the World Wide Web, listserv, or gopher address and contains an annotation describing its content and focus. In recognition of the rapidly changing nature of Internet sites, free updates are provided via the Web (www.lu.com/Internet_Resource_Directory).

412. Polly, Jean Armour. **The Internet Kids Yellow Pages.** Berkeley, CA: Osborne/McGraw Hill, 1996. 812p. ISBN 0-07-882197-7.

If funds allow purchasing only one of the Internet directories, this is the most useful. It is organized so that children, as well as adults, can locate Internet sites by title, theme, or subject.

413. Wolff, Michael. **Net Guide: Your Complete Guide to the Internet and Online Services.** New York: Dell Books, 1997. 800p. ISBN 0-4402-2390-3.

This is an easy-to-use guide to the Internet and other online sources.

THE INTERNET

The World Wide Web

Perhaps the most popular, most innovative access to information via the computer is the World Wide Web. Access points, primarily the home page sites, are proliferating virtually at the speed of light. Conversely, the number of Web sites that discontinue after only a short time online is also a point of consideration. A caveat is offered at this point; although all of these sites were active at the time this manuscript was being prepared for publication, they may have fallen by the wayside by the time the book is published. The good news is that, via search engines such as WebCrawler, Yahoo, Lycos, Excite, AltaVista, or Magellan, citations to ongoing as well as new Web sites are easily located.

This list of Web sites, listservs, and e-mail addresses is only a representative list. Although the Web sites listed below are directly related to children's literature, some also have a specialized focus. These include Web sites on multicultural literature, children's classics, authors, and even on such delightful subjects as Pooh Corners.

Another caveat—Web crawling can become addictive!

414. American Library Association Web Sites
http://www.ala.org

Perhaps best place for the Web searcher to start when looking for information about children's books and authors is with the ALA home page. It will no doubt save time and frustration for the novice World Wide Web user. Recommended sites include:

414.1. The Caldecott Medal Awards
http://www.ala.org/alsc/caldecott.html

414.2. The Newbery Medal Awards
http://www.ala.org/alsc/newbery.html

Here you'll find the most complete information on the latest medal winners, as well as the retrospective winners.

414.3. Cool Sites for Kids
http://www.ala.org/alsc/children.links.html

"Reading & Writing," "Facts & Learn," and "Just for Fun" promise help with those assigned school reports and much more. Don't miss it!

414.4. KidsConnect
http://www.ala.org/ICONN/AskC.html

This is an excellent on-line answering and referral service for young people.

414.5. **The Librarian's Guide to Cyberspace for Parents & Kids**
http://www.ala.org/parentspage/greatsites/50.html
This Web site is a guide to fifty plus great sites for children and parents. The presentation is attractive and the recommended sites are chosen to reflect children's interests. They range from topics such as "Bill Nye the Science Guy" to "Children's Television Workshop."

414.6. **Notable Books for Children**
http://www.ala.org/alsc/notable97.html
A complete list of highly recommended books for 1997.

414.7. **700+ Great Sites**
http://www.ala.org/parentspage/greatsites/amazing.html
The subtitle of this site announces that it is an "Amazing, Spectacular, Mysterious, Colorful Web Site For Kids and the Adults Who Care For Them"— and it lives up to its promise.

415. **The Arthur Page**
http://pbs.org/wgbh/pages/arthur
There is fun galore for the fans of Marc Brown's Arthur series.

416. **AskEric Home Page**
http://ericir.syr.edu//AskEric
This site provides educational information with a personal touch.

417. **Berit's Best Sites for Children**
http://db.cochran.com/li_toc:theoPage.db
What a gem! Recommended as a good place to start a search.

418. **The Big Busy House**
http://www.harperchildrens.com/index.htm
This attractively illustrated site guides the reader to information on children's books published by HarperCollins.

419. **The BookWire Electronic Children's Book Index**
http://www.bookwire.com/links/readingroom/echildbooks.html
An easy-to-use index to full-text classic literature for children, from Louisa May Alcott to Mark Twain.

420. **Caldecott Medal Awards**
http://www.ils.unc.edu/award/chome.html
This site offers a colorful presentation on the award winners, each with a book description and a picture of the dust jacket. A history of the medals and an explanation of how the winners are selected are also included.

421.   **Carol Hurst's Children's Literature Site**

http://www.carolhurst.com

This site provides access to literature for children from a variety of perspectives, including her interesting reviews of children's books.

422.   **Children's Best-Sellers**

http://www.bookwire.com/pw/bsl/childrens/current.childrens.html

Looking for current best sellers? *Publishers Weekly* provides information on best-sellers, including picture books, fiction and nonfiction books, and paperbacks.

423.   **Children's Book Council**

http://www.CBCbooks.org

CBC presents an attractively illustrated multidirectional Web page. It addresses the interests of publishers, teachers, librarians, booksellers, parents, authors, and illustrators.

424.   **Children's Literature: A Newsletter for Adults**

http://www.parentsplace.com/readroom/children

This home page is designed to enhance children's literacy via recommended best children's books currently available.

425.   **Children's Literature: Treasure Island: Classic Books for Teens**

http://jollyroger.com/treasureisland.html

The discussion of the classics is opened up to, as the site originator says, "children and teenagers of all ages seeking to talk about cool books."

426.   **Children's Literature & Language Arts Resources**

http://falcon.jmu.edu/~ramseyil/childlit.htm

Bibliographies, listservs, biographies of authors and illustrators, and multicultural literature are included.

427.   **Children's Literature Authors and Illustrators**

http://www.ucet.ufl.edu/~jbrown/chauth.html

Readers looking for Web sites on authors and illustrators of children's books are sure to find it here. Great!

428.   **Children's Literature Sampler**

http://funnelweb.utcc.utk.edu//~estes/estes.html

Although this site has not been updated recently, it is still recommended as a good source of information about books and related materials for children through grade eight.

429.   **The Children's Literature Web Guide**
http://www.ucalgary.ca/~dkbrown
This comprehensive, well-organized guide provides extensive information on all aspects of children's literature, as well as links to booksellers and publishers. Readers are encouraged to set aside plenty of time to browse this excellent Web site.

430.   **Children's Multicultural Literature**
http://www.members.aol.com/mcsing29/index.html
A selected list of recommended multicultural books.

431.   **Digital Librarian: A Librarian's Choice of the Best of the Web**
http://www.servtech.com/public/mvail/digital.html
An amazing array of items for the librarian, including media for children.

432.   **Electronic Resources for Youth Services**
http://www.ccn.cs.dal.ca/~aa331/childlit.html
A well-designed searchable site that links with a variety of Web resources.

433.   **Fairrosa's Cyber Library**
http://users.interport.net/~fairrosa/lists/index.html
This site serves as an excellent exploration of the fascinating world of children's literature. Access to articles, book reviews, a reading room, and information on authors and illustrators is just a beginning.

434.   **Goosebumps**
http://place.scholastic.com/goosebumps/index.htm
This is a site that will tickle the fancy of all the Goosebumps fans.

435.   **Internet Public Library Web Site**
http://ipl.org/youth
The Internet Public Library is a colorful site that provides information about authors of books for children, books for reluctant readers, and more.

    435.1.   **Ask the Author**
    http://ipl.sils.umich.edu/youth

    435.2.   **Book Lists for Reluctant Readers**
    http://ipl.org/youth/WorldReading

436.   **Internet School Library Media Center**
http://falcon.jmu.edu/~ramseyil
Here is a chance to visit many sites for teachers and librarians.

437. **KidLit Web Site**
   http://isit.com/kidlit
   or
   http://www.mgfx.com/kidlit
   Children and teachers will find this an excellent resource for various kinds of information . It covers authors and writers, art, and interesting sites, done in coordination with The Nature Company, on butterflies and birds.

438. **Kids' Action**
   http://www.ran.org/ran/kids_action/index.html
   Children are encouraged to be concerned with ecology, especially regarding the rainforest. Recommended reading and activities are presented.

439. **Kids' Corner**
   http://kids.ot.com
   This is an interactive guide to kids' art, puzzles, web surfing, and more.

440. **Kids' Web**
   http://www.npac.syr.edu/textbook/kidsweb
   and
   http://www.npac.syr.edu/textbook/kidsweb/literature.html
   The goal of this Web site, targeted for children in grades K-12, is "to present students with a subset of the Web that is simple to navigate." The literature site includes authors, book, and guides to reading and online stories. Give it a try.

441. **LM_NET**
   http://ericir.syr.edu/lm_net
   The Web site for the listserv for school library media specialists to exchange ideas and discuss issues.

442. **The Magic School Bus**
   http://place.scholastic.com/magicschoolbus/index.htm
   This site gives a chance for children to follow Ms. Frizzle in all of her escapades!

443. **Multicultural Resources**
   http://falcon.jmu.edu/~ramseyil/multipub.htm
   A good source for locating multicultural resources for adults and children.

444. **Native American Indian Resources**
   http://indy4.fdl.cc.mn.us/~isk/books/bookmenu.html
   Paula Giese, a Native American, maintains this attractively illustrated site. In addition to the recommended book section is a provocative one, called "baddies," which discusses stereotyping in children's and adult books.

445. **Newbery Classroom Homepage**
     http://www.rci.rutgers.edu/~mjoseph/newbery.html
     A guide to interesting and dynamic Web pages for children's and young adult literature.

446. **Newbery Medal Awards**
     http://www.ils.unc.edu/award/nhome.html
     This site offers a colorful presentation on the award winners, each with a book description and a picture of the dust jacket. A history of the medals and an explanation of how the winners are selected are also included.

447. **Notable Children's Trade Books in the Field of Social Studies**
     http://www.CBCbooks.org
     and
     http://www.ncss.org

448. **Outstanding Science Trade Books for Children**
     http://www.CBCbooks.org
     and
     http://www.nsta.org
     The Children's Book Council provides quick access to current recommended social studies and science books for children.

449. **NSLS: North Suburban Library System**
     http://www.nslsilus.org
     This home page of the North Suburban Library System in Wheeling, Illinois, presents a wide variety of information sources, including a cleverly illustrated and presented "Just For Kids" page.

450. **The Page at Pooh Corner**
     http://www.public.iastate.edu/~jmilne/pooh.html
     This page is dedicated to the discussion of Winnie the Pooh stories and its author, A. A. Milne.

451. **Parents and Children Together Online**
     http://www.indiana.edu/~eric_rec/fl/ras.html
     Parents and Children Together, a magazine produced by the Family Literacy Center of ERIC Clearinghouse for Reading, English and Communications, is now available online.

452. **Reading Rainbow Reading List**
     http://www.pbs.org/readingrainbow
     This a good site for keeping current with the Public Broadcasting System's Reading Rainbow programs.

453. **Vandergrift's Children's Literature Page**
      http://www.scils.rutgers.edu/special/kay/childlit.html
      Kay Vandergrift discusses various aspects of children's literature on her
      home page. Subjects include the impact of literature on children, realistic fiction
      historical fiction, biography, and more. Highlighted within the text are Web sites
      that relate to the topic being discussed. This is a well-written, interesting site that
      anyone concerned in children's literature will appreciate.
      Other special sites are:

> 453.1. **Kay Vandergrift's Special Interest Page**
>   http://www.scils.rutgers.edu/special/kay/kay.hp2.html
>
> 453.2. **Selected List of Multimedia Publishers, Producers, and
>   Distributors**
>   http://www.scils.rutgers.edu/special/kay/mediacatalog.html
>
> 453.3. **Snow White**
>   http://www.scils.rutgers.edu/special/kay/snowwhite.html
>
> 453.4. **Vandergrift's Feminist Page**
>   http://www.scils.rutgers.edu/special/kay/feminist.html

454. **Winnie-the-Pooh**
      http:www.penguin.com/usa/pooh/index/html
      Try this if you a Pooh fan. It's lots of fun!

Representative Author Web Sites

455. **Avi**
      http://.avi-writer.com
      Prepare for lots of fun, but, watch out for the weasel wonk!

456. **Chris Van Allsburg: Share the Spirit '95!**
      http://www.hmco.com/polarexpress/VanAllsburg.html
      You've enjoyed his Jumanji and The Polar Express, now learn more about
      this highly popular author/illustrator.

457. **Jan Brett's Home page**
      http://www.janbrett.com
      Brett presents the reader with lots of interesting places to explore—everything
      from trolls to armadillos.

458. **Judy Blume's Home Base**
      http://www.judyblume.com
      Come and meet this ever-popular writer.

459. **Lewis Carroll Collection**
     http://www.users.interport.net/~fairrosa/carroll.html
     A great visit with this award-winning author.

460. **Lois Lowry**
     http://www.bdd.com/teachers/lowr.html
     This is a chance to visit with the two-time winner of the Newbery Award.

461. **Maurice Sendak**
     http://falcon.jmu.edu/~ramseyil/sendak.html
     Here you will have a brief visit with the author.

462. **The Official Eric Carle's Web Site**
     http://www.eric-carle.com
     Be ready for some fun!

463. **Katherine Paterson's Web Site**
     http://www.terabithia.com/index.html
     You will have a pleasant visit with this two-time Newbery Medal winner.

464. **Patricia Polacco: A Woman's Voice Remembering**
     http://www.scils.rutgers.edu/special/kay/polacco.html
     An interesting visit with the author at an attractively illustrated site

465. **Virginia Hamilton**
     http://www.virginiahamilton.com
     and
     http://members.aol.com/bodeep/index.html

466. **Jane Yolan**
     http://ipl.org/youth/AskAuthor/Yolen.html
     Yolan shares her many talents and comments with children.

Listservs, Gopher Sites, and E-Mail Addresses

467. **Bank Street College Child Study Children's Book Committee**
     E-mail address: lindag@bnk1.bnkst.edu
     This address can be used as a good source to ask for recommendations of children's books.

468. **BOOKBRAG**
To subscribe: BookBrag-request@scholastic.com.
Leave subject line blank
Type on message line: subscribe BookBrag first name, last name
This is useful for reviews of new children's books.

469. **Childlit**
To subscribe: listserv@smithers.rutgers.edu
Leave subject line blank
Type on message line: subscribe child_lit
This is a discussion devoted to the exchange of information, analysis, and opinions related to children's literature, past and present.

470. **Children's Literature Center**
Gopher address: gopher://marvel.loc.gov/11/research/reading.rooms/children
This site provides access to the Children's Literature Center of the Library of Congress, describes resources, and also offers a chat center.

471. **Cooperative Children's Book Center (CCBC)**
To subscribe: listserv@ccbc.soemadison.wisc.edu
Type on subject line: subscribe ccbc-net first name, last name
Leave message line blank
This listserv provides a discussion of children's books and issues in literature for children, directed by the center's book examination center and research library staff at the University of Wisconsin at Madison's School of Education. Each month a specific subject is targeted for discussion online.

472. **Electronic Children's Books**
Gopher address: gopher://lib.nmsu.edu/11/.subjects/Education/.childlit/.childbooks
At this address, the reader will find an index of many sites related to children's literature.

473. **Folklore**
To subscribe: listserv@tamvml.tamu.edu
Leave the subject line blank
Type on message line: SUBSCRIBE folklore first name, last name
This listserv is recommended for people interested in good discussions on folklore and folk literature.

474. **Kidlit-L**
> To subscribe: listserv@bingvmb.cc.binghamton.edu
> Leave subject line blank
> Type on message line: subscribe KIDLIT-L first name, last name
> This is a discussion group interested in children's reading and the exchange of ideas on reading promotion.

475. **Kidsphere**
> To subscribe: kidsphere-request@vms.cis.pitt.edu
> Leave subject line blank
> Type on message line: subscribe Kidsphere first name, last name
> The purpose of Kidsphere is to set up an international network for the use of children and teachers.

476. **LM_NET**
> To subscribe: listserv@LISTSERV.syr.edu
> Leave subject line blank
> Type on message line: subscribe LM_NET first name last name
> This is a discussion group open to school library media specialists worldwide, designed for the exchange of ideas and issues related to school library media centers.

477. **PUBYAC**
> To subscribe: majordomo@nysernet.org
> Leave subject line blank
> Type on message line: subscribe PUBYAC first name, last name
> A discussion of services and issues for public librarians serving children and young adults.

478. **STORYTELL**
> E-mail address: STORYTELL-REQUEST@TWU.EDU
> To subscribe:STORYTELL-REQUEST@venus.twu.edu
> Leave subject line blank
> This is a site for storytellers and those interested in storytelling.

Author/Title Index

Reference is to entry number.
Numbers followed by an n refer to citations in annotations.

A to Zoo: Subject Access to Children's Picture Books, 72, 240

AASL (American Association of School Librarians), 388

ACEI (Association for Childhood Education International), 390

Accept Me As I Am: Best Books of Juvenile Nonfiction on Impairments and Disabilities, 104, 105n

Ada, Alma Flor, 119

Adamson, Lynda G., 201-4

Adoption Literature for Children and Young Adults: An Annotated Bibliography, 184

Adventuring with Books: A Booklist for Pre-K–Grade 6, 16

Africa in Literature for Children and Young Adults: An Annotated Bibliography of English-Language Books, 167

Against Borders: Promoting Books for a Multicultural World, 137

The Aging Adult in Children's Books and Nonprint Media: An Annotated Bibliography, 179

AJL (Association of Jewish Libraries), 392

ALA (American Library Association), 389

Alexander, Sharon, 191

Alphabet: A Handbook of ABC Book sand Book Extensions for the Elementary Classroom, 188

Alphabet Books as a Key to Language Patterns: An Annotated Action Bibliography, 189

ALSC (Association for Library Service to Children), 10, 19, 354

Alternative Press Publishers of Children's Books: A Directory, 225

American Association of School Librarians (AASL), 388

American History for Children and Young Adults: An Annotated Bibliographic Index, 210, 246

American Indian Reference Books for Children and Young Adults, 161

American Indian Resource Manual, 158

American Indian Stereotypes in the World of Children: A Reader and Bibliography, 160

American Library Association (ALA), 389

American Library Association Web Sites, 414

American Writers for Children: 1900-1960, 293.1

American Writers for Children Before 1900, 293.2

American Writers for Children Since 1960: Fiction, 293.3

American Writers for Children Since 1960: Poets, Illustrators, and Non-Fiction Authors, 293.4

Ammon, Bette D., 9

Anatomy of Wonder 4: A Critical Guide to Science Fiction, 172

Anderson, Marcella F., 97

Anderson, Vicki, 120-21, 157, 238, 261

Appraisal: Science Books for Young People, 336

Apseloff, Marilyn Fain, 17

Arbuthnot, May Hill, 18

The Art of Children's Picture Books: A Selective Reference Guide, 74

The Arthur Page (Web site), 415
Arthur Rackham Collection, 384
Arthur Rackham: His Life and Work,
    384n
*Artists of the Page: Interviews with
    Children's Book Illustrators*,
    300
Ash, Lee, 378
Ask the Author (Web site), 435.1
AskEric Home Page, 416
Association for Childhood Education
    International (ACEI), 390
Association for Library Service to
    Children (ALSC), 10, 19, 354
Association of Jewish Libraries
    (AJL), 392
Austin, Mary C., 122, 166
Author a Month series, 301n
Authors of Books for Young People,
    312
*AV Guide: The Learning Media
    Newsletter*, 372
*AV Market Place: The Complete
    Directory of Audio, Audio
    Visual, Computer Systems,
    Film, Video, Programming,
    with Industry Yellow Pages*,
    355
Avi (Web site), 455
*Award-Winning Books for Children
    and Young Adults, 1990-1991*, 2
Azarnoff, Pat, 98

Banja, Judith Rogers, 303
Bank Street College Child Study
    Children's Book Committee
    (E-mail), 467
Barker, Keith, 20
Barron, Neil, 172
Barstow, Barbara, 21
*Basic Collection of Children's Books
    in Spanish*, 152.1
Baskin, Barbara H., 62, 99
Basta, Margo McLoone, 233

*Behind the Covers: Interviews with
    Authors and Illustrators of
    Books for Children and Young
    Adults*, 304
Beilke, Patricia, 149, 164
Benfield, Cynthia Mayer, 41
Berger, Laura Standley, 310
Berit's Best Sites for Children (Web
    site), 417
Bernstein, Joanne E., 111
*Best Books for Children: Preschool
    Through Grade 6*, 31
*The Best High/Low Books for
    Reluctant Readers*, 68
The Best in Children's Books, 55
*The Best of Bookfinder: A Guide to
    Children's Literature About
    Interests and Concerns of
    Youth Aged 1-18*, 102
*Best of the Best for Children: Books,
    Magazines, Videos, Audio,
    Software, Toys, Travel*, 27, 358
*The Best of the Latino Heritage: A
    Guide to the Best Juvenile
    Books About Latino People and
    Cultures*, 152.5
*The Best Science and Technology
    Reference Books for Young
    People*, 217, 228
*The Best Science Books for Children:
    A Selected and Annotated List
    of Science Books for Children
    Age Five Through Twelve*, 222
*The Best Toys, Books and Videos for
    Kids 1997: 1,000+ Kid-Tested
    Classics and New Products*, 53,
    107
*Best Videos for Children and Young
    Adults: A Core Collection for
    Libraries*, 359
*Beyond Fact: Nonfiction for Children
    and Young People*, 22
*Beyond Picture Books: A Guide to
    First Readers*, 21
The Big Busy House (Web site), 418

Bilingual Books in Spanish and English for Children, 150

Bingham, Jane M., 223, 285

The Birthday Book: Birthdates, Birthplaces and Biographical Sources for American Authors and Illustrators of Children's Books, 303

Bishop, Rudine Sims, 123. *See also* Sims, Rudine

The Black American in Books for Children: Readings in Racism, 143

Black Authors and Illustrators of Children's Books: A Biographical Dictionary, 145, 305

The Black Experience in Children's Books, 118n, 142

Blackburn, G. Meredith, 248

Blake, Barbara, 165

Blishen, Edward, 80

Bodart, Joni Richards, 81

Bolgehold, Betty D., 52

Book Links: Connecting Books, Libraries and Classrooms, 317

Book Lists for Reluctant Readers (Web site), 435.2

Book Review Digest, 257

Book Review Index, 258

Book World, 349

Bookbird: World of Children's Books, 318

BOOKBRAG (Listserv), 468

*Bookbrain*Bookwhiz*, 367

The Bookfinder, Volume 4: When Kids Need Books: Annotations of Books Published 1983 Through 1986, 102n, 103

Booklist, 337

Bookpeople: A First Album, 301

Bookpeople: A Second Album, 301n, 302

Books and Real Life: A Guide for Gifted Students and Teachers, 64

Books by African-American Authors and Illustrators: For Children and Young Adults, 148

Books for Children, 385n

Books for Children to Read Alone, 60

Books for the Gifted, 62

Books for the Gifted Child, 63

Books in Spanish for Children and Young Adults: An Annotated Guide, 152.3

Books Kids Will Sit Still For: The Complete Read-Aloud Guide, 83

Books That Build Character: A Guide to Teaching Your Child Moral Values Through Stories, 181, 271

Books to Help Children Cope with Separation and Loss: An Annotated Bibliography, 111

Books to Read Aloud with Children of All Ages, 82, 113n

Booktalking the Award Winners 3, 81

The BookWire Electronic Children's Book Index (Web site), 419

Bowker's Complete Video Directory, 1995, 356

Boyd, Alex, 124

Braille Book Review, 338

Branton, Ann, 251

Brazouski, Antoinette, 173

Breen, Karen, 286

Brenner, Barbara, 52

Brodie, Carolyn S., 131, 200.1

Brown, Dorothy A., 66

Brown, Jean E., 208

Brown, Muriel W., 11

Brown, Risa, 141

Bulletin of the Center for Children's Books, 55n, 339

Cain, Melissa, 280

The Caldecott Medal Awards (Web site), 414.1, 420

Carlin, Margaret F., 100

Carmody, Barbara, 361

*Carol Hurst's Children's Literature
    Site* (Web site), 421
Carpenter, Humphrey, 234
Carr, Jo, 22
Carroll, Frances Laverne, 174, 175
Carruth, Gorton, 235
Cascardi, Andrea E., 23
Catholic Library Association, 393
CBC (The Children's Book Council,
    Inc.), 1, 114, 423
*CBC Features: Containing News of
    the Children's Book World,*
    319
CD-ROMs for Kids: Booklist*'s Best
    Bets,* 373
Cech, John, 293.1
Cecil, Nancy Lee, 136, 176
*Celebrate the World: Twenty Tellable
    Folktales for Multicultural
    Festivals,* 183
Celebrate with Books, 117n
Child Study Children's Book
    Committee at Bank Street
    College, 113
*Childhood Education: Infancy
    Through Early Adolescence,*
    320
Childlit (Listserv), 469
Children and Books, 284
*Children & Books I: African
    American Story Books and
    Activities for All Children,* 144
*Children of Promise: African-American
    Literature and Art for Young
    People,* 147
Children Who Can Read, but Don't,
    116n
*Children's Authors and Illustrators:
    An Index to Biographical
    Dictionaries,* 287
Children's Best Sellers (Web site),
    422
*Children's Book Awards
    International: A Directory of
    Awards and Winners, from
    Inception Through 1990,* 6

The Children's Book Council, Inc.
    (CBC), 1, 114, 423
*Children's Book Illustration and
    Design,* 289-90
Children's Book Review Index, 259
*Children's Book Review Index,
    Master Cumulation,
    1985-1994,* 259.1
Children's Book Review Service, 340
Children's Books, 118n
*Children's Books: Awards & Prizes:
    Including Prizes and Awards
    for Young Adult Books, 1996,*
    1, 394n
Children's Books and Their Creators,
    307
*Children's Books in Print: An
    Author, Title, and Illustrator
    Index to Books for Children
    and Young Adults,* 264, 368n
*Children's Books of International
    Interest,* 28
Children's Books of the Year, 113n
*Children's Books on Ancient Greek
    and Roman Mythology: An
    Annotated Bibliography,* 173
Children's Books Too Good to Miss,
    18
Children's Catalog, 265, 268n
Children's Choices, 37n, 115n
Children's Classics to Read Aloud,
    80
Children's Fiction Sourcebook, 34
Children's Folklore Review, 341
*Children's Jukebox: A Subject Guide
    to Musical Recordings and
    Programming Ideas for
    Songsters Ages One to Twelve,*
    365
Children's Literature, 321
*Children's Literature: A Guide to the
    Criticism,* 277
*Children's Literature: A Newsletter
    for Adults* (Web site), 424
*Children's Literature: An Issues
    Approach,* 273

The Children's Literature: Annual of the Modern Language Association Division of Children's Literature and the Children's Literature Association, 274

Children's Literature: Treasure Island: Classic Books for Teens (Web site), 425

Children's Literature Abstracts, 275

Children's Literature & Language Arts Resources (Web site), 426

Children's Literature Assembly of NCTE, 395

Children's Literature Association (CLA), 396

Children's Literature Association Quarterly, 322

Children's Literature Authors and Illustrators (Web site), 427

Children's Literature Awards and Winners: A Directory of Prizes, Authors, and Illustrators, 7

Children's Literature Center (Gopher site), 470

Children's Literature for All God's Children, 195

Children's Literature for Health Awareness, 106

Children's Literature in Education, 323

Children's Literature in the Elementary School, 282

Children's Literature Review: Excerpts from Reviews, Criticisms, and Commentary on Books for Children and Young People, 276, 309n

Children's Literature Sampler (Web site), 428

The Children's Literature Web Guide (Web site), 429

Children's Magazine Guide, 313

Children's Media Market Place, 357

Children's Multicultural Literature (Web site), 430

Children's Reading Round Table of Chicago (CRRT), 397

Children's Reference PLUS, 21n, 31n, 63n, 67n, 72n, 84n, 85n, 94n, 99n, 105n, 110n, 111n, 134n, 178n, 182n, 215n, 220n, 286n, 368

Children's Religious Books: An Annotated Bibliography, 186

The Children's Song Index, 1978-1993, 251

Children's Television Workshop, 398

Children's Video Report, 374

Choices: A Core Collection for Young Reluctant Readers, 24

Choosing Books for Children: A Commonsense Guide, 32

Choosing Books for Young People: A Guide to Criticism and Bibliography: 1976-1984, 30

Choosing the Right Book for the Right Child at the Right Time, 52

Choosing Your Children's Books: 2 to 5 Years, 57

Choosing Your Children's Books: 5 to 8 Year, 58

Choosing Your Children's Books: 8 to 12 Years, 59

A Chorus of Cultures: Developing Literacy Through Multicultural Poetry, 119

Chris Van Allsburg: Share the Spirit '95 (Web site), 456

Cianciolo, Patricia, 70

CLA (Children's Literature Association), 396

Classic Myths to Read Aloud, 90

Classics to Read Aloud to Your Children, 91

The Cleveland Public Library, 117

Colborn, Candy, 25

Collected Perspectives: Choosing and Using Books for the Classroom, 280

Comfort, Claudette Hegel, 12

Commire, Anne, 288, 309

A Comprehensive Guide to Children's Literature with a Jewish Theme, 154

The Computer Museum Guide to the Best Software for Kids: More Than 200 Reviews for Windows, Macintosh, and DOS Computers, Including the Best CD-ROMs, 363

Connecting Cultures: A Guide to Multicultural Literature for Children, 140

Contemporary Authors, 296.1n

Contemporary Spanish-Speaking Writers and Illustrators for Children and Young Adults: A Biographical Dictionary, 153, 306

Cool Sites for Kids (Web site), 414.3

Cooper, Ilene, 199

Cooperative Children's Book Center, 380, 471

Cordier, Mary Hurlbut, 205, 207

The Coretta Scott King Awards Book: From Vision to Reality, 15

Council on Interracial Books for Children, 399

Counting Books Are More Than Numbers: An Annotated Action Bibliography, 190

Crawford, Elizabeth D., 296.6

Criscoe, Betty, 2

A Critical Handbook for Children's Literature, 279

CRRT (Children's Reading Round Table of Chicago), 397

Cuddigan, Maureen, 101

Cullinan, Bernice E., 26, 281

Culturally Diverse Library Collections for Children, 141

Cultures Outside the United States in Fiction: A Guide to 2,875 Books for Librarians and Teachers K-9, 120

Cummins, Julie, 289, 290

Dale, Doris Cruger, 150

Davis, Enid, 154

Day, Frances Ann, 125, 151, 291, 292

Day, Serenna F., 260

The de Grummond Children's Literature Collection, 381

De Montreville, Doris, 296.5-96.6

de Usabel, Frances, 158

Death and Dying in Children's and Young People's Literature: A Survey and Bibliography, 187

Developing Multicultural Awareness Through Children's Literature: A Guide for Teachers and Librarians, Grades K-8, 136

Developing Resiliency Through Children's Literature: A Guide for Teachers and Librarians, K-8, 176

Dictionary of American Children's Fiction, 1859-1959: Books of Recognized Merit, 3.1

Dictionary of American Children's Fiction, 1960-1984: Books of Recognized Merit, 3.2

Dictionary of American Children's Fiction, 1985-1989: Books of Recognized Merit, 3.3

Dictionary of American Children's Fiction, 1990-1994: Books of Recognized Merit, 3, 5n

Dictionary of British Children's Fiction: Books of Recognized Merit, 4, 5n

Dictionary of Children's Fiction from Australia, Canada, India, New Zealand, and Selected African Countries: Books of Recognized Merit, 5

Dictionary of Literary Biography: Children's Writers Series, 293

Digital Librarians: A Librarian's Choice of the Best of the Web (Web site), 431

Distinguished Children's Literature: The Newbery & Caldecott Winners—The Books and Their Creators, 12

Dogs, Cats, and Horses: A Resource Guide to the Literature for Young People, 194

Dolan, Nancy, 312

Doll, Carol A., 200.2

Donavin, Denise Perry, 27, 358

Dreyer, Sharon Spredemann, 102-3

Dunhouse, Mary Beth, 224

E for Environment, 220

Eastern Europe in Children's Literature: An Annotated Bibliography of English-Language Books, 170

Easy Reading: Book Series and Periodicals for Less Able Readers, 69

Eaton, Dawn, 312

Educator's Companion to Children's Literature, Volume 1: Mysteries, Animal Tales, Books of Humor, Adventure Stories, and Historical Fiction, 45

Educator's Companion to Children's Literature, Volume 2: Folklore, Contemporary Realistic Fiction, Fantasy, Biographies, and Tales from Here and There, 46

Egoff, Sheila A., 177

El-Hi Textbooks and Serials in Print, 1995, 266

Electronic Children's Books (Gopher site), 472

Electronic Resources for Youth Services (Web site), 432

The Elementary School Library Collection: A Guide to Books and Other Media. 20th ed. Phases 1-2-3, 267

The Elizabeth Nesbitt Room, 386

Elleman, Barbara, 28

Elliott, Alison, 363

Elliott, Emory, 226

Encyclopedias, Atlases & Dictionaries, 237n

Estes, Glenn E., 293.2-93.4

Estes, Sally, 29

Ettlinger, John R. T., 30

Exciting, Funny, Scary, Short, Different, and Sad Books Kids Like About Animals, Science, Sports, Families, Songs, and Other Things, 174

Explorers and Exploration: The Best Resources from Grade 5 Through 9, 213

Exploring the Great Lakes States Through Literature, 200.4

Exploring the Mountain States Through Literature, 200.6

Exploring the Northeast States Through Literature, 200.3

Exploring the Pacific States Through Literature, 200.2

Exploring the Plains States Through Literature, 200.1

Exploring the Southeast States Through Literature, 200.7

Exploring the Southwest States Through Literature, 200.5

Exploring the United States Through Literature Series, 200

Eyeopeners! How to Choose and Use Children's Books About Real People, Places and Things, 38

Eyeopeners II: Children's Books to Answer Children's Questions About the World Around Them, 39

Fairrosa's Cyber Library (Web site), 433

Fakih, Kimberly Olson, 178

Families in Transition: An Annotated Bibliography, 192

Fantasy Literature for Children and Young Adults: An Annotated Bibliography, 182

Fenton, Ann D., 229

Fiction, Folklore, Fantasy, & Poetry for Children, 1876-1985, 239

Fiction Index to Readers 10-16: Subject Access to Over 8,200 Books (1960-1990), 238

Fiction Sequels for Readers, 10 to 16: An Annotated Bibliography, 261

Field, Carolyn, 270

Fifteen Centuries of Children's Literature: An Annotated Chronology of British and American Works in Historical Context, 223

The Fifth Book of Junior Authors and Illustrators, 296.7

Fisher, Janet, 245

Fisher, Margery, 294

The Five Owls: A Publication for Readers Personally and Professionally Involved in Children's Literature, 324

Folklore (Listserv), 473

For Reading Out Loud! A Guide to Sharing Books with Children, 86

Foudray, Rita Schock, 11

The Fourth Book of Junior Authors and Illustrators, 296.6

Frantz, Pollyanne, 251

Freeman, Judy, 83, 84

Frey, O. Diane, 200.3

Friedberg, Joan Brest, 104-5

From Page to Screen: Children's and Young Adult Books on Film and Video, 364

Fuller, Muriel, 296.4

Gagne, Kathleen Dunne, 111

Gallant, Jennifer Jung, 359

Garraty, John A., 236

Gath, Tracy, 214

Gender Positive! A Teachers' and Librarians' Guide to Nonstereotyped Children's Literature, K-8, 191

Gillespie, Cindy S., 109, 272

Gillespie, John T., 31, 85

Gilliland, Hap, 159

Girls Are People Too! A Bibliography of Nontraditional Female Roles in Children's Books, 185

Glisson, Peg, 24

Global Voices, Global Vision: A Core Collection of Multicultural Books, 133

Good Books to Grow On: A Guide to Building Your Child's Library from Birth to Age 5, 23

Goosebumps (Web site), 434

Graves, Bonnie G., 69

Graves, Michael F., 69

Great Books Foundation, 400

Great New Nonfiction Reads, 47

Green, Diana Huss, 360

Growing Pains: Helping Children Deal with Everyday Problems Through Reading, 101

A Guide to Children's Books About Asian Americans, 165

Guide to Multicultural Resources: 1997/1998, 124

A Guide to Non-Sexist Children's Books, Volume II: 1976-1985, 199

Hahn, Harley, 410

Hall, Susan, 71

Handbook for the Newbery Medal and Honor Books, 1980-1989, 9

Hanson, Mary Beth, 101

Harley Hahn's Internet and Web Yellow Pages, 1998, 410

Harris, Karen, 62, 99

Harris, Violet J., 119

Hauser, Paula, 63

Haycraft, Howard, 296.3
Hayden, Carla D., 126
*Health, Illness, and Disability: A
    Guide to Books for Children
    and Young Adults*, 98
Hearne, Betsy, 32, 55
Helbig, Alethea K., 3-6, 127
Helmer, Dona, 231
Helping Children Through Books,
    108
Hendrickson, Linnea, 277
*Hey! Listen to This: Stories to Read
    Aloud*, 95
*High Interest-Easy Reading: An
    Annotated Booklist for Middle
    School and Senior High
    School*, 33
*High/Low Handbook: Encouraging
    Literacy in the 1990s*, 67
*High/Scope Buyer's Guide to
    Children's Software*, 361
Hill, Donna, 296.5
Hirschfelder, Arlene B., 160
*A Hispanic Heritage: A Guide to
    Juvenile Books About Hispanic
    People and Cultures*, 152.2
Historical Children's Collection, 387
Hobson, Margaret, 34
Hohmann, Charles, 361
Holtze, Sally Holmes, 296.1,
    296.7-96.8
Homa, Linda L., 267
Hopkins, Lee Bennett, 119, 295
*The Horn Book Guide to Children's
    and Young Adult Books*, 278,
    342
Horn Book Index, 260
*The Horn Book Magazine:
    Recommending Books for
    Children and Young Adults*,
    343
Horner, Catherine Townsend, 179-80
Horning, Kathleen T., 128-29, 225
*Horse Stories: An Annotated
    Bibliography for All Ages*, 197

*Hospitalized Children and Books: A
    Guide for Librarians, Families,
    and Caregivers*, 97
*How to Grow a Young Reader: A
    Parent's Guide to Books for
    Kids*, 42
Huck, Charlotte, 282

*Immigrants in the United States in
    Fiction: A Guide to 705 Books
    for Librarians and Teachers,
    K-9*, 121
*Index to Children's Plays in
    Collections: 1975-1984*, 256
*Index to Collective Biographies for
    Young Readers*, 286
*An Index to Fairy Tales, 1987-1992:
    Including 310 Collections of
    Fairy Tales, Folktales, Myths,
    and Legends with Significant
    Pre-1987 Titles Not Previously
    Indexed*, 244
*An Index to Historical Fiction for
    Children and Young*, 245
*Index to Poetry for Children and
    Young People 1988-1992: A
    Title, Subject, Author, and First
    Line Index to Poetry in
    Collections for Children and
    Young People*, 248
*Index to Songs on Children's
    Recordings*, 255
Indian Children's Books, 159
*The Indian Subcontinent in Literature
    for Children and Young Adults:
    An Annotated Bibliography of
    English-Language Books*, 168
*The Information Please Kids'
    Almanac*, 233
Information Books for Children, 20
*International Directory of Children's
    Literature*, 224
International Reading Association
    (IRA), 35-37, 115, 401
The Internet Kids Yellow Pages, 412
Internet Public Library Web Site, 435

*The Internet Resource Directories for
    K-12 Teachers and Librarians:
    97/98*, 411
*Internet School Library Media
    Center* (Web site), 436
Introducing Bookplots, 85n
IRA (International Reading
    Association), 35-37, 115, 401

Jan Brett's Home Page, 457
Jane Yolan (Web site), 466
*Japan Through Children's
    Literature: An Annotated
    Bibliography*, 169
Jenkins, Esther C., 166, 122
Jenson, Julie, 16
Jewish Book Council, 155, 402
Jones, Dolores Blythe, 7, 379
*Journal of Youth Services in
    Libraries*, 325
Judy Blume's Home Page, 458
The Junior Book of Authors,
    296.2-96.3
The Junior Book of Authors and
    Illustrators Series, 296
Junior DISCovering Authors, 369
Juniorplots, 85n
Juvenile and Young Adult Author
    Series, 298
*The Juvenile Novels of World War II:
    An Annotated Bibliography*,
    209

*Kaleidoscope: A Multicultural
    Booklist for Grades K-8*, 123
Kaminski, Robert, 93, 139
Karp, Rashelle S., 249, 250
Kastan, David Scott, 226
Katherine Paterson's Web Site, 463
Katz, Bill, 314
Katz, Linda Steinberg, 314
*Kay Vandergrift's Special Interest
    Page* (Web site), 453.1
Kennedy, Dayann M., 215
The Kerlan Collection, 382

*The Kerlan Collection Manuscripts
    and Illustrations for Children's
    Books: A Checklist*, 382n
Khorana, Meena, 167-68
KidLit Web Site, 437
Kidlit-L (Listserv), 474
Kids' Action (Web site), 438
Kids' Corner (Web site), 439
*Kids' Favorite Books: Children's
    Choices: 1989-1991*, 35
Kids Pick the Best Videos, 362
Kids' Web (Web site), 440
KidsConnect, 414.4
Kidsphere (Listserv), 475
Kiefer, Barbara, 282
Kilpatrick, William, 181, 271
Kimmel, Margaret Mary, 86
Kimmel, Sue, 61
Kingman, Lee, 13
*Kirkus Reviews: A Pre-publication
    Review Service*, 344
Klatt, Mary J., 173
Kobrin, Beverly, 38-39
Kohn, Rita, 227
Kovacs, Deborah, 297
Kruse, Ginny Moore, 128-29
Kuipers, Barbara J., 161
Kunitz, Stanley J., 296.2-96.3

Lanasa, Philip J., 2
Landsberg, Michele, 40
Language Arts, 326
*The Latest and Greatest Read-
    Alouds*, 88
*Latina and Latino Voices in
    Literature for Children and
    Teenagers*, 151, 292
*A Latino Heritage: A Guide to
    Juvenile Books About Latino
    People and Cultures*, 152.4
Latino/Hispanic Heritage Series, 152
Latrobe, Kathy Howard, 200.4
Laughlin, Jeannine L., 100
Laughlin, Kay, 251

Learning About . . . the Holocaust: Literature and Other Resources for Young People, 208

Lenz, Millicent, 216

Let's Read About Finding Books They'll Love to Read, 26

Levine, Evan, 362

Lewis Carroll Collection (Web site), 459

The Librarian's Guide to Cyberspace for Parents & Kids (Web site), 414.5

Library Talk: The Magazine for Elementary School Librarians, 327

LiBretto, Ellen V., 67

Libros en Español Para Pequenos, 118n

Liggett, Twila C., 41

Light a Candle!: The Jewish Experience in Children's Books, 118n

Lima, Carolyn, 72, 240

Lima, John A., 72, 240

Lindgren, Merri, 130

Lindskoog, John, 42

Lindskoog, Kathryn, 42

The Lion and the Unicorn: A Critical Journal of Children's Literature, 328

Lipson, Eden Ross, 43

A List of Stories to Tell and Read Aloud, 87, 118n

Literature and the Child, 281

Literature Connections to American History, K-6: Resources to Enhance and Entice, 201

Literature Connections to American History, 7-12: Resources to Enhance and Entice, 202

Literature Connections to World History, 202n

Literature for Children About Asians and Asian Americans: Analysis and Annotated Bibliography, with Additional Reading for Adults, 166

The Literature of Delight: A Critical Guide to Humorous Books for Children, 178

LM_NET (Listserv), 476

LM_NET (Web site), 441

Lois Lowry (Web site), 460

Los Angeles Times Book Review, 350

Lukins, Rebecca J., 279

Lynn, Ruth Nadelman, 182

MacCann, Donnarae, 143

MacDonald, Eleanor Kay, 206

MacDonald, Margaret Read, 183

Madden, Jennifer, 34

Magazines for Children: A Guide for Parents, Teachers, and Librarians, 315, 316n

Magazines for Kids & Teens: A Resource for Parents, Teachers, Librarians, and Kids!, 316

Magazines for School Libraries, 314n

Magazines for Young People, 314

The Magic School Bus (Web site), 442

Magill, Frank N., 241, 298

Mahoney, Ellen, 44

Major Authors and Illustrators for Children and Young Adults: A Selection of Sketches from Something About the Author, 299

Makino, Yasuko, 169

Malinowsky, H. Robert, 217, 228

Manna, Anthony L., 106, 200.1

Many Faces, Many Voices: Multicultural Literary Experiences for Youth, 131

Marantz, Kenneth A., 73-74, 132, 300

Marantz, Sylvia S., 73-75, 132, 300

Marquardt, Dorothy A., 196, 311, 312

Master Index to Summaries of Children's Books, 242

Masterplots II: Juvenile and Young Adult Biography Series, 298

Masterplots II: Juvenile and Young Adult Fiction Series, 241

Maurice Sendak (Web site), 461

McCabe-Bran, Chica, 361

McElmeel, Sharron L., 45-47, 88, 301-2

McGovern, Edythe, 48

Meacham, Mary, 174-75

Media & Methods: Educational Products, Technologies & Programs for Schools and Universities, 329, 375

Meet the Authors and Illustrators: 60 Creators of Favorite Children's Books Talk About Their Works, 297

Michele Landsberg's Guide to Children's Books: With a Treasury of More Than 350 Great Children's Books, 40n

Middle and Junior High School Library Catalog, 268

Middleplots 4: A Book Talk Guide for Use with Readers 8-12, 85

Miles, Susan G., 184

Miller, Betty Davis, 195

Miller, Elizabeth B., 411

Miller, William G., 378

Miller-Lachmann, Lyn, 133-34

Miranker, Cathy, 363

Moir, Hughes, 280

Moll, Patricia Buerke, 144

Montanaro, Ann R., 76

More Books Kids Will Sit Still For: A Read-Aloud Guide, 84

More Classics to Read Aloud to Your Children, 92

More Exciting, Funny, Scary, Short, Different, and Sad Books Kids Like About Animals, Science, Sports, Families, Songs, and Other Things, 175

More Junior Authors, 296.4

More Kids' Favorite Books: A Compilation of Children's Choices: 1992-1994, 36

More Notes from a Different Drummer: A Guide to Juvenile Fiction Portraying the Disabled, 99, 104n

Moss, Joyce, 60, 364

Mother Goose Comes First: An Annotated Guide to Best Books and Recordings for Your Preschool Child, 61

Muller, Helen, 48

Mullins, June B., 104-5

The Multicolored Mirror: Cultural Substance in Literature for Children and Young Adults, 130

Multicultural Folktales: Stories to Tell Young Children, 93, 139

Multicultural Literature for Children: A Selected Listing of Books by and About People of Color, Vol. 1: 1980-1990, 128

Multicultural Literature for Children: A Selected Listing of Books by and About People of Color, Vol. 2: 1991-1996, 129

Multicultural Picture Books: Art for Understanding Others, 75

Multicultural Resources (Web site), 443

Multicultural Voices in Contemporary Literature: A Resource for Teachers, 125, 292

Multiethnic Children's Literature, 135

Multimedia CD-ROM Reviews on the World Wide Web, 370

Munroe, Mary Hovas, 303
The Museum of Science and Industry Basic List of Children's Science Books, 1988, 219

Naden, Corrine J., 31, 85
Nakamura, Joyce, 287, 308
National Braille Association, Inc., 403
National Council of Teachers of English, 404
Native American Indian Resources (Web site), 444
Native Americans in Children's Literature, 163
Native Americans in Fiction: A Guide to 765 Books for Librarians and Teachers K-9, 157
The Neal-Schuman Index to Finger-Plays, 252
Nelson, Gail A., 63
Net Guide: Your Complete Guide to the Internet and Online Services, 413
The New Advocate, 330
The New York Public Library: Office of Branch Libraries, 118
New York Times Book Review, 351
The New York Times Parent's Guide to the Best Books for Children, 43
The Newbery and Caldecott Awards: A Guide to the Medal and Honor Books, 10
Newbery and Caldecott Medal and Honor Books in Other Media, 14, 112, 366
Newbery and Caldecott Medal Books, 1976-1985, 13
Newbery and Caldecott Medalists and Honor Winners: Bibliographies and Resource Materials Through 1991, 11
Newbery Classroom Homepage, 445
The Newbery Medal Awards (Web site), 414.2, 446

Newman, Joan E., 185
Nodelman, Perry, 49-51, 77
Norton, Donna E., 283
Notable Books for Children (Web site), 414.6
Notable Children's Books: 1976-1980, 19
Notable Children's Films and Videos, Filmstrips, and Recordings, 1973-1986, 354
Notable Children's Trade Books in the Field of Social Studies, 114n, 447
NSLS: North Suburban Library System (Web site), 449
Nuclear Age Literature for Youth: The Quest for a Life-Affirming Ethic, 216

The Official Eric Carle's Web Site, 462
Olexer, Marycile E., 253
Once Upon . . . a Time for Young People and Their Books: An Annotated Resource Guide, 227
Oppenheim, Joan F., 52-53, 107
Oppenheim, Stephanie, 53, 107
Our Family, Our Friends, Our World: An Annotated Guide to Significant Multicultural Books for Children and Teenagers, 134
Outstanding Science Trade Books for Children, 114n, 448
The Oxford Companion to Children's Literature, 234

The Page at Pooh Corner (Web site), 450
Palmer, Eileen C., 256
Paperback Books for Children, 113n
Parents and Children Together Online (Web site), 451
Parents' Choice: A Review of Children's Media, 376

Parents' Choice: A Sourcebook of the Very Best Products to Educate, Inform, and Entertain Children of All Ages, 360

Parents' Choice Foundation, 405

Patricia Polacco: A Woman's Voice Remembering (Web site), 464

Pauses: Autobiographical Reflections of 101 Creators of Children's Books, 295

Pearl, Patricia, 108, 186

Peoples of the American West: Historical Perspectives Through Children's Literature, 205

Perez-Stable, Maria A., 205, 207

Perkins, Agnes Regan, 3-6, 127

Peterson, Carolyn Sue, 229

Pettus, Eloise S., 242

Pflieger, Pat, 243

Phelan, Carolyn, 218

Phelan, Patricia, 33

The Phoenix Award of the Children's Literature Association: 1990-1994, 6

Photography in Books for Young People, 196, 311

Picture Books for Children, 70

Picture Books for Gifted Programs, 65, 78

Picture Books for Looking and Learning: Awakening Visual Perceptions Through the Art of Children's Books, 73

Pilla, Marianne Laino, 68

Play Index, 254

Play, Learn, and Grow: An Annotated Guide to the Best Books and Materials for Very Young Children, 56

Plays for Children and Young Adults: An Evaluative Index and Guide, 249

Plays for Children and Young Adults: An Evaluative Index and Guide, Supplement 1, 1989-1994, 250

Poetry Anthologies for Children and Young People, 253

Polette, Nancy, 64, 65, 78

Polly, Jean Armour, 412

Pop-up and Movable Books: A Bibliography, 76

Popular Reading for Children, III: A Collection of Booklist *Columns*, 29

Portraying Persons with Disabilities: An Annotated Bibliography of Fiction for Children and Teenagers, 110

Portraying Persons with Disabilities: An Annotated Bibliography of Nonfiction for Children and Teenagers, 105

Povsic, Frances F., 170-71

Preller, James, 297

Price, Anne, 268

Prichard, Mari, 234

Primaryplots 2: A Book Talk Guide for Use with Readers Ages 4-8, 85n, 94

Promoting World Understanding Through Literature, K-8, 122

Prosak-Beres, Leslie, 280

Public Library Association, 406

PUBYAC (Listserv), 477

Puckett, Katharyn, 79

Pyles, Marian S., 187

Ramirez, Gonzalo, Jr., 135

Ramirez, Jan L., 135

Rasinski, Timothy V., 109, 272

The Read-Aloud Handbook, 96

Read It Again! Multicultural Books for the Primary Grades, 138

The Reader's Adviser: The Best in Reference Works, British Literature and American Literature, 226

Reading Aloud to Your Children, 116n

Reading As We Grow, 117n

Reading for the Love of It: Best Books for Young Readers, 40

Reading for Young People series, 200n

Reading Is Fun!, 116n

Reading Is Fundamental, Inc., 116, 407

The Reading Rainbow Guide to Children's Books: The 101 Best Titles, 41

Reading Rainbow Reading List (Web site), 452

The Reading Teacher: A Journal of the International Reading Association, 331

Ready, Set, Read: Best Books to Prepare Preschoolers, 44

Recreating the Past: A Guide to American and World Historical Fiction for Children and Young Adults, 203

Reference Books for Children, 229

Reference Books for Children's Collections, 230

Reference Books for Young Readers: Authoritative Evaluation of Encyclopedias, Atlases, and Dictionaries, 237

A Reference Guide to Historical Fiction for Children and Young Adults, 204

A Reference Guide to Modern Fantasy for Children, 243

Reference Sources for Children's and Young Adult Literature, 231

Reid, Rob, 365

Research and Professional Resources in Children's Literature: Piecing a Patchwork Quilt, 232

Richardson, Selma K., 315

Richey, Virginia H., 79

Richter, Bernice, 219

Riggle, Judith, 21

Roberts, Patricia L., 136, 176, 188-91

Robertson, Debra E. J., 110

Rochman, Hazel, 89, 137

Roeber, Jane A., 158

Roginski, Jim, 304

Rollins, Deborah, 231

Rollock, Barbara, 145, 305

Roman, Susan, 262

Rosenberg, Judith K., 263

Roser, Nancy L., 16

Rothlein, Liz, 138

Rubin, Janet E., 208

Rudman, Masha Kabakow, 111, 273

Russell, William F., 90-92

Ryder, Randall J., 69

Sader, Marion, 237

Sadler, Judith DeBoard, 192

Salluzzo, Sharon, 24

A Sampler of Jewish American Folklore, 156

San Francisco Chronicle Review, 352

Saniga, Richard D., 100

Schlessinger, Bernard S., 250

Schlessinger, June H., 249-50

Schliesman, Megan, 129

Scholt, Grayce, 223

Schomburg Center for Research in Black Culture, 383

Schon, Isabel, 152.1-52.5, 153, 306

School Library Journal: The Magazine of Children's, Young Adult, & School Librarians, 332, 377

School Library Media Activities Monthly, 333

Sciara, Frank J., 149, 164

Science and Children, 345

Science & Technology in Fact and Fiction: A Guide to Young Adult Books, 215

Science Books and Films, 346

Science Books and Films: Best Books for Children, 1992-95, 214

Science Books for Children: Selections from Booklist, 221

Science Books for Young People, 218

Seale, Doris, 162

Segel, Elizabeth, 86

The Selected Children's Judaica Collection, 155

Selected List of Multimedia Publishers, Producers, and Distributors (Web site), 453.2

Selecting Materials for and About Hispanic and East Asian Children and Young People, 149, 164

Senick, Gerard J., 308

Seniorplots, 85n

Sensitive Issues: An Annotated Guide to Children's Literature K-6, 109, 272

Sequences: An Annotated Guide to Children's Fiction in Series, 262

700+ Great Sites (Web site), 414.7

The Seventh Book of Junior Authors and Illustrators, 296.2

Shadow and Substance: Afro-American Experience in Contemporary Children's Fiction, 146

Sharkey, Paulette Bochnig, 14, 112, 366

Sharp, Pat Tipton, 200.5

Sherman, Gale W., 9

Sherman, Josepha, 156

Short, Kathy G., 232

Siegel, Alice, 233

Sierra, Judy, 93, 139

Signals: Approaches to Children's Books, 334

Silvey, Anita, 307

Sims, Rudine, 146. *See also* Bishop, Rudine Sims

Sinclair, Patti K., 220

The Single-Parent Family in Children's Books: An Annotated Bibliography, 189

The Sixth Book of Junior Authors and Illustrators, 296.8

Slapin, Beverly, 162

Smith, Henrietta M., 15

Smith, Laura, 8

Smith, Sharyl G., 200.6

Snow, Barbara, 255

Snow White (Web site), 453.3

Social Education: The Official Journal of the National Council of the Social Studies, 347

Something About the Author: Autobiographical Series, 288n, 296.1n, 308

Something About the Author: Facts and Pictures About Contemporary Authors and Illustrators of Books for Young People, 309

Sosa, Marian, 214

The Soviet Union in Literature for Children and Young Adults, 171

Spangler, Stella S., 215

Special Collections in Children's Literature: An International Directory, 379

Spencer, Pam, 54

Spirt, Diana L., 30

Sprug, Joseph W., 244

Stephens, Elaine C., 208

Stoll, Donald R., 316

Storey, Dee, 193

STORYTELL (Listserv), 478

Stott, Jon C., 163

Strickland, Charlene, 194

Subject Collections: A Guide to Special Book Collections and Subject Emphasis as Reported by University, College, Public, and Special Libraries and Museums in the United States and Canada, 378

Subject Guide to Children's Books in Print: 1995, 269, 368n

Sukiennik, Adelaide W., 104-5

Sullivan, Charles, 147

Survival Themes in Fiction for Children and Young People, 198

Sutherland, Zena, 55, 284

Sutton, Roger, 55

Synons, Cynthia Wolford, 106

Tales of Love and Terror: Booktalking the Classics, Old and New, 89

Taylor, Desmond, 209

Teachers' Choices, 115n

Teachers' Favorite Books for Kids: Teachers' Choices, 1989-1993, 37

They Wrote for Children Too: An Annotated Bibliography of Children's Literature by Famous Writers for Adults, 17

They're Never Too Young for Books: A Guide to Children's Books for Ages 1 to 8, 48

The Third Book of Junior Authors, 296.5

This Land Is Our Land: A Guide to Multicultural Literature for Children and Young Adults, 127

Thomas, James L., 56

Thomas, Rebecca L., 94, 140

Thomas, Virginia Coffin, 195

Through Indian Eyes: The Native Experience in Books for Children, 162

Through the Eyes of a Child: An Introduction to Children's Literature, 283

Totten, Herman, 141

Touchstones: Fairy Tales, Fables, Myths, Legends and Poetry: Reflections on the Best in Children's Literature, 50

Touchstones: Picture Books: Reflections on the Best in Children's Literature, 51, 77

Touchstones: Reflections on the Best in Children's Literature, 49

Trefny, Beverly Robin, 256

Trelease, Jim, 95-96

Tribune Books, 353

Twentieth-Century Children's Writers, 285n, 310

Twins in Children's and Adolescent Literature: An Annotated Bibliography, 193

Understanding Abilities, Disabilities, and Capabilities: A Guide to Children's Literature, 100

Understanding American History Through Children's Literature: Instructional Units and Activities for Grades K-8, 207

U.S. Board on Books for Young People, 408

Using Picture Storybooks to Teach Literary Devices: Recommended Books for Children and Young Adults, 71

Values in Selected Children's Books of Fiction and Fantasy, 270

Van Meter, Vandelia, 210-11, 246-47

Vandergrift's Children's Literature Page (Web site), 453

Vandergrift's Feminist Page (Web site), 453.4

Vanderworf, Mary Ann, 215

Variety's Video Directory PLUS, 371

Veltze, Linda, 200.7

Venture into Cultures: A Resource Book of Multicultural Materials and Programs, 126

Virginia Hamilton (Web site), 465

Walter, Virginia A., 212

War and Peace Literature for Children and Young Adults: A Resource Guide to Significant Issues, 212

Ward, Martha E., 196, 311-12

Wear, Terri A., 197
The WEB: Wonderfully Exciting Books, 348
Weiss, Jacqueline Shachter, 270
Welton, Ann, 213
Wenzel, Duane, 219
What Do Children Read Next? A Reader's Guide to Fiction for Children, 25
What Do Young Adults Read Next? A Reader's Guide to Fiction for Young Adults, 54
White, Valerie, 57-59
Who's Who in Children's Books, 294
Wilcox, Leah, 44
Wild, Terri Christman, 138
Wilkin, Binnie Tate, 198
Williams, Helen F., 148
Wilms, Denise Mureko, 199, 221
Wilson, George, 60, 364
A Window into History: Family Memory in Children's Literature, 206
Winkel, Lois, 61
Winnie-the-Pooh (Web site), 454
Wolfe, Gregory, 181, 271
Wolfe, Kathryn, 222
Wolfe, Michael, 413
Wolfe, Suzanne M., 181, 271
Wood, Irene, 373
Woodward, Gloria, 143

Wordless/Almost Wordless Picture Books: A Guide, 79
World History for Children and Young Adults: An Annotated Bibliographic Index, 211, 247
A World of Books: An Annotated Reading List for ESL/EFL Students, 66
Worlds Within: Children's Fantasy from the Middles Ages to Today, 177
Writers for Children: Critical Studies of Major Authors Since the Seventeenth Century, 285

Yaakon, Juliette, 268
YALSA (Young Adult Library Services Association), 409
Yesterday's Authors of Books for Children: Facts & Pictures About Authors and Illustrators of Books for Young People, from Early Times to 1960, 285n, 288
Young Adult Library Services Association (YALSA), 409
Young Children, 335
Young People's Books in Series: Fiction and Non-Fiction, 1975-1991, 263
The Young Reader's Companion, 235
The Young Reader's Companion to American History, 236

Subject Index

Reference is to entry number.

AASL (American Association of
    School Librarians), 388
ACEI (Association for Childhood
    Education International), 390
Adoption literature, 184
Adventure stories, 45
African American literature, 142-48
    art, 147
    biography, authors and illustra-
        tors, 145, 305
    stereotyping in children's books,
        143
African literature, 167
Afro American literature. *See* African
    American literature
AJL (Association of Jewish
    Libraries), 392
ALA (American Library
    Association), 389
ALSC (Association for Library
    Service to Children), 391
Alphabet books, 188-89
Alternative press, 225
American Association of School
    Librarians (AASL), 388
American history. *See* United States,
    history
American Indian literature. *See*
    Native American literature
American Library Association
    (ALA), 389
Animal stories, 45
    cats, 194
    dogs, 194
    horses, 194, 197
Asian literature. *See* Literature of
    East Asian cultures; Literature
    of Southeast Asian cultures
Asian American literature, 165-66
Association for Childhood Education
    International (ACEI), 390

Association for Library Service to
    Children (ALSC), 391
Association of Jewish Libraries
    (AJL), 392
Associations, professional, 113-16,
    388-409. *See also* names of
    individual organizations
Audio, 27, 358
Author and illustrator biographies.
    See Biographies, authors and
    illustrators
Awards, honors, and prizes, 1-15
    British Commonwealth, 4-5
    Caldecott Medal and Honor
        Books, 10-14, 112, 366,
        414.1, 420
    Coretta Scott King Award, 15
    international, 8
    Newbery Medal and Honor
        Books, 9-14, 112, 366,
        414.2, 445-46
    Phoenix Award, 6

Beginning readers, 21, 23, 44, 56-58,
    61
Best books, 16-61. *See also* Awards,
    honors, and prizes
Bibliographies, commercial, 264-69
Bilingual books, Spanish, 150
Biographies, authors and illustrators,
    285-312
    African American, 305
    CD-ROM, 370
    collective biographies, 286
    dictionaries, 293-94, 310
        African American, 305
        Hispanic/Latino, 306
    indexes, 286-87
    multicultural, 291-92
    photographers, 312

181

Black literature. *See* African American literature

Book reviews. *See* Children's literature; Indexes

Books, early childhood. *See* Early childhood, books for

Books of international interest, 8

Booktalking, 81, 85, 89, 94. *See also* Read-aloud books

Braille books for children, 112, 338

British literature for children. *See* Awards, honors, and prizes

Caldecott Medal and Honor Books, 10-14, 112, 366, 414.1, 420

Catholic Library Association, 393

Cats. *See* Animal stories

CBC (The Children's Book Council), 114, 394

CD-ROMs, 367-71, 373

Child Study Children's Book Committee at Bank Street College, 113

The Children's Book Council (CBC), 114, 394

Children's literature
  critical guides, 276-77, 279
  research, 232
  reviews, 30, 276-80
  special collections, 378-87
    centers, 384-87
    directories, 378-79
    research collections, 380-83
  textbooks, 281-84

Children's Literature Assembly of NCTE, 395

Children's Literature Association (CLA), 396

Children's magazines. *See* Periodicals

Children's Reading Round Table of Chicago (CRRT), 397

Children's Television Workshop (CTW), 398

CLA (Children's Literature Association), 396

Classic literature, 49-51, 80, 90-92

Commercial bibliographies. *See* Bibliographies, commercial

Coretta Scott King Awards, 15

Council on Interracial Books for Children, 399

Counting books, 190

Criticism, children's books. *See* Children's literature, critical guides

CRRT (Children's Reading Round Table of Chicago), 397

CTW (Children's Television Workshop), 398

Death and dying in children's literature. *See* Sensitive issues

Dictionaries and encyclopedias, 234-37
  biography, 293-94, 310
    African American, 305
    Hispanic/Latino, 306
  literature, 224

Disabled children. *See* Special needs children

Divorce and separation. *See* Moral and ethical values in children's literature

Dogs. *See* Animal stories

Early childhood, books for, 23, 44, 48, 56-57, 61

Ecology. *See* Environmental issues in children's literature

EFL (English as a Foreign Language). *See* High/low reading books

Encyclopedias. *See* Dictionaries and encyclopedias

English as a Foreign Language (EFL). *See* High/low reading books

English as a Second Language (ESL). *See* High/low reading books

Environmental issues in children's literature, 220

ESL (English as a Second Language).
  See High/low reading books
Ethics in children's literature. *See*
  Moral and ethical values in
  children's literature
Ethnic literature. *See* Multicultural
  literature
European literature. *See* Literature of
  Eastern European cultures
Explorers and exploration, 213

Fables. *See* Fairy tales, myths,
  legends, fables
Fairy tales, myths, legends, fables,
  46, 50, 239, 244. *See also*
  Folktales; Mythology
Family relationships, 192
Fantasy literature, 46, 177, 182, 239,
  243
Films, 214, 346, 354, 364. *See also*
  Videos
Finger plays, index, 252
First readers. *See* Beginning readers
Folklore. *See* Folktales
Folktales, 46, 93, 244. *See also* Fairy
  tales, myths, legends, fables
  index, 239
  multicultural, 139, 183
Free and inexpensive guides to best
  books, 113-18

Geography, United States. *See* United
  States, literature by geographic
  location
Gifted, 62-65
  picture books, 65, 77
Great Books Foundation, 400
Greek mythology. *See* Mythology
Growing up, 101-2, 176. *See also*
  Realistic literature

Handicapped children. *See* Special
  needs children
Health awareness, 98, 106, 108
High/low reading books, 24, 33,
  66-69

ESL/EFL books, 66
  reluctant readers, 24, 68-69
Hispanic/Latino literature, 149-53
  authors and illustrators, 153
Historical literature, 45, 173, 201-13
  biography, authors and illustra-
    tors, 223, 306
  dictionaries and encyclopedias,
    236
  indexes, 245-47
Holocaust, literature of the, 208
Honor Books. *See* Awards, honors,
  and prizes
Horse stories. *See* Animal stories
Hospital libraries. *See* Pediatric
  libraries
Humor in children's books, 174-75,
  178

Illustration in children's books,
  289-90
Indexes
  biography, 286-87
  book reviews, 257-60
  fairy tales, folklore, myths, 239,
    241
  fantasy, 239, 243
  fiction, 238-39, 241, 261
  finger plays, 252
  historical literature, 223, 245-47
  picture books, 240
  plays, 249-50, 254, 256
  plot summaries, 242
  poetry, 239, 248
  series and sequels, 261-63
  songs, 251, 255
India, literature of the cultures, 168
Indian literature. *See* Native
  American literature
Informational literature, 20, 22,
  38-39, 47, 104-5
International book awards. *See*
  Awards, honors, and prizes
International Reading Association
  (IRA), 115, 401

Internet. *See* Listservs, gopher sites, e-mail addresses; World Wide Web sites
IRA (International Reading Association), 115, 401
Issues in literature for children, 273. *See also* Moral and ethical values in children's literature; Sensitive issues

Jewish Book Council, 402
Jewish literature, 154-56
Journals. *See* Periodicals

Large print books, 112
Latino literature. *See* Hispanic/Latino literature
Legends. *See* Fairy tales, myths, legends, fables
Listservs, gopher sites, e-mail addresses
  children's literature, 467-78
    folklore, 473
    storytelling, 478
  resource guides, 410-13
Literature of East Asian cultures, 164-66, 169
Literature of Southeast Asian cultures, 164-66
Literature of Eastern European cultures, 170
Literature of the cultures of India, 168

Magazines. *See* Periodicals
Masterplots
  biography, 298
  fiction, 241
Modern fantasy. *See* Fantasy literature
Moral and ethical values in children's literature, 270-71
Multicultural folktales. *See* Multicultural literature

Multicultural literature. *See also* African literature; Hispanic/Latino literature; Jewish literature; Literature of East Asian cultures; Literature of Eastern European cultures; Literature of Southeast Asian cultures; Literature of the cultures of India; Soviet Union, literature
  biography, 291-92, 306
  folktales, 139, 183
  picture books, 93, 132
  poetry, 119
  read-aloud stories, 139
Multiethnic literature. *See* Multicultural literature
Mystery stories, 45
Mythology, Greek and Roman, 173. *See also* Fairy tales, myths, legends, fables

National Braille Association, Inc., 403
National Council of Teachers of English (NCTE), 404
Native American literature, 157-62
  folktales, 157
  stereotyping in books for children, 160, 162
NCTE (National Council of Teachers of English), 404
Newbery Medal and Honor Books, 9-14, 112, 366, 414.2, 445-46
Nonsexism in children's books. *See* Sexism and sex roles in children's literature
Nonfiction books. *See* Informational literature
Nonprint media
  audio, 27, 358
  CD-ROMs, 367-71, 373
    books on, 367-68
    biography, 369
    multimedia reviews, 370
    reference books, 368
    video directory, 371

directories
  general, 355, 357, 360
  video, 356
films, 214, 346, 354, 364
filmstrips, 354
Newbery and Caldecott Medal
    and Honor Books, 112, 366
recordings, 61, 354, 365
reviewing sources, 372-77
  video, 374
software, 27, 358, 361, 363
songs, 255
toys, 27, 53, 358
videos, 27, 53, 354, 358-59, 362,
    364
Nontraditional female roles, 185
North American Indian literature. *See*
    Native American literature
Nuclear age literature, 216
Number books. *See* Counting books

Older adults as portrayed in
    children's books, 179

Parents' Choice Foundation, 405
Peace literature in children's books.
    See War and peace literature
Pediatric libraries, 97-98
Periodicals
  book reviewing journals, 336-48
    folklore, 341
    science, 345-46
  directories, 313
  newspaper reviews, 349-53
  professional journals, 317-35
  recommended children's maga-
    zines, 27
  selection aides, 314-16
Personal development. *See* Realistic
    literature, fiction and nonfiction
Phoenix Award, 6
Photography in children's books, 196
Physical handicaps. *See* Special
    needs children
Picture books, 70-79
  alphabet books, 188-89
  art, 73

for the gifted, 65
multicultural, 75
subject access to, 72, 240
wordless books, 79
Pioneer and frontier life. *See* United
    States, history, fiction and
    nonfiction
PLA (Public Library Association),
    406
Plays, indexes, 249-50, 254, 256
Poetry, 50
  indexes, 239, 248
Pop-up and movable books, 76
Preschool children, books for. *See*
    early childhood, books for
Prizes for children's literature. *See*
    Awards, honors, and prizes
Professional associations, 113-16,
    388-409. *See also* names of
    individual organizations
Public Library Association (PLA),
    406

Racism in children's literature. *See*
    Stereotyping in children's books
Read-aloud books, 80-96
  award books, 81
  booktalking guides, 81, 85, 89, 94
  classics, 80, 90-92
  multicultural folktales, 93
Reading Is Fundamental, Inc. (RIF),
    116, 407
Reading Rainbow books, 41
Realistic literature, fiction and
    nonfiction, 46
  death and dying, 187
  nontraditional families, 192
  personal development, 161,
    570-72
  portrayal of older adults, 179
  resiliency/strength of character,
    176
  single-parent families, 180
  survival themes, 198
Recordings, 61, 255, 354, 365
Reference sources
  almanacs, 233

Reference sources (*cont.*)
  atlases, 237
  bibliographies, 229-31, 237
  children's literature, 226
      bibliographies, print and non-
          print, 227, 231, 234-35
  dictionaries and encyclopedias, 237
  on CD-ROMS, 368
Religious literature for children,
    154-56, 186, 195
Reluctant readers, books for. *See*
    High/low reading books
Reminiscences, historical. *See* United
    States, history
Research collections. *See* Children's
    literature
Resiliency in children's literature.
    See Realistic literature, fiction
    and nonfiction
Reviewing sources, of nonprint
    media, 372-77
Reviews. *See* Children's literature,
    reviews
RIF (Reading Is Fundamental, Inc.),
    116, 407
Roman mythology. *See* Mythology
Russian literature. *See* Soviet Union,
    literature

Science and technology, 214-22
  films, 214, 346
  nuclear age literature, 216
  reference books, 217, 228
Science fiction, 172
Selection aids. *See* Bibliographies,
    commercial
Sensitive issues, 101, 108-9, 272
  death and dying, 187
  separation and loss, 111
Senior citizens. *See* Older adults as
    portrayed in children's books
Series and sequels
  fiction, 261-63
  nonfiction, 263
Sexism and sex roles in children's
    literature, 185, 191, 199
  nontraditional roles, 185

Single-parent families, 180
Software, 27, 358, 363
  high/low guides, 361
Songs for children, 251
  index, 251
  on recordings, 255, 365
Soviet Union, literature, 171
Special collections of children's
    literature. *See* Children's
    literature, special collections
Special needs children, 97-112
  nonbook formats, 107, 112
  nonfiction, 104-5
  pediatric libraries, 97
Stereotyping in children's books
  African Americans, 143
  gender positive characterizations,
    191
  Native Americans, 160, 162

Technology literature. *See* Science
    and technology
Textbooks, 281-84
Toys, 27, 53, 358
Traditional literature. *See* Folktales
Transitional families. *See* Family
    relationships
Twins in literature for children, 193

United States, literature by
    geographic location, 200
  Great Lakes states, 200.4
  Mountain states, 200.6
  Northeast states, 200.3
  Pacific states, 200.2
  Plains states, 200.1
  Southeast states, 200.7
  Southwest states 200.5
United States, history, fiction and
    nonfiction, 201-3, 205-7, 210
  indexes, 223, 246
  family chronicles, 206
U.S. Board on Books for Young
    People (USBBY), 408
USBBY (U.S. Board on Books for
    Young People), 408

Videos, 27, 53, 354, 356, 358-59, 362, 364, 371, 374. *See also* Films

War and peace literature, 212
Wordless/almost wordless books, 79
World history, fiction and nonfiction, 210, 203-4, 211
   index, 247
World War II
   fiction, 209
   Holocaust, 208
World Wide Web sites, 414-67
   authors and illustrators, 427, 435.1, 455-66

Caldecott Medal and Honor Books, 414.1, 420
classics, 425
multicultural literature, 430, 443
   Native American, 444
Newbery Medal and Honor Books, 414.2, 445-46
Reading Rainbow, 452
for reluctant readers, 435.2
science, 448
social sciences, 447

YALSA (Young Adult Library Services Association), 409
Young Adult Library Services Association (YALSA), 409